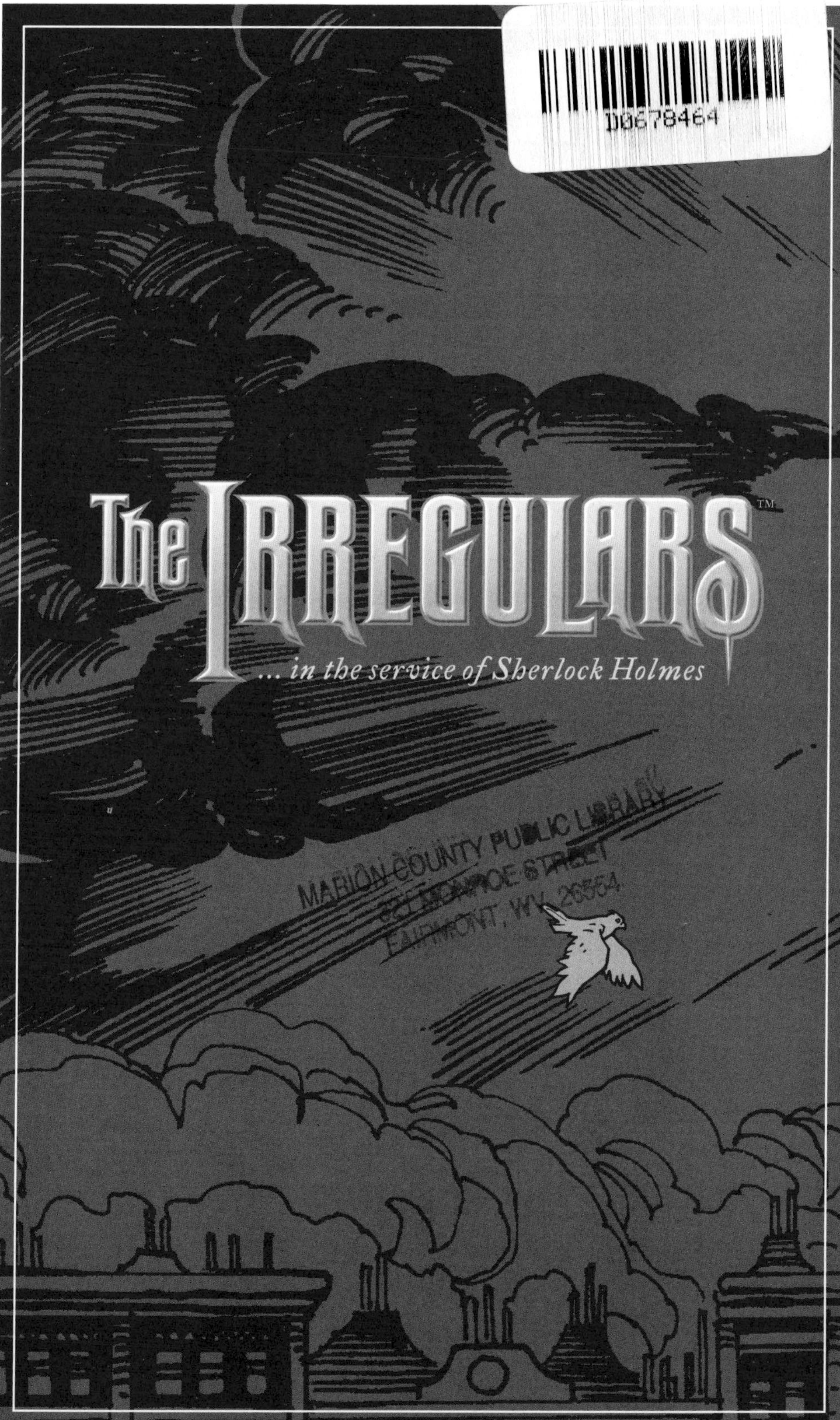
The Irregulars™
... in the service of Sherlock Holmes

PUBLISHER
Mike Richardson

EDITOR
Mike Carriglitto

COLLECTION DESIGNER
Amy Arendts

ART DIRECTOR
Lia Ribacchi

*Special Thanks to David Campiti at Glasshouse Graphics
and to Scott Allie for his guidance and support.*

THE IRREGULARS

Published by
Dark Horse Books
A division of Dark Horse Comics, Inc.
10956 SE Main Street
Milwaukie, OR 97222

darkhorse.com

To find a comics shop in your area, call the Comic Shop Locator Service
toll-free at 1-888-266-4226

First edition: February 2005
ISBN: 1-59307-303-8

10 9 8 7 6 5 4 3 2 1
Printed in Canada

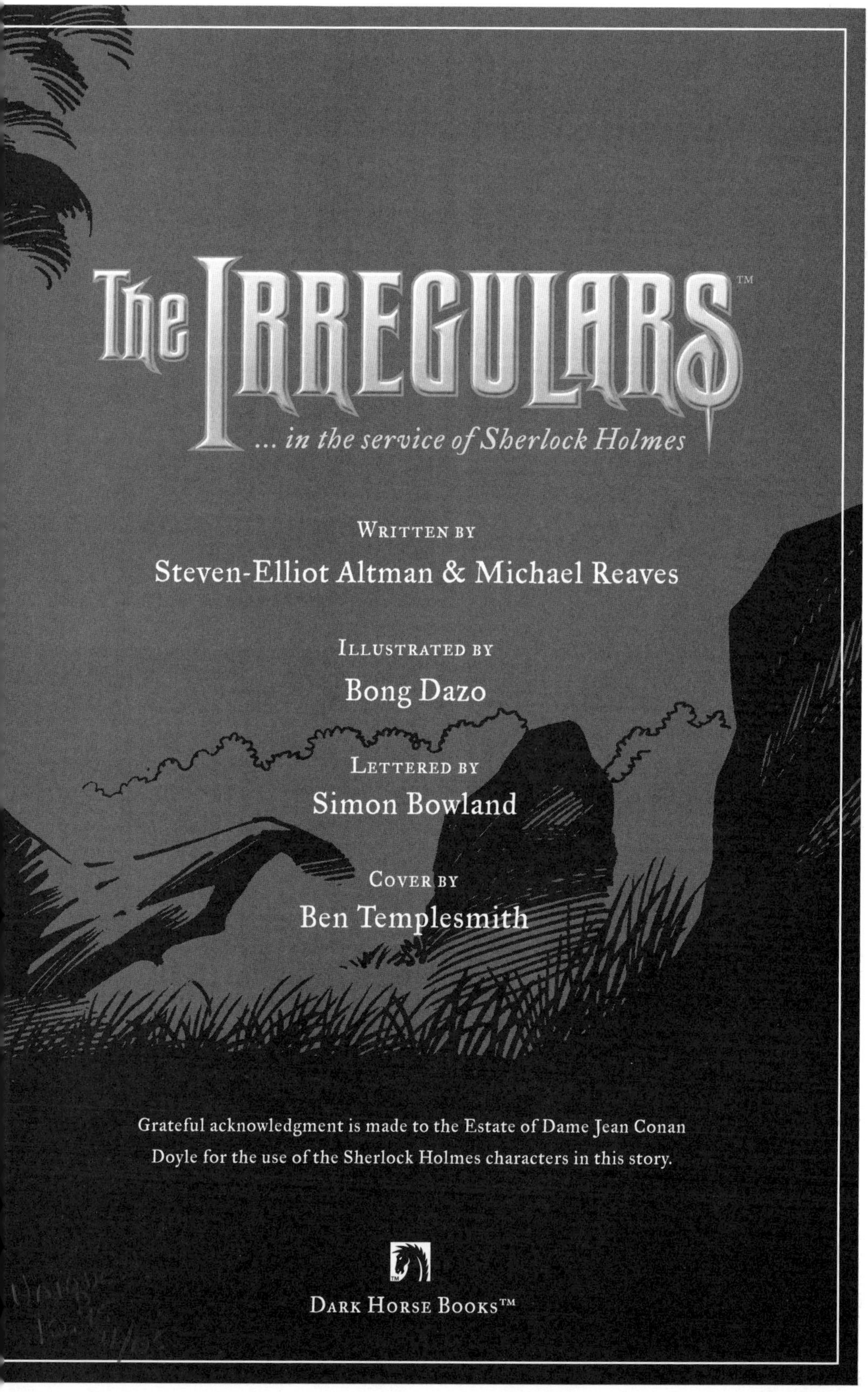

The IRREGULARS™

... in the service of Sherlock Holmes

Written by

Steven-Elliot Altman & Michael Reaves

Illustrated by

Bong Dazo

Lettered by

Simon Bowland

Cover by

Ben Templesmith

Grateful acknowledgment is made to the Estate of Dame Jean Conan Doyle for the use of the Sherlock Holmes characters in this story.

Dark Horse Books™

{ DRAMATIS PERSONAE }

Mr. Sherlock Holmes
The world's greatest detective

Dr. John Watson
A retired army surgeon

Inspector Lestrade
An officer of Scotland Yard

Professor James Moriarty
The Napoleon of crime

Miss Irene Adler
An American opera singer

Jack Springer
A mysterious visitor

The **BAKER STREET IRREGULARS**

Wiggins
The band's leader

Molly
A clever matchstick girl

Patch
A pickpocket and escapist

James
An accomplished artist

Burke
A protégé of Dr. Watson

Puck
A singular child

Toby
The best nose in London

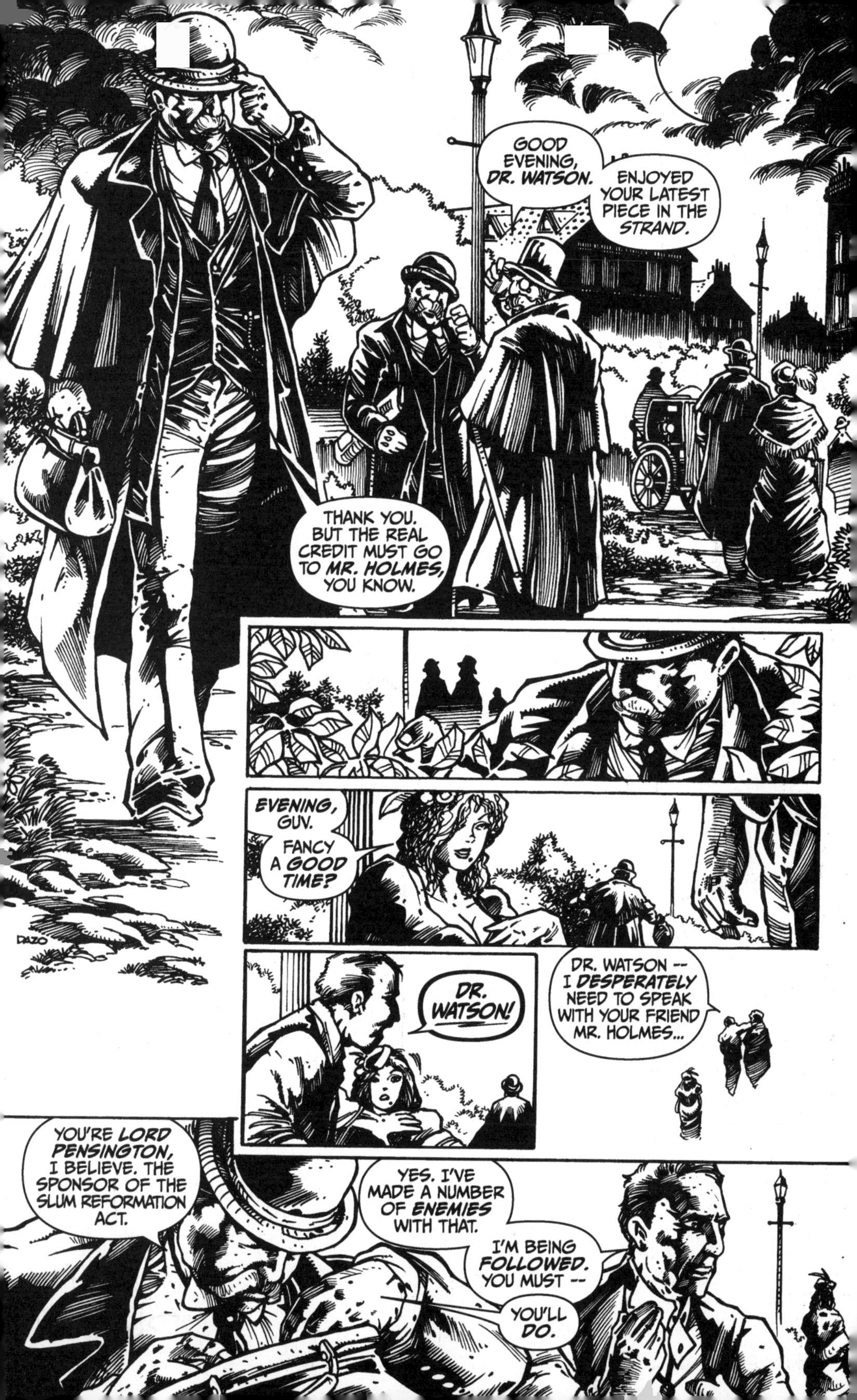
GOOD EVENING, DR. WATSON.
ENJOYED YOUR LATEST PIECE IN THE STRAND.
THANK YOU. BUT THE REAL CREDIT MUST GO TO MR. HOLMES, YOU KNOW.
EVENING, GUV.
FANCY A GOOD TIME?
DAZO
DR. WATSON!
DR. WATSON -- I DESPERATELY NEED TO SPEAK WITH YOUR FRIEND MR. HOLMES...
YOU'RE LORD PENSINGTON, I BELIEVE. THE SPONSOR OF THE SLUM REFORMATION ACT.
YES. I'VE MADE A NUMBER OF ENEMIES WITH THAT.
I'M BEING FOLLOWED. YOU MUST --
YOU'LL DO.

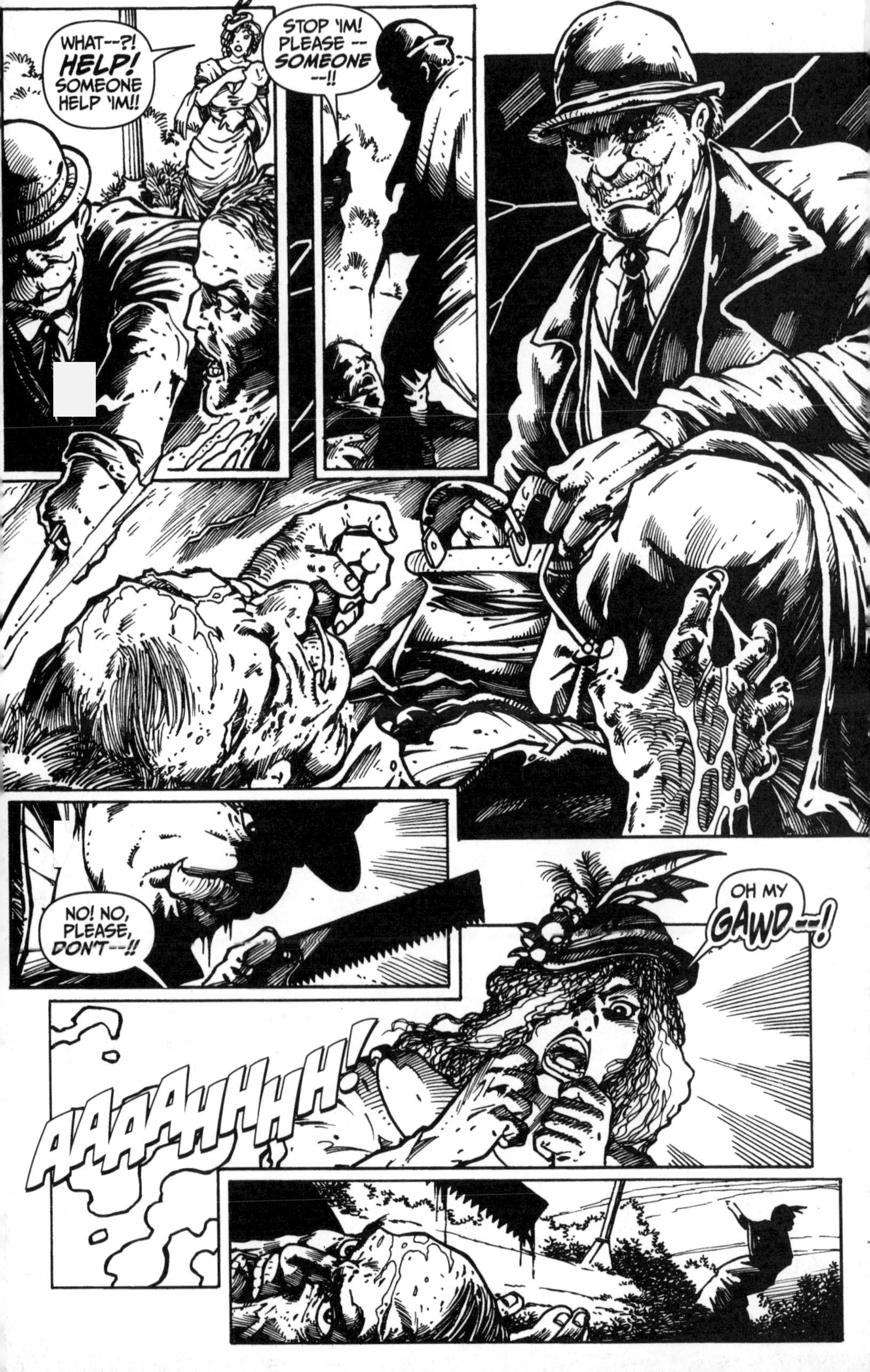
WHAT--?! HELP! SOMEONE HELP 'IM!!
STOP 'IM! PLEASE -- SOMEONE --!!
NO! NO, PLEASE, DON'T--!!
OH MY GAWD--!
AAAAHHHHH!

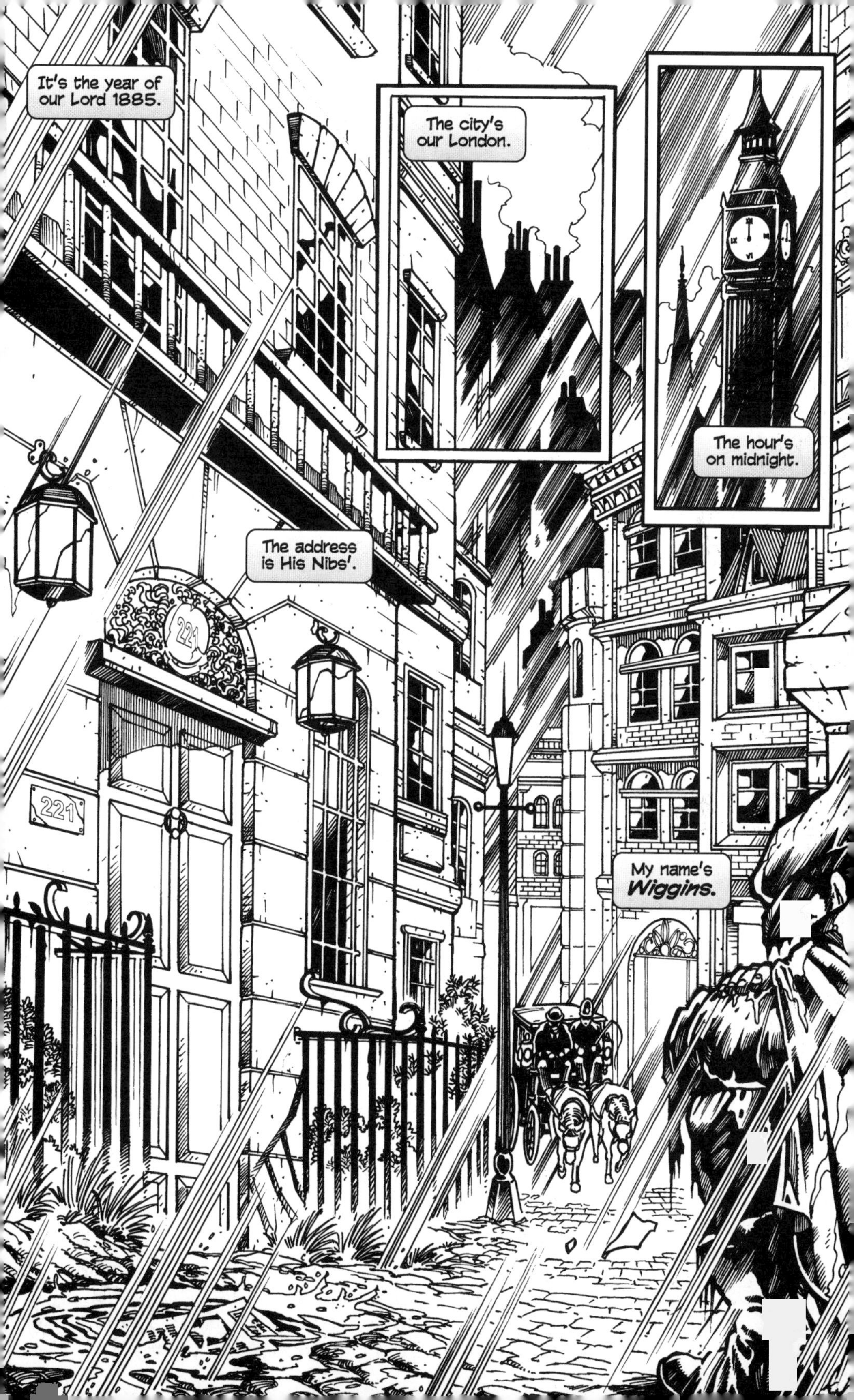
It's the year of our Lord 1885.
The city's our London.
The hour's on midnight.
The address is His Nibs'.
221
221
My name's *Wiggins.*

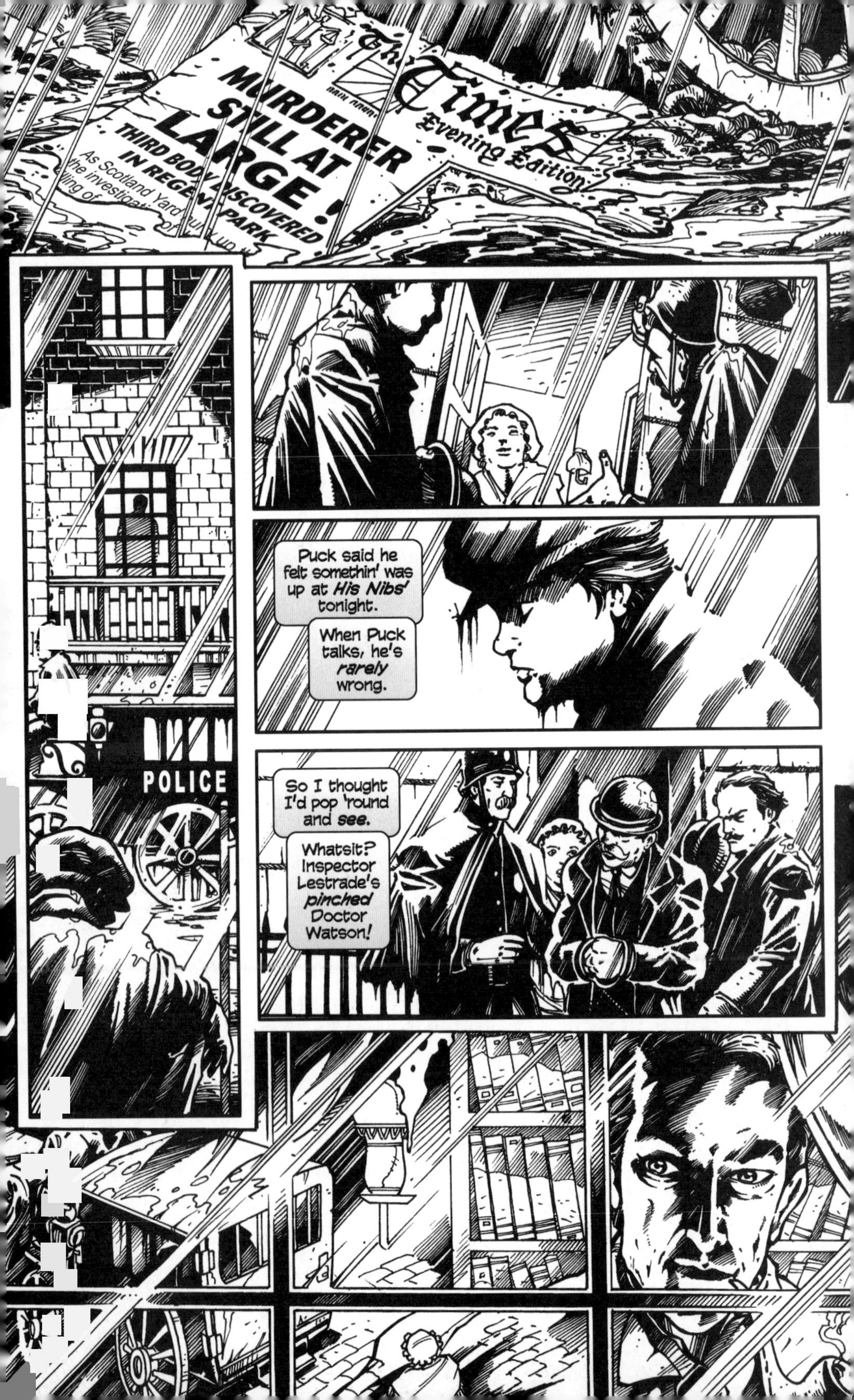

The Times
Evening Edition
MURDERER STILL AT LARGE!
THIRD BODY DISCOVERED
As Scotland Yard
POLICE
Puck said he felt somethin' was up at *His Nibs'* tonight.
When Puck talks, he's *rarely* wrong.
So I thought I'd pop 'round and *see*.
Whatsit? Inspector Lestrade's *pinched* Doctor Watson!

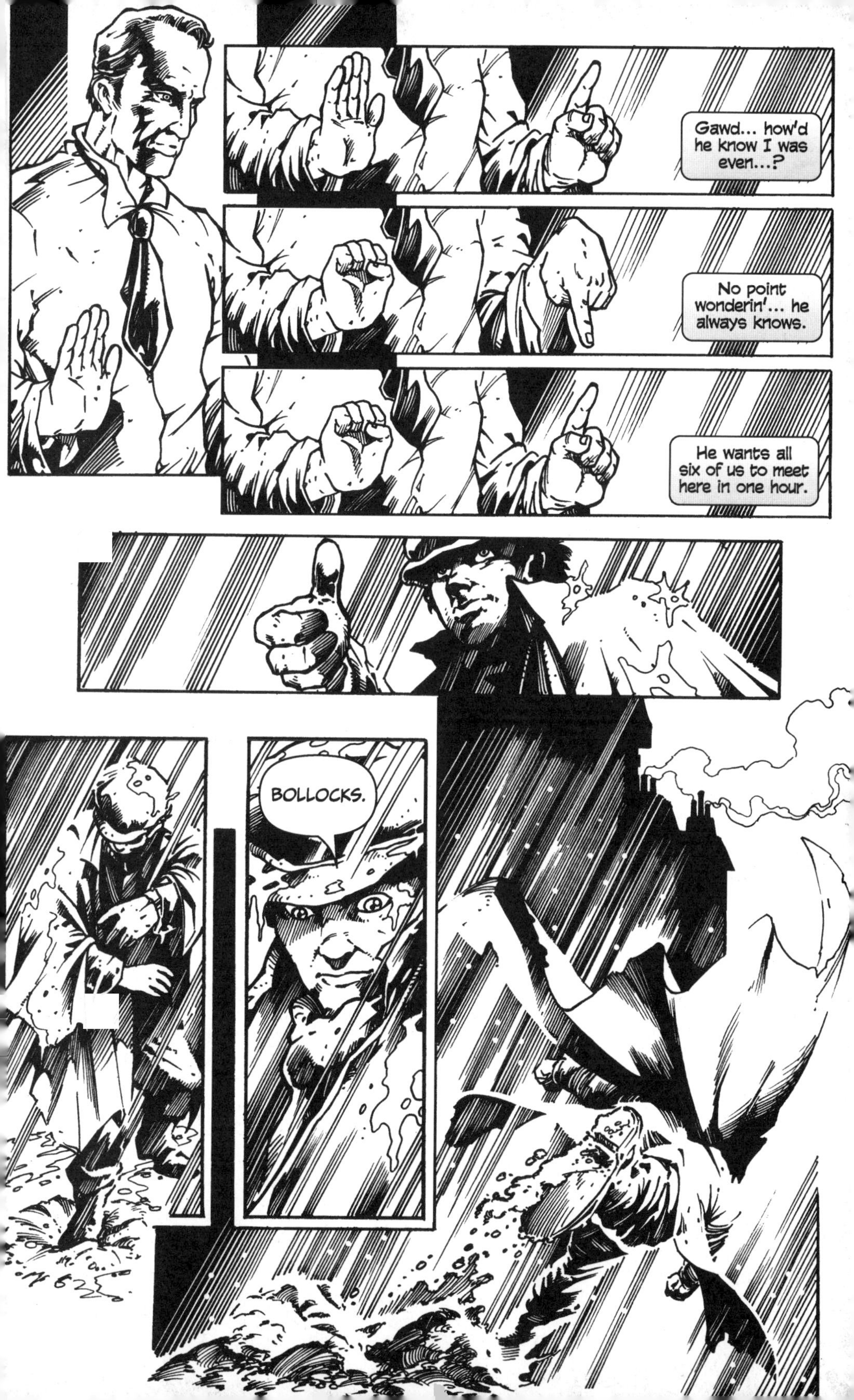
Gawd... how'd he know I was even...?
No point wonderin'... he always knows.
He wants all six of us to meet here in one hour.
BOLLOCKS.

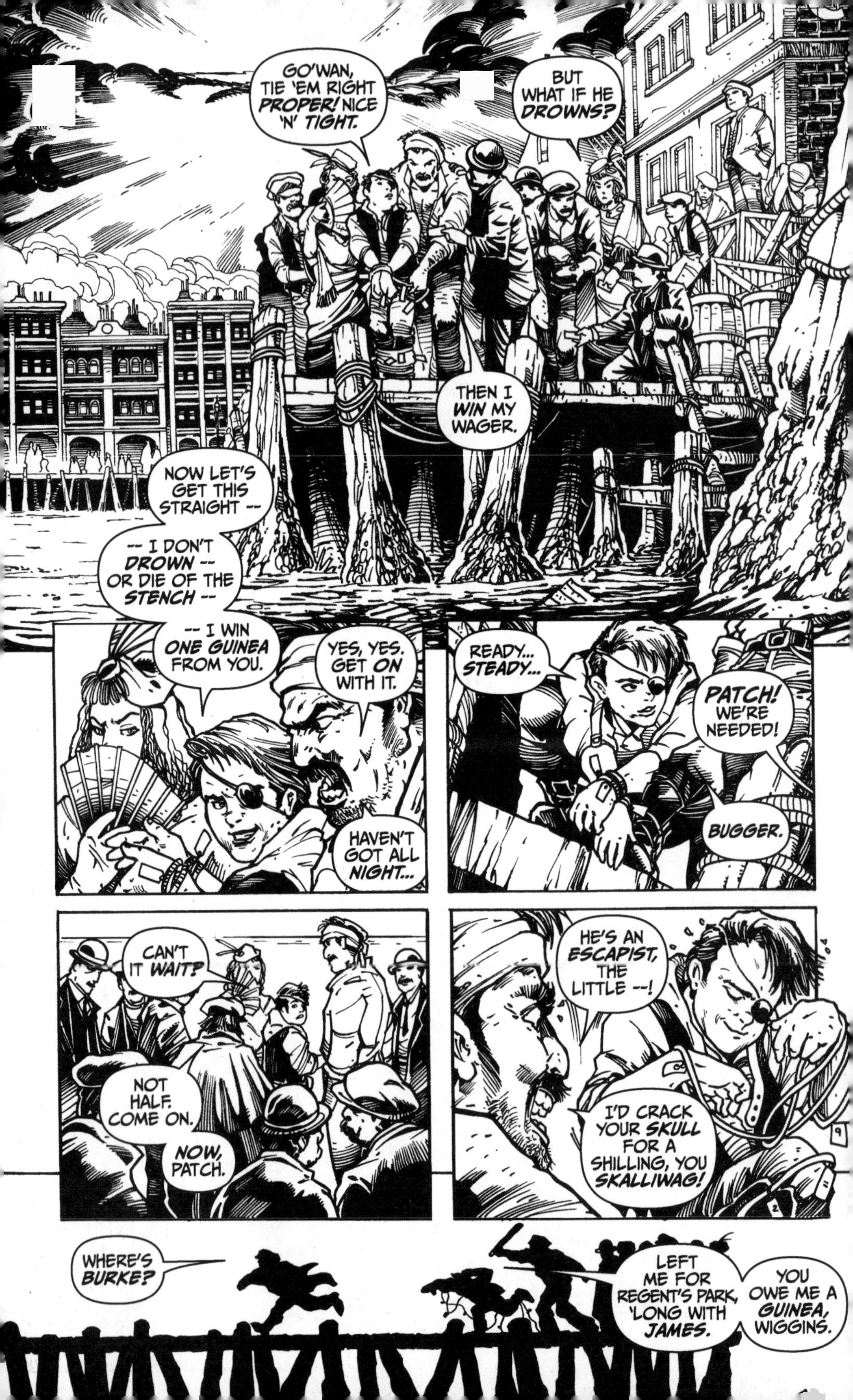
GO'WAN, TIE 'EM RIGHT PROPER! NICE 'N' TIGHT.
BUT WHAT IF HE DROWNS?
THEN I WIN MY WAGER.
NOW LET'S GET THIS STRAIGHT --
-- I DON'T DROWN -- OR DIE OF THE STENCH --
-- I WIN ONE GUINEA FROM YOU.
YES, YES. GET ON WITH IT.
HAVEN'T GOT ALL NIGHT...
READY... STEADY...
PATCH! WE'RE NEEDED!
BUGGER.
CAN'T IT WAIT?
NOT HALF. COME ON.
NOW, PATCH.
HE'S AN ESCAPIST, THE LITTLE --!
I'D CRACK YOUR SKULL FOR A SHILLING, YOU SKALLIWAG!
WHERE'S BURKE?
LEFT ME FOR REGENT'S PARK, 'LONG WITH JAMES.
YOU OWE ME A GUINEA, WIGGINS.

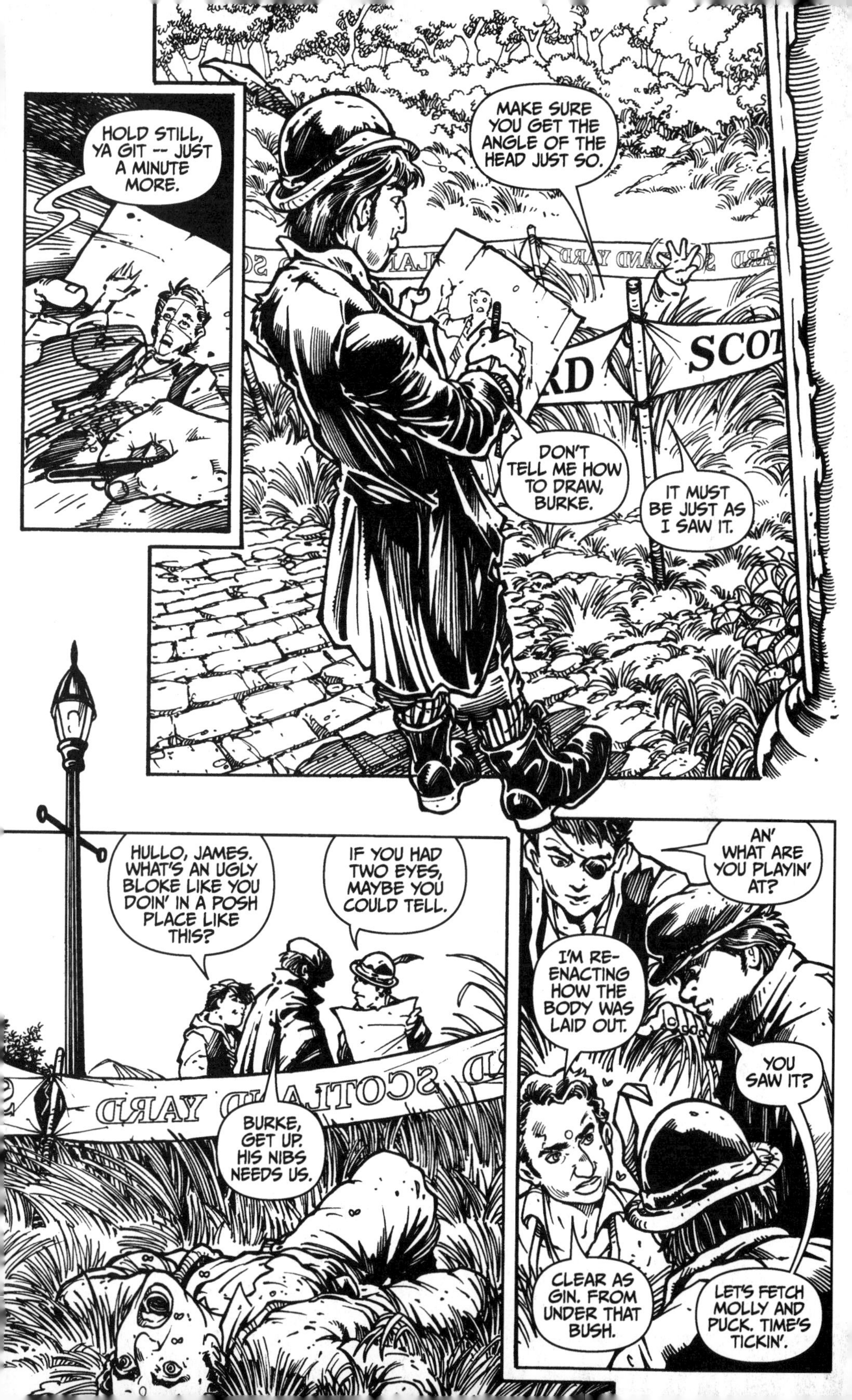
HOLD STILL, YA GIT -- JUST A MINUTE MORE.
MAKE SURE YOU GET THE ANGLE OF THE HEAD JUST SO.
DON'T TELL ME HOW TO DRAW, BURKE.
IT MUST BE JUST AS I SAW IT.
SCOTLAND YARD
HULLO, JAMES. WHAT'S AN UGLY BLOKE LIKE YOU DOIN' IN A POSH PLACE LIKE THIS?
IF YOU HAD TWO EYES, MAYBE YOU COULD TELL.
BURKE, GET UP. HIS NIBS NEEDS US.
AN' WHAT ARE YOU PLAYIN' AT?
I'M RE-ENACTING HOW THE BODY WAS LAID OUT.
YOU SAW IT?
CLEAR AS GIN. FROM UNDER THAT BUSH.
LET'S FETCH MOLLY AND PUCK. TIME'S TICKIN'.

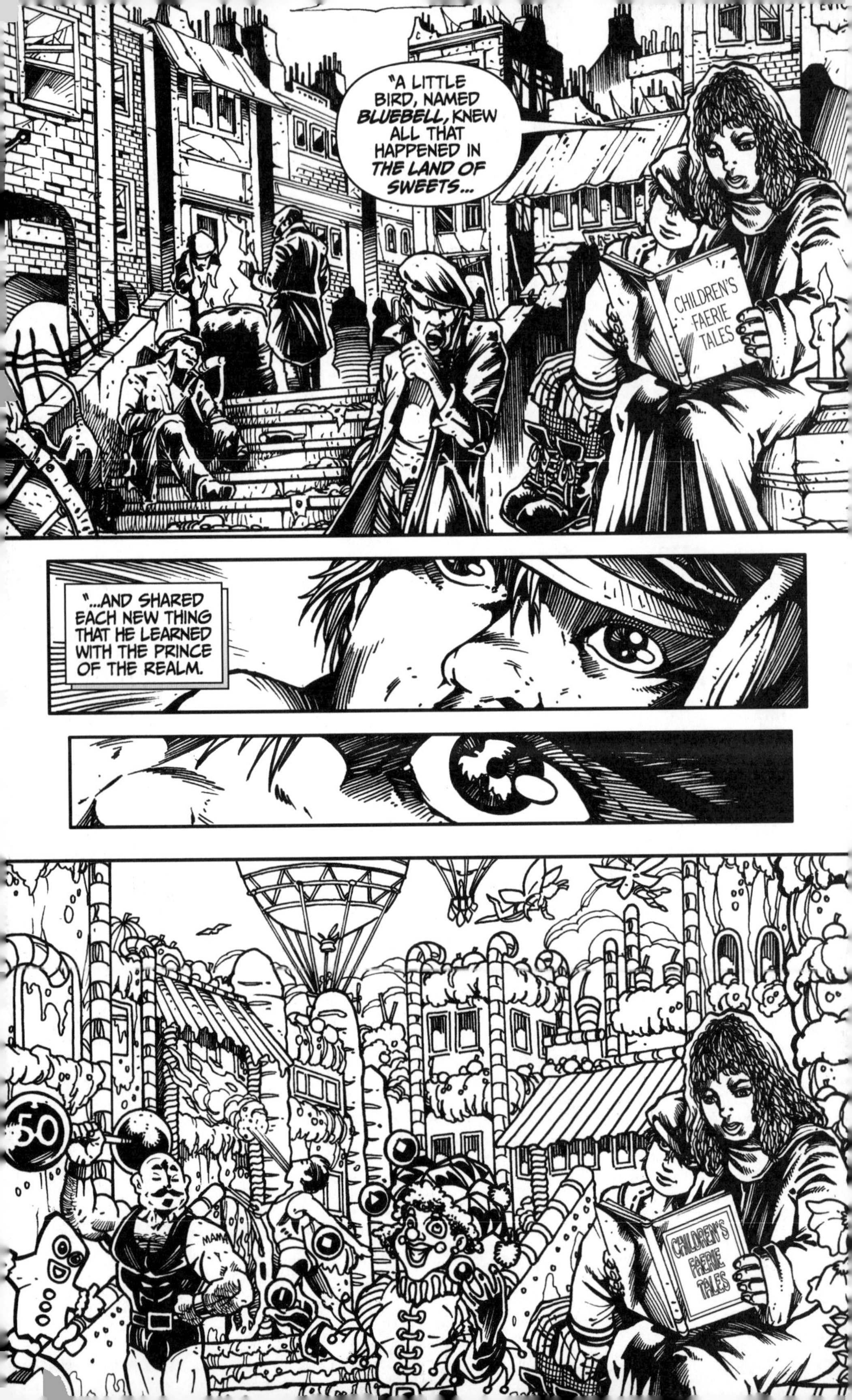
"A LITTLE BIRD, NAMED BLUEBELL, KNEW ALL THAT HAPPENED IN THE LAND OF SWEETS...
CHILDREN'S FAERIE TALES
"...AND SHARED EACH NEW THING THAT HE LEARNED WITH THE PRINCE OF THE REALM.
50
MAMA
CHILDREN'S FAERIE TALES

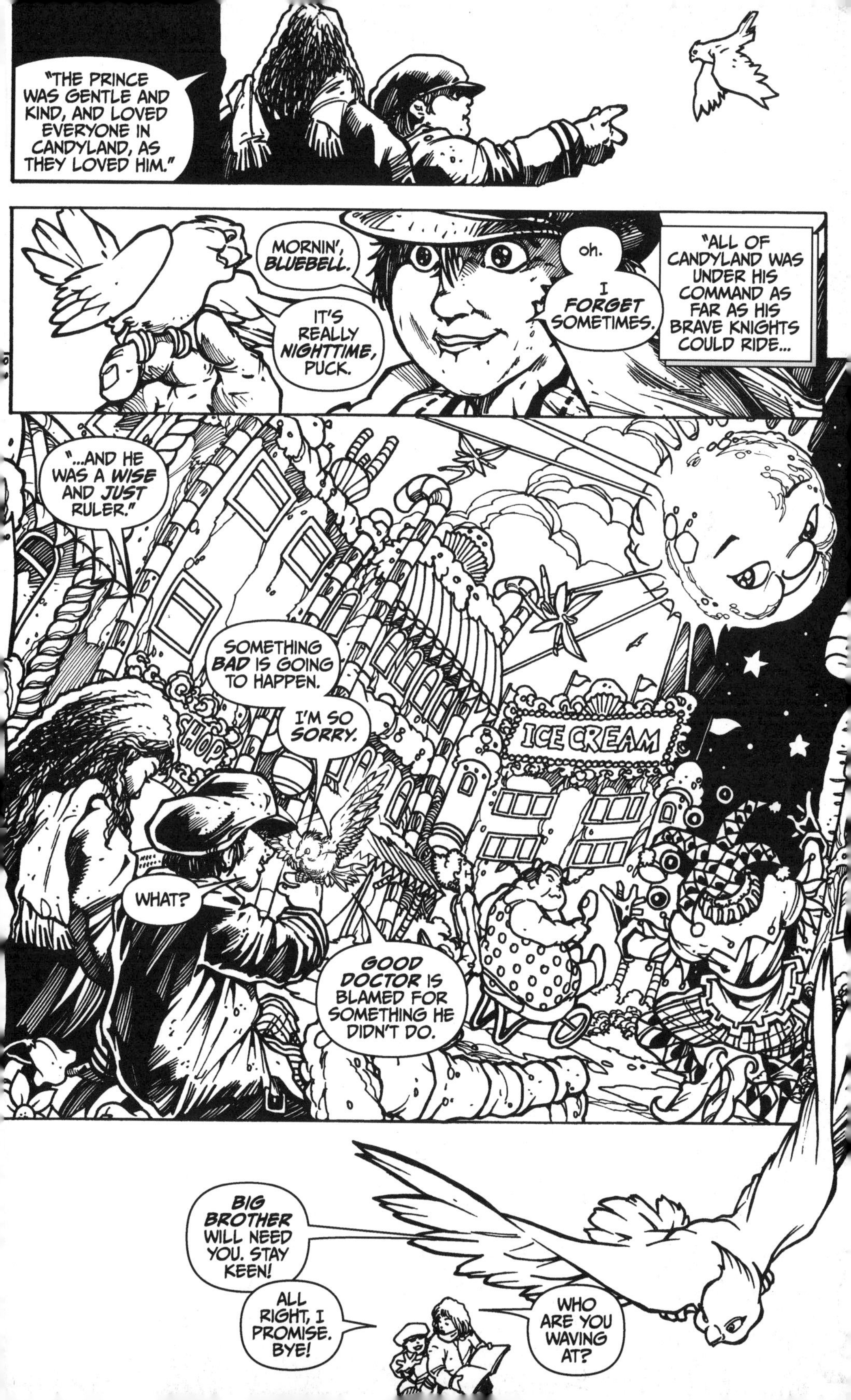
"THE PRINCE WAS GENTLE AND KIND, AND LOVED EVERYONE IN CANDYLAND, AS THEY LOVED HIM."
MORNIN', BLUEBELL.
IT'S REALLY NIGHTTIME, PUCK.
oh.
I FORGET SOMETIMES.
"ALL OF CANDYLAND WAS UNDER HIS COMMAND AS FAR AS HIS BRAVE KNIGHTS COULD RIDE...
"...AND HE WAS A WISE AND JUST RULER."
SOMETHING BAD IS GOING TO HAPPEN.
I'M SO SORRY.
SHOP
ICE CREAM
WHAT?
GOOD DOCTOR IS BLAMED FOR SOMETHING HE DIDN'T DO.
BIG BROTHER WILL NEED YOU. STAY KEEN!
ALL RIGHT, I PROMISE. BYE!
WHO ARE YOU WAVING AT?

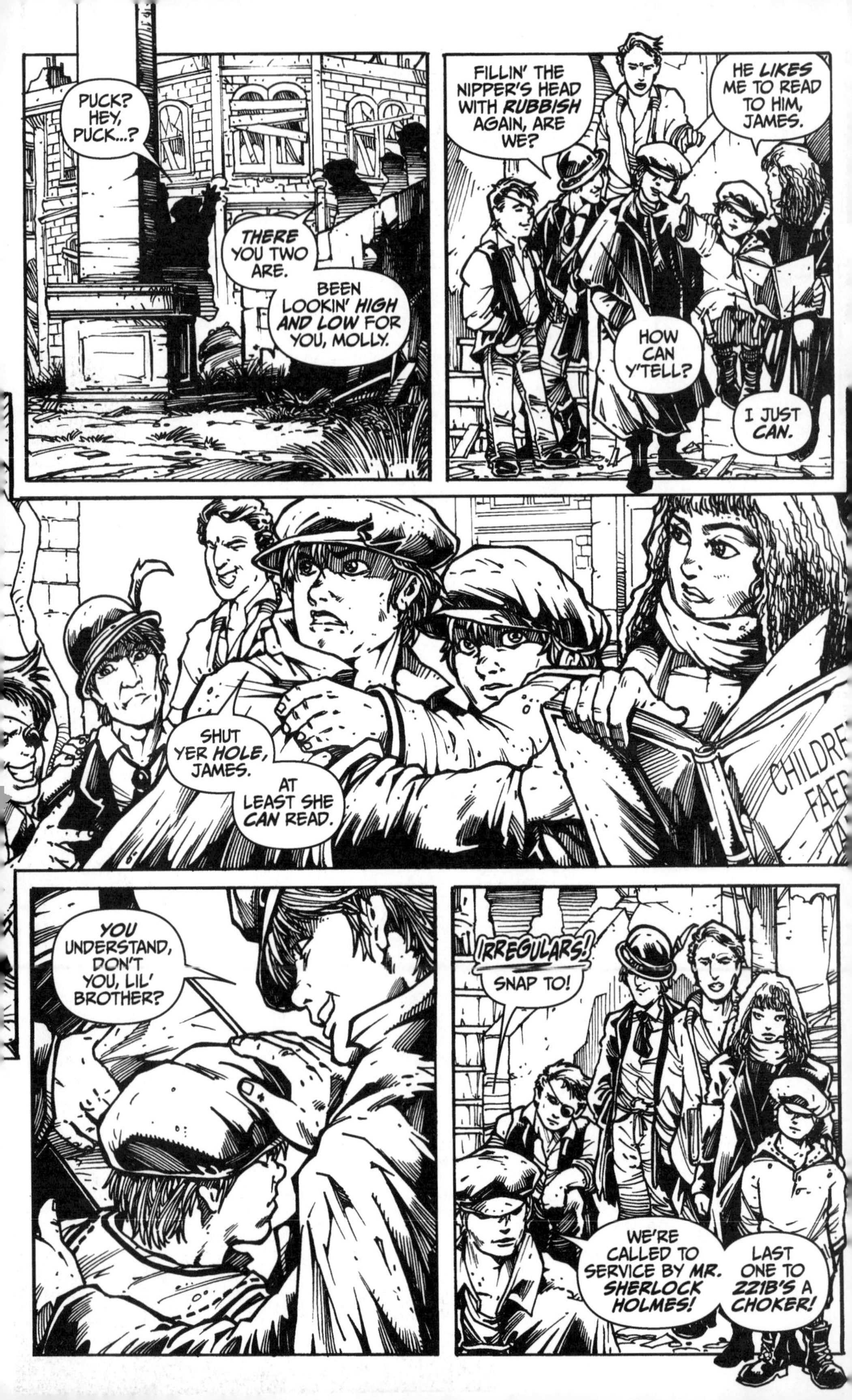
PUCK? HEY, PUCK...?
THERE YOU TWO ARE.
BEEN LOOKIN' HIGH AND LOW FOR YOU, MOLLY.
FILLIN' THE NIPPER'S HEAD WITH RUBBISH AGAIN, ARE WE?
HE LIKES ME TO READ TO HIM, JAMES.
HOW CAN Y'TELL?
I JUST CAN.
SHUT YER HOLE, JAMES.
AT LEAST SHE CAN READ.
YOU UNDERSTAND, DON'T YOU, LIL' BROTHER?
IRREGULARS!
SNAP TO!
WE'RE CALLED TO SERVICE BY MR. SHERLOCK HOLMES!
LAST ONE TO 221B'S A CHOKER!

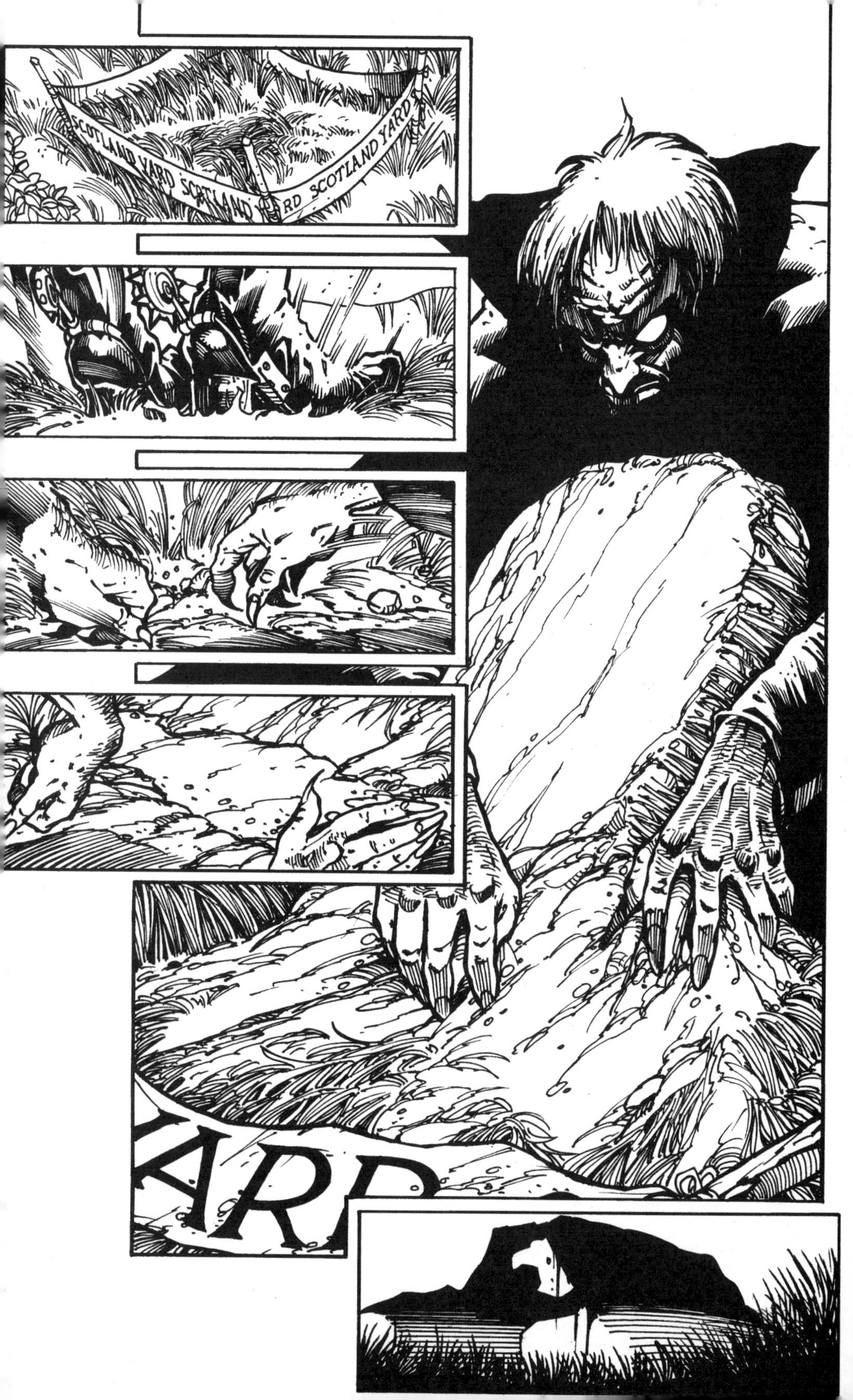
SCOTLAND YARD SCOTLAND YARD SCOTLAND
RD SCOTLAND YARD
ARD

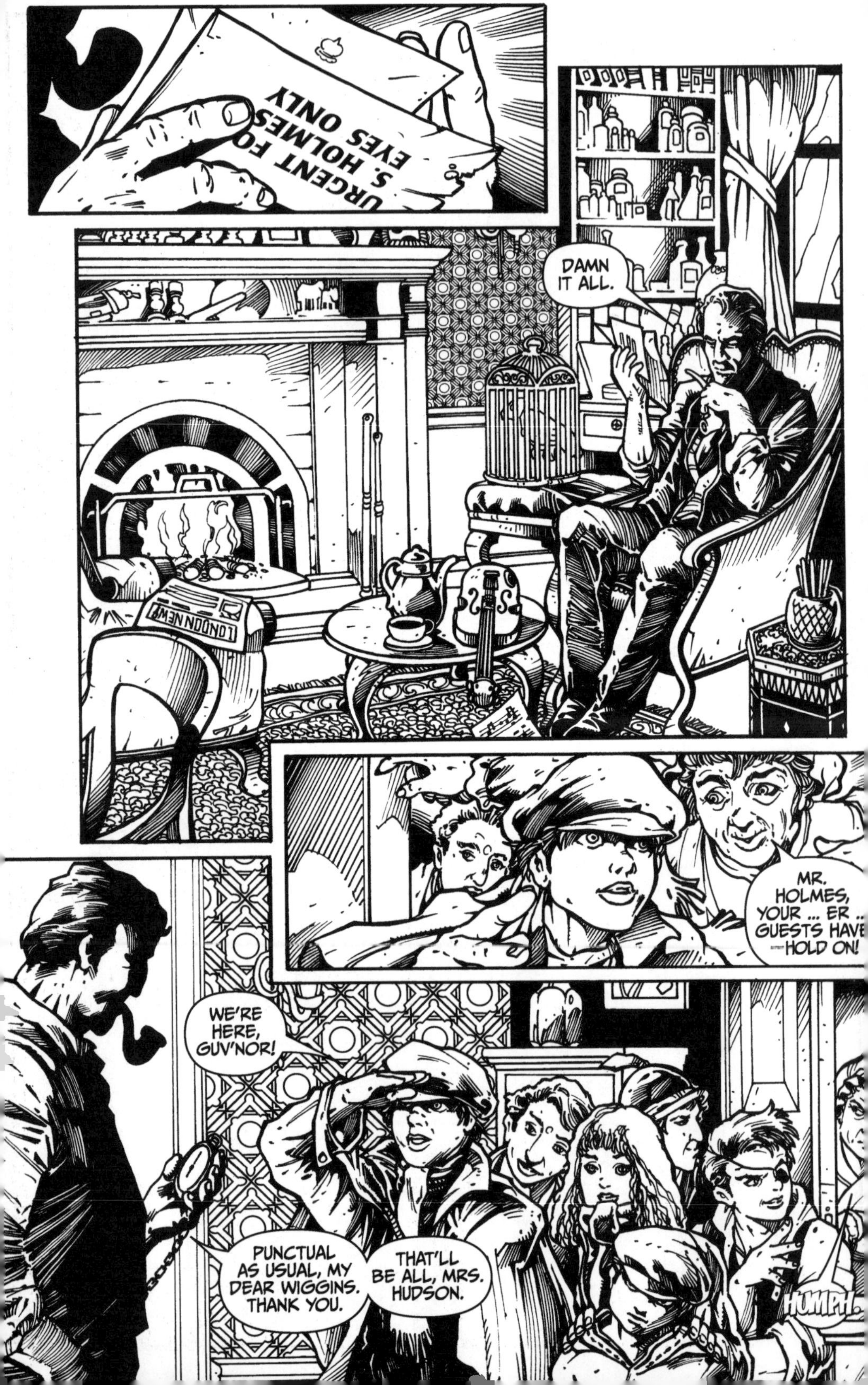
URGENT FO
S. HOLMES
EYES ONLY
DAMN IT ALL.
LONDON NEWS
MR. HOLMES, YOUR ... ER ... GUESTS HAVE
HOLD ON!
WE'RE HERE, GUV'NOR!
PUNCTUAL AS USUAL, MY DEAR WIGGINS. THANK YOU.
THAT'LL BE ALL, MRS. HUDSON.
HUMPH.

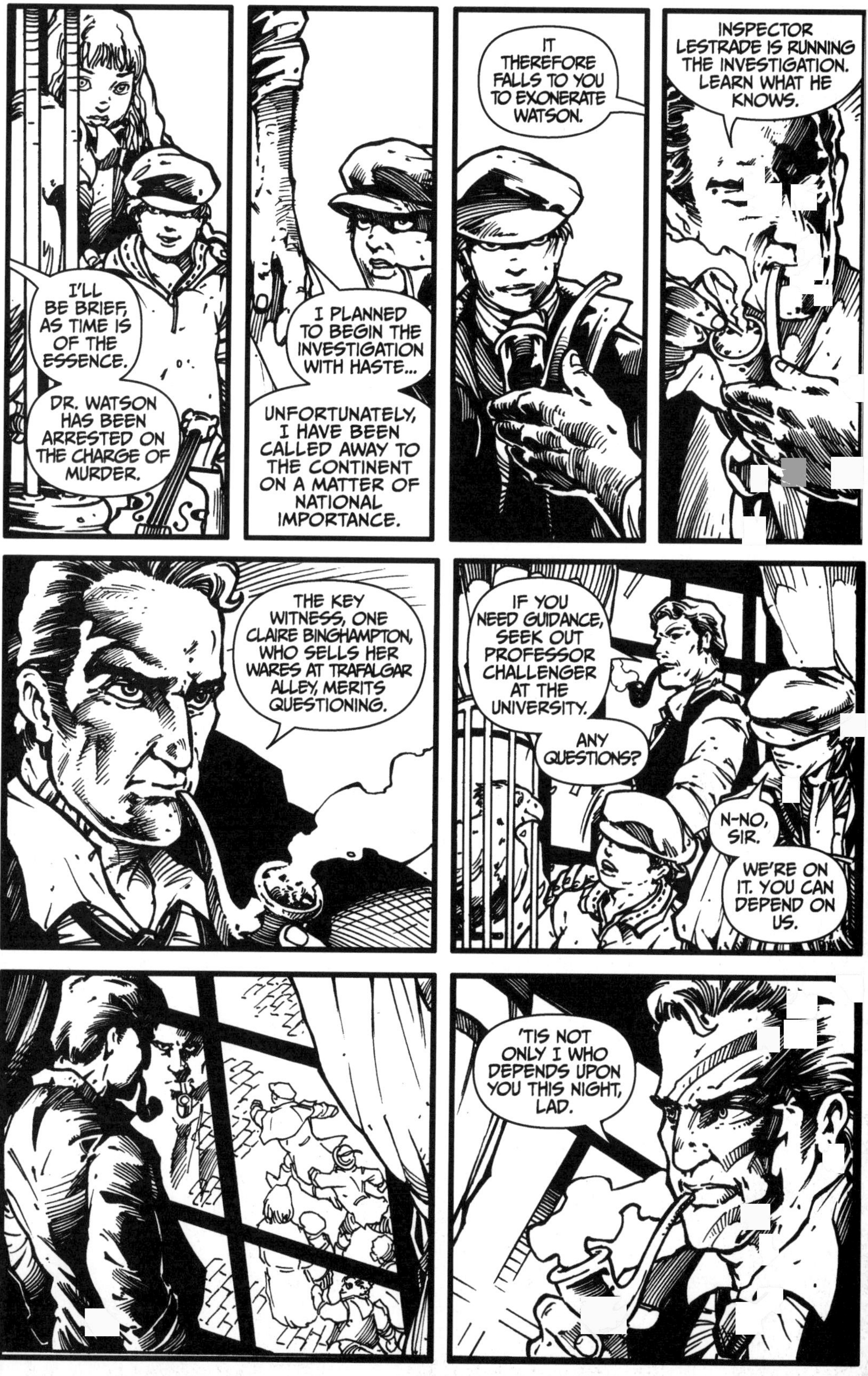
I'LL BE BRIEF, AS TIME IS OF THE ESSENCE.
DR. WATSON HAS BEEN ARRESTED ON THE CHARGE OF MURDER.
I PLANNED TO BEGIN THE INVESTIGATION WITH HASTE...
UNFORTUNATELY, I HAVE BEEN CALLED AWAY TO THE CONTINENT ON A MATTER OF NATIONAL IMPORTANCE.
IT THEREFORE FALLS TO YOU TO EXONERATE WATSON.
INSPECTOR LESTRADE IS RUNNING THE INVESTIGATION. LEARN WHAT HE KNOWS.
THE KEY WITNESS, ONE CLAIRE BINGHAMPTON, WHO SELLS HER WARES AT TRAFALGAR ALLEY, MERITS QUESTIONING.
IF YOU NEED GUIDANCE, SEEK OUT PROFESSOR CHALLENGER AT THE UNIVERSITY.
ANY QUESTIONS?
N-NO, SIR.
WE'RE ON IT. YOU CAN DEPEND ON US.
'TIS NOT ONLY I WHO DEPENDS UPON YOU THIS NIGHT, LAD.

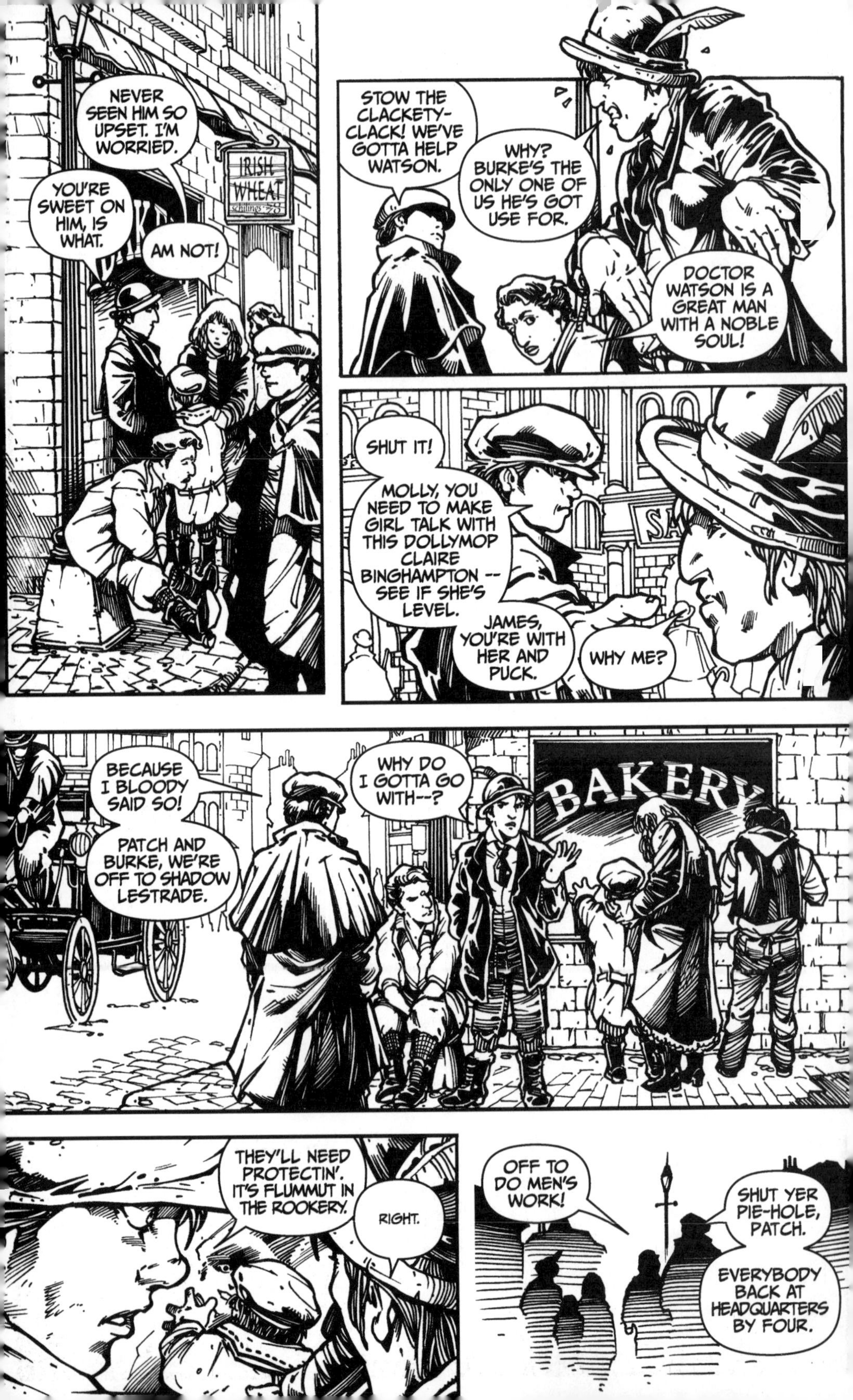
NEVER SEEN HIM SO UPSET. I'M WORRIED.
YOU'RE SWEET ON HIM, IS WHAT.
AM NOT!
IRISH WHEAT
STOW THE CLACKETY-CLACK! WE'VE GOTTA HELP WATSON.
WHY? BURKE'S THE ONLY ONE OF US HE'S GOT USE FOR.
DOCTOR WATSON IS A GREAT MAN WITH A NOBLE SOUL!
SHUT IT!
MOLLY, YOU NEED TO MAKE GIRL TALK WITH THIS DOLLYMOP CLAIRE BINGHAMPTON -- SEE IF SHE'S LEVEL.
JAMES, YOU'RE WITH HER AND PUCK.
WHY ME?
BECAUSE I BLOODY SAID SO!
PATCH AND BURKE, WE'RE OFF TO SHADOW LESTRADE.
WHY DO I GOTTA GO WITH--?
BAKERY
THEY'LL NEED PROTECTIN'. IT'S FLUMMUT IN THE ROOKERY.
RIGHT.
OFF TO DO MEN'S WORK!
SHUT YER PIE-HOLE, PATCH.
EVERYBODY BACK AT HEADQUARTERS BY FOUR.

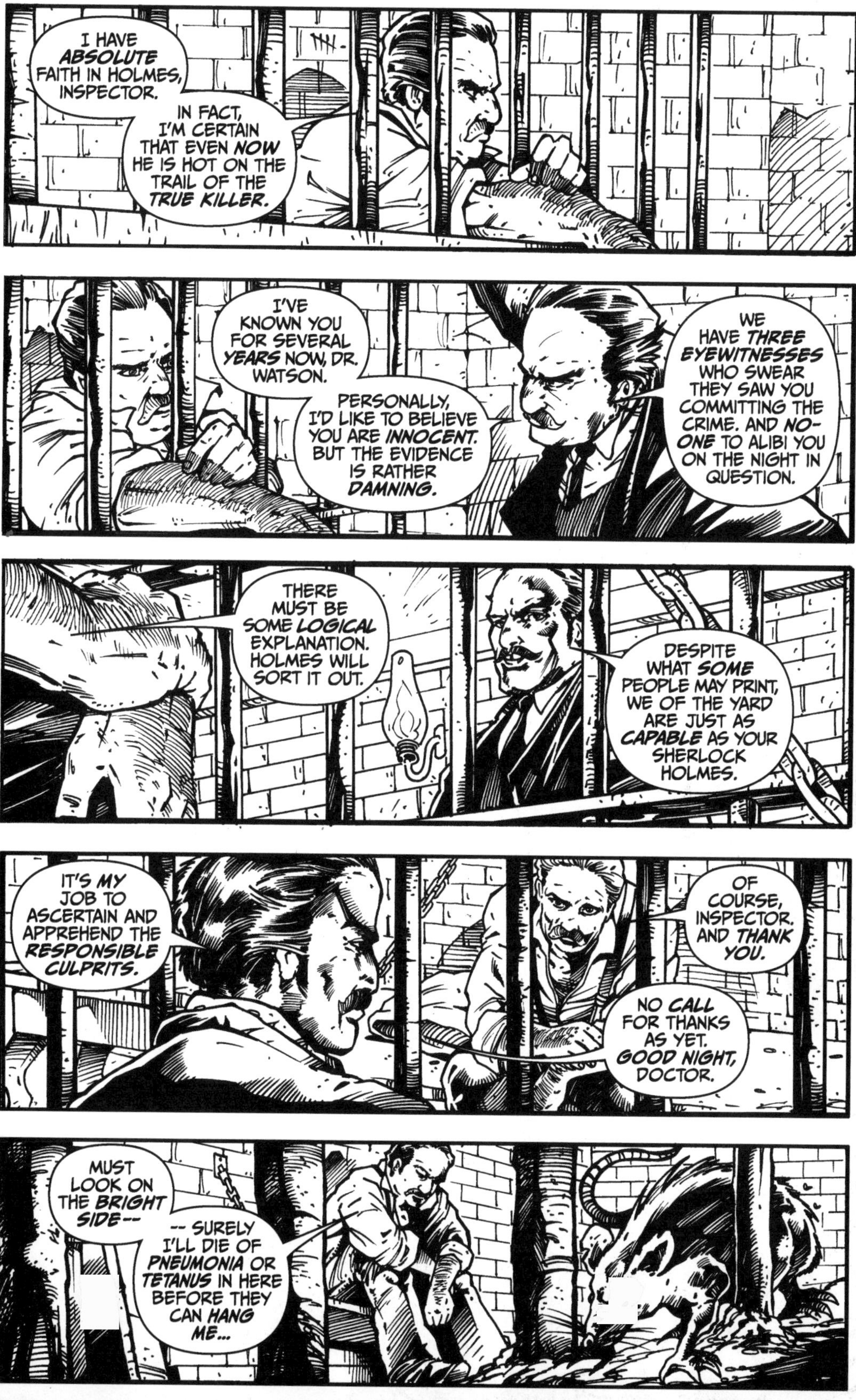
I HAVE ABSOLUTE FAITH IN HOLMES, INSPECTOR.
IN FACT, I'M CERTAIN THAT EVEN NOW HE IS HOT ON THE TRAIL OF THE TRUE KILLER.
I'VE KNOWN YOU FOR SEVERAL YEARS NOW, DR. WATSON.
PERSONALLY, I'D LIKE TO BELIEVE YOU ARE INNOCENT. BUT THE EVIDENCE IS RATHER DAMNING.
WE HAVE THREE EYEWITNESSES WHO SWEAR THEY SAW YOU COMMITTING THE CRIME. AND NO-ONE TO ALIBI YOU ON THE NIGHT IN QUESTION.
THERE MUST BE SOME LOGICAL EXPLANATION. HOLMES WILL SORT IT OUT.
DESPITE WHAT SOME PEOPLE MAY PRINT, WE OF THE YARD ARE JUST AS CAPABLE AS YOUR SHERLOCK HOLMES.
IT'S MY JOB TO ASCERTAIN AND APPREHEND THE RESPONSIBLE CULPRITS.
OF COURSE, INSPECTOR. AND THANK YOU.
NO CALL FOR THANKS AS YET. GOOD NIGHT, DOCTOR.
MUST LOOK ON THE BRIGHT SIDE--
-- SURELY I'LL DIE OF PNEUMONIA OR TETANUS IN HERE BEFORE THEY CAN HANG ME...

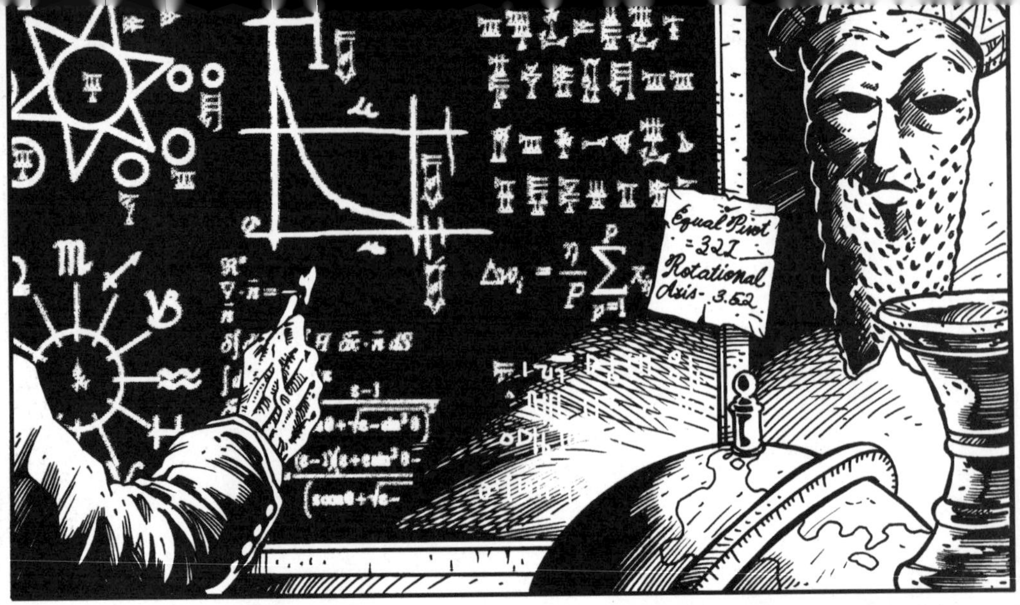
Equal Pivot = 327
Rotational Axis - 3.52

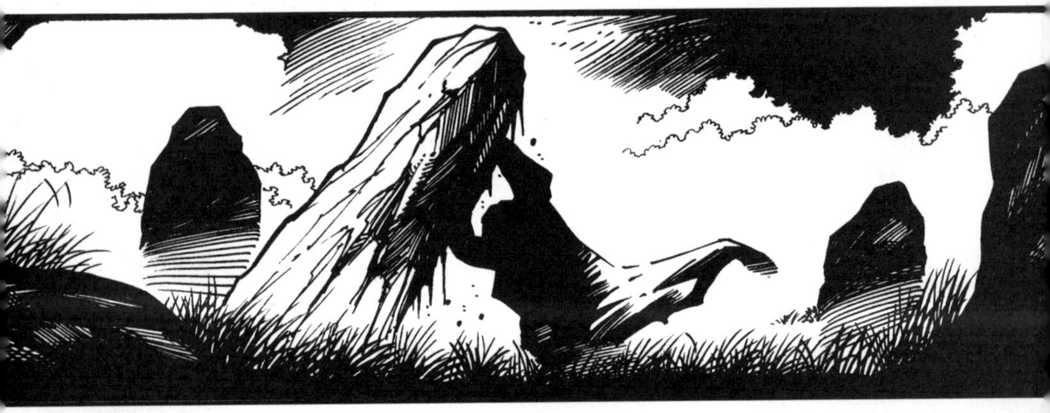

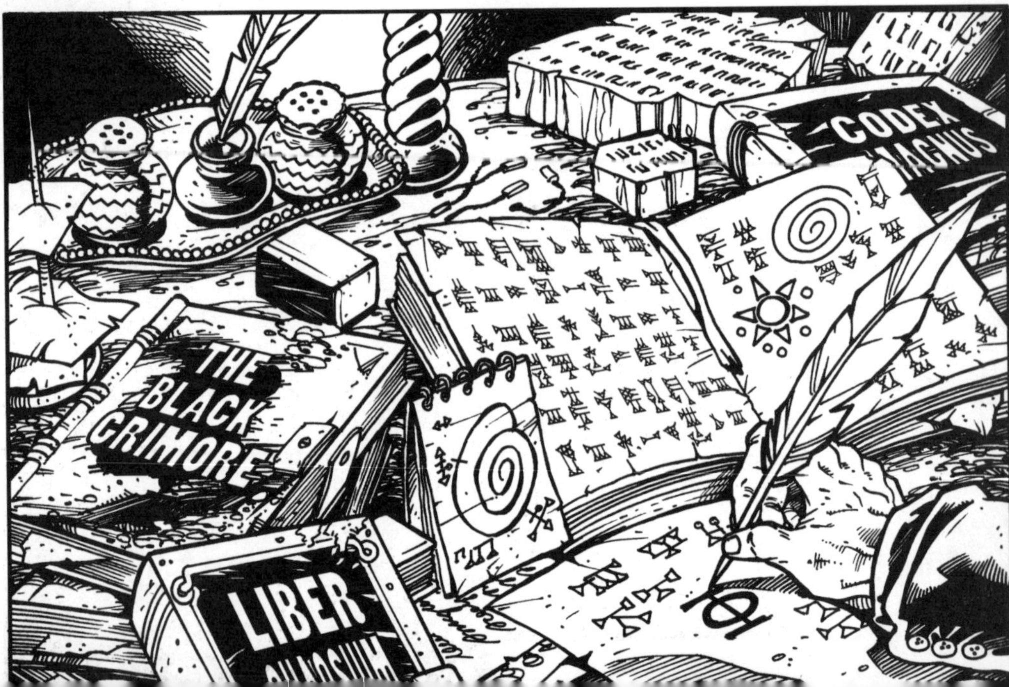
CODEX
THE BLACK GRIMORE
LIBER

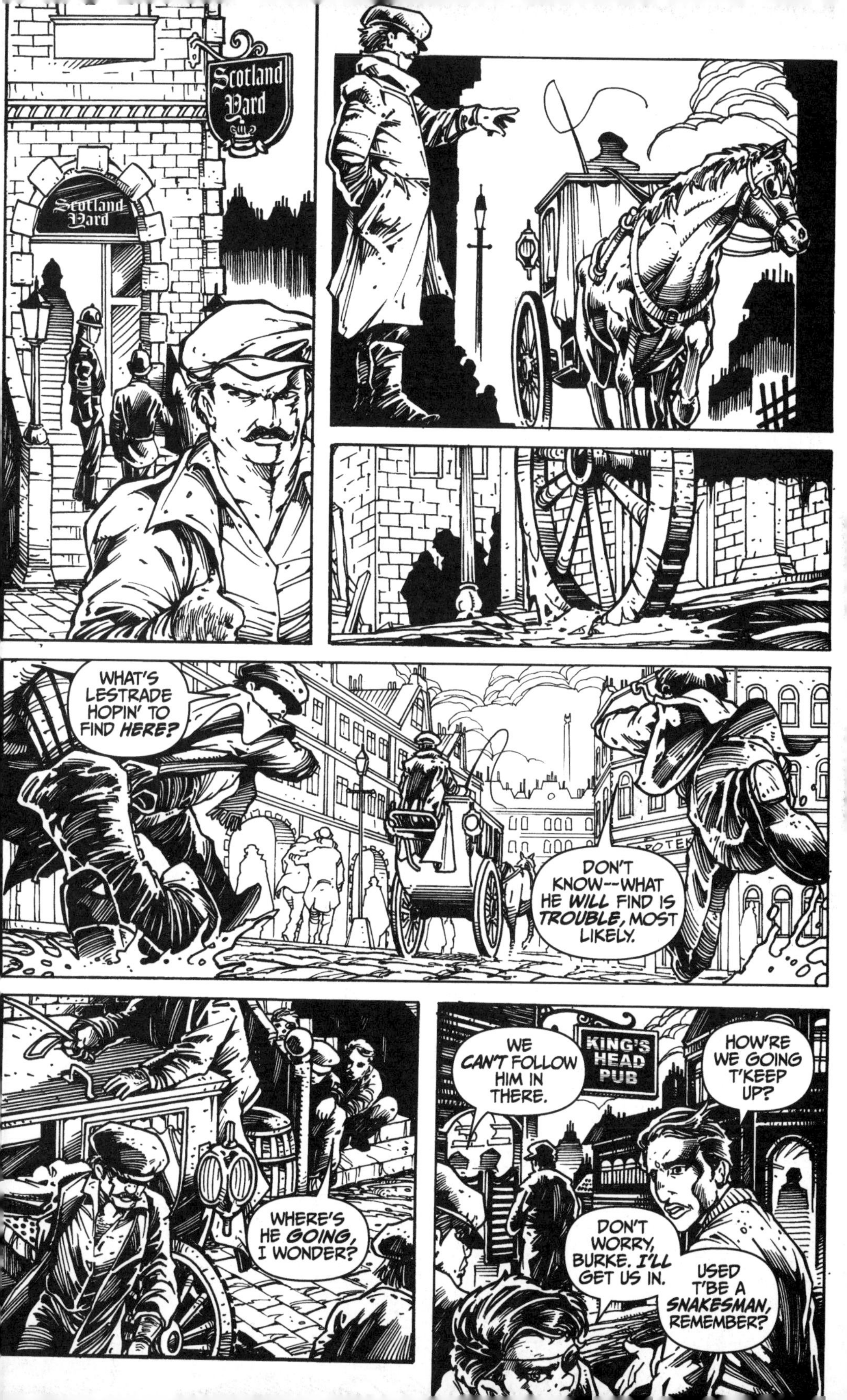

Scotland Yard
Scotland Yard
WHAT'S LESTRADE HOPIN' TO FIND HERE?
DON'T KNOW--WHAT HE WILL FIND IS TROUBLE, MOST LIKELY.
WHERE'S HE GOING, I WONDER?
WE CAN'T FOLLOW HIM IN THERE.
KING'S HEAD PUB
HOW'RE WE GOING T'KEEP UP?
DON'T WORRY, BURKE. I'LL GET US IN.
USED T'BE A SNAKESMAN, REMEMBER?

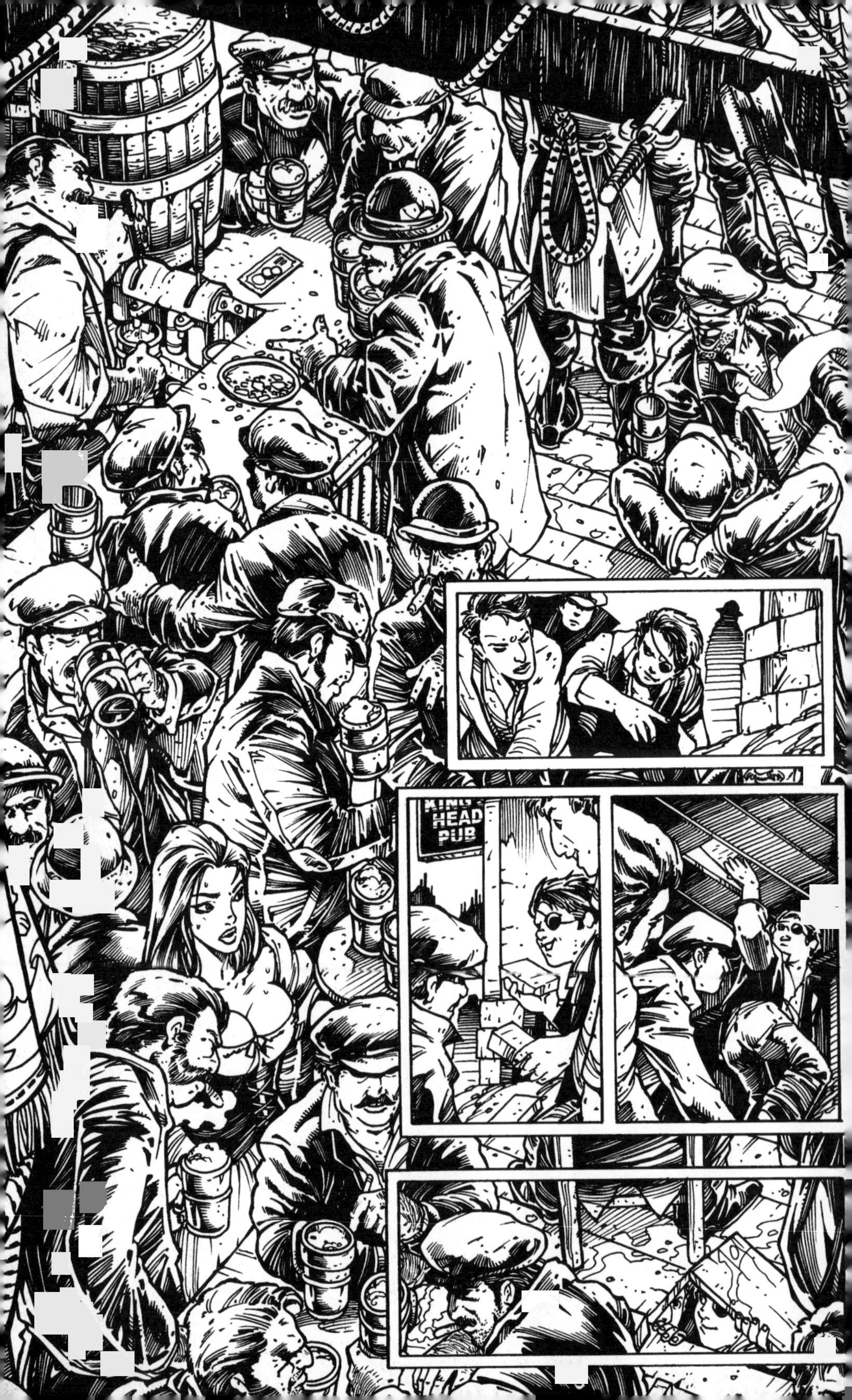
KING'S HEAD PUB

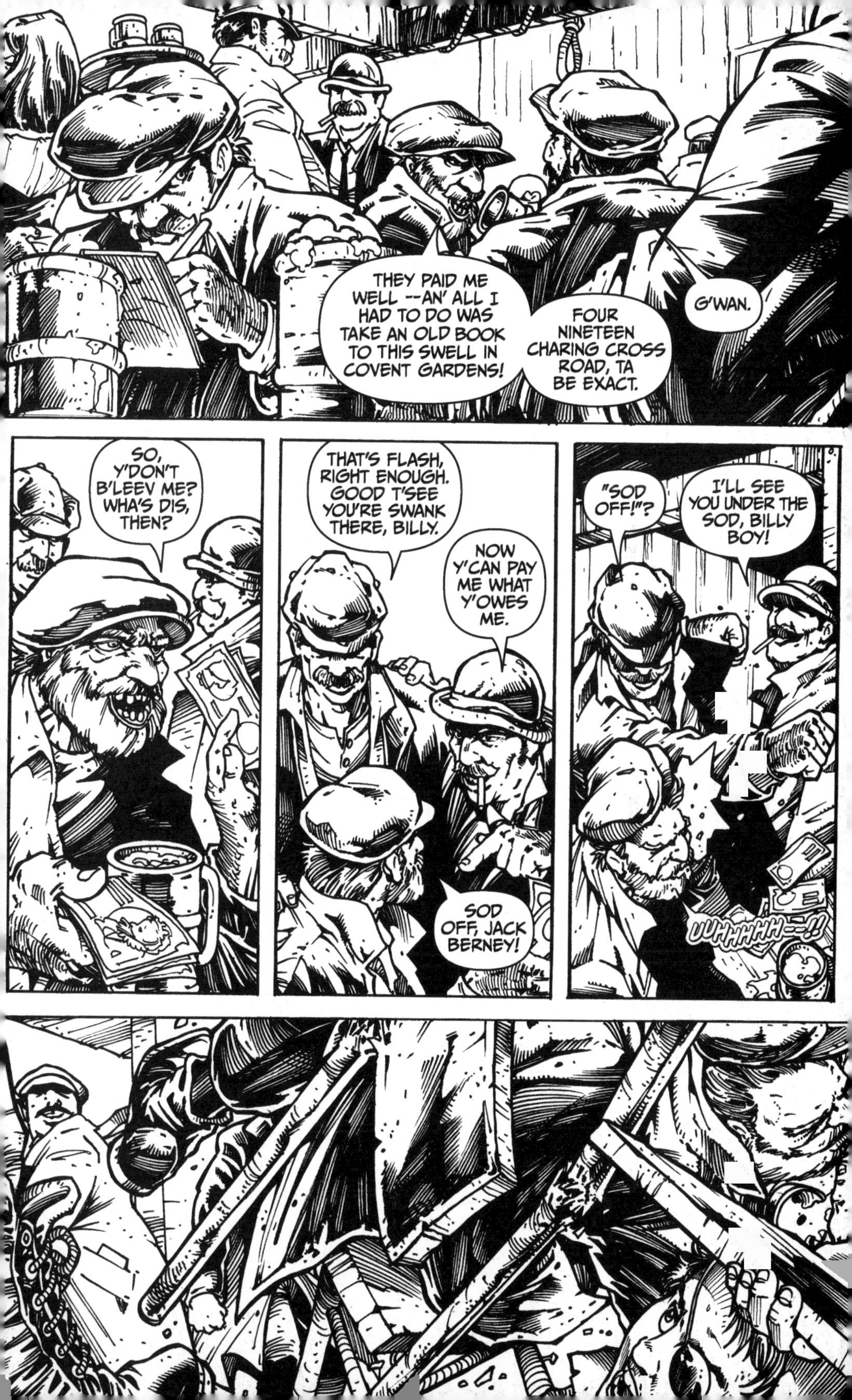
THEY PAID ME WELL --AN' ALL I HAD TO DO WAS TAKE AN OLD BOOK TO THIS SWELL IN COVENT GARDENS!
FOUR NINETEEN CHARING CROSS ROAD, TA BE EXACT.
G'WAN.
SO, Y'DON'T B'LEEV ME? WHA'S DIS, THEN?
THAT'S FLASH, RIGHT ENOUGH. GOOD T'SEE YOU'RE SWANK THERE, BILLY.
NOW Y'CAN PAY ME WHAT Y'OWES ME.
SOD OFF, JACK BERNEY!
"SOD OFF!"?
I'LL SEE YOU UNDER THE SOD, BILLY BOY!
UUHHHHH--!!

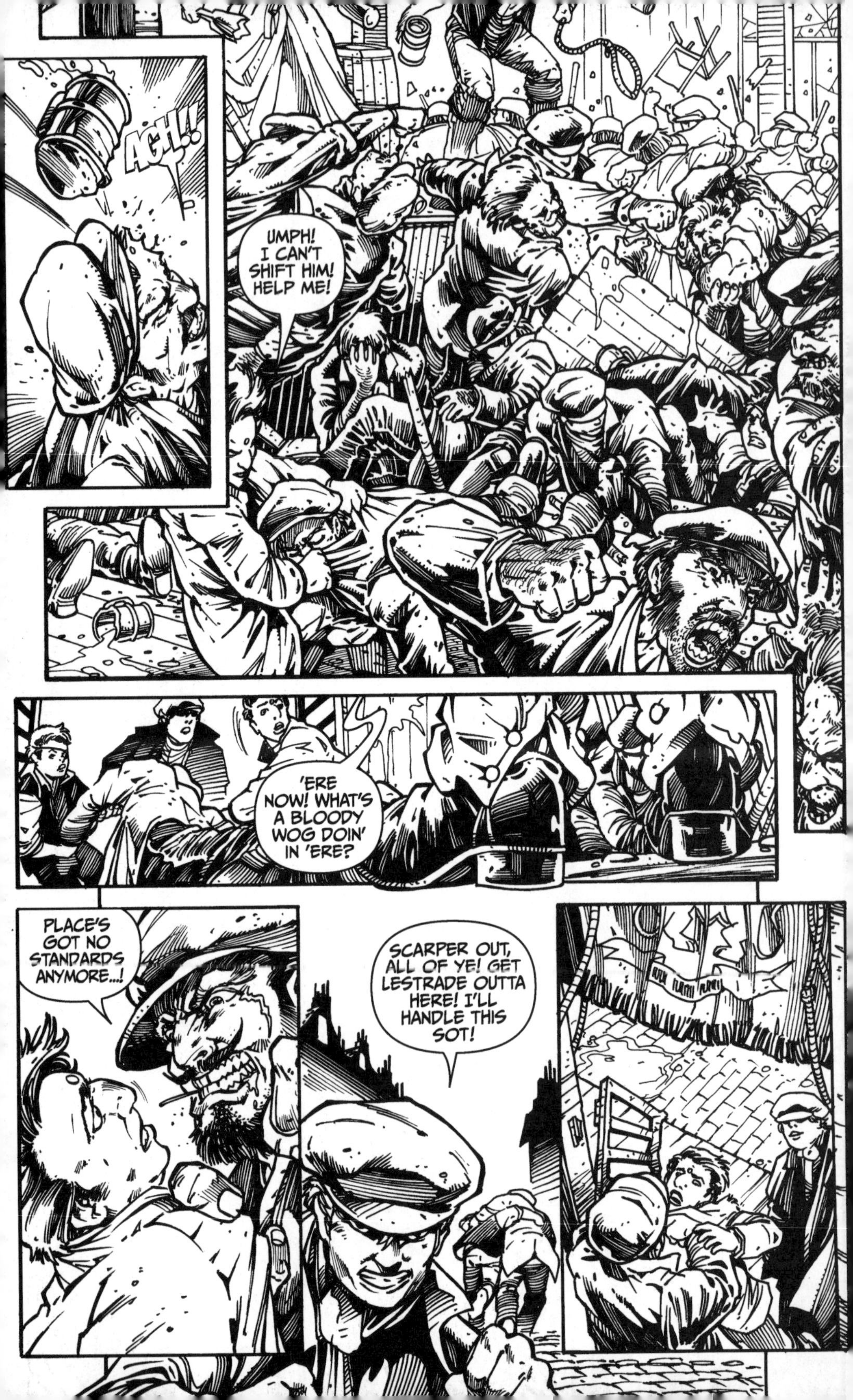
ACH!!
UMPH! I CAN'T SHIFT HIM! HELP ME!
'ERE NOW! WHAT'S A BLOODY WOG DOIN' IN 'ERE?
PLACE'S GOT NO STANDARDS ANYMORE...!
SCARPER OUT, ALL OF YE! GET LESTRADE OUTTA HERE! I'LL HANDLE THIS SOT!

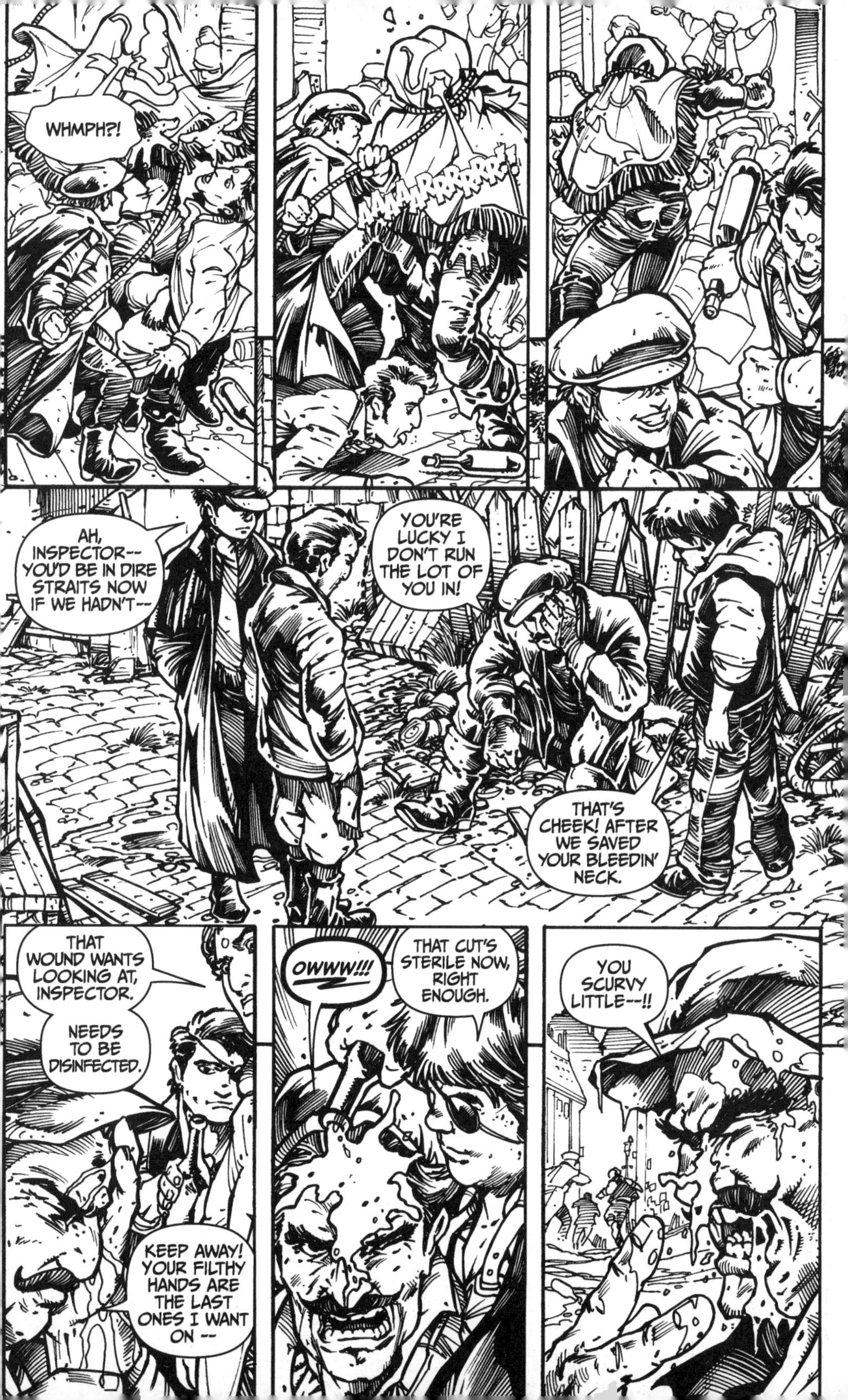
WHMPH?!
AAAAARRRRRRR?!
AH, INSPECTOR-- YOU'D BE IN DIRE STRAITS NOW IF WE HADN'T--
YOU'RE LUCKY I DON'T RUN THE LOT OF YOU IN!
THAT'S CHEEK! AFTER WE SAVED YOUR BLEEDIN' NECK.
THAT WOUND WANTS LOOKING AT, INSPECTOR.
NEEDS TO BE DISINFECTED.
KEEP AWAY! YOUR FILTHY HANDS ARE THE LAST ONES I WANT ON --
OWWW!!!
THAT CUT'S STERILE NOW, RIGHT ENOUGH.
YOU SCURVY LITTLE--!!

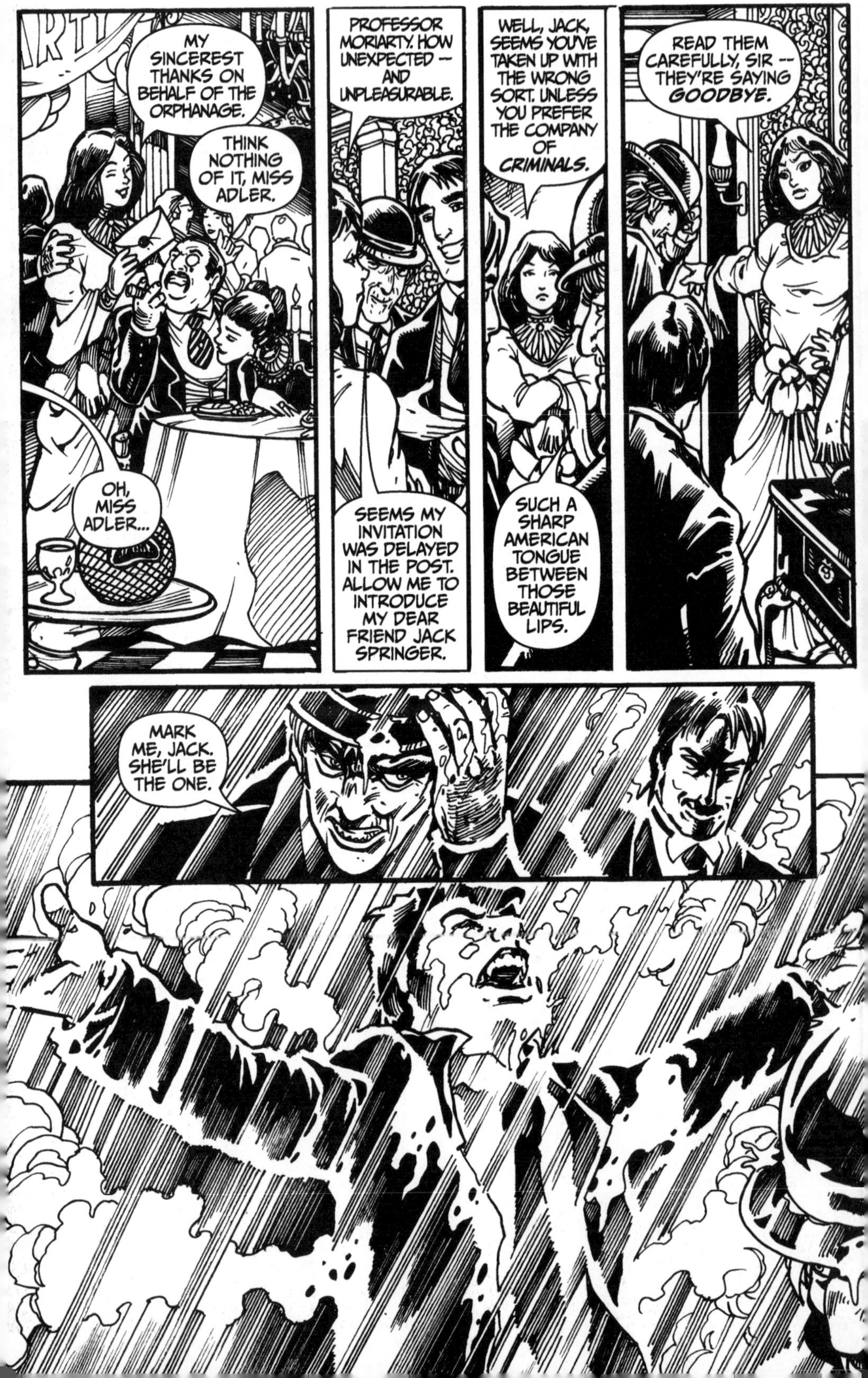
MY SINCEREST THANKS ON BEHALF OF THE ORPHANAGE.
THINK NOTHING OF IT, MISS ADLER.
OH, MISS ADLER...
PROFESSOR MORIARTY. HOW UNEXPECTED -- AND UNPLEASURABLE.
SEEMS MY INVITATION WAS DELAYED IN THE POST. ALLOW ME TO INTRODUCE MY DEAR FRIEND JACK SPRINGER.
WELL, JACK, SEEMS YOU'VE TAKEN UP WITH THE WRONG SORT. UNLESS YOU PREFER THE COMPANY OF CRIMINALS.
SUCH A SHARP AMERICAN TONGUE BETWEEN THOSE BEAUTIFUL LIPS.
READ THEM CAREFULLY, SIR -- THEY'RE SAYING GOODBYE.
MARK ME, JACK. SHE'LL BE THE ONE.

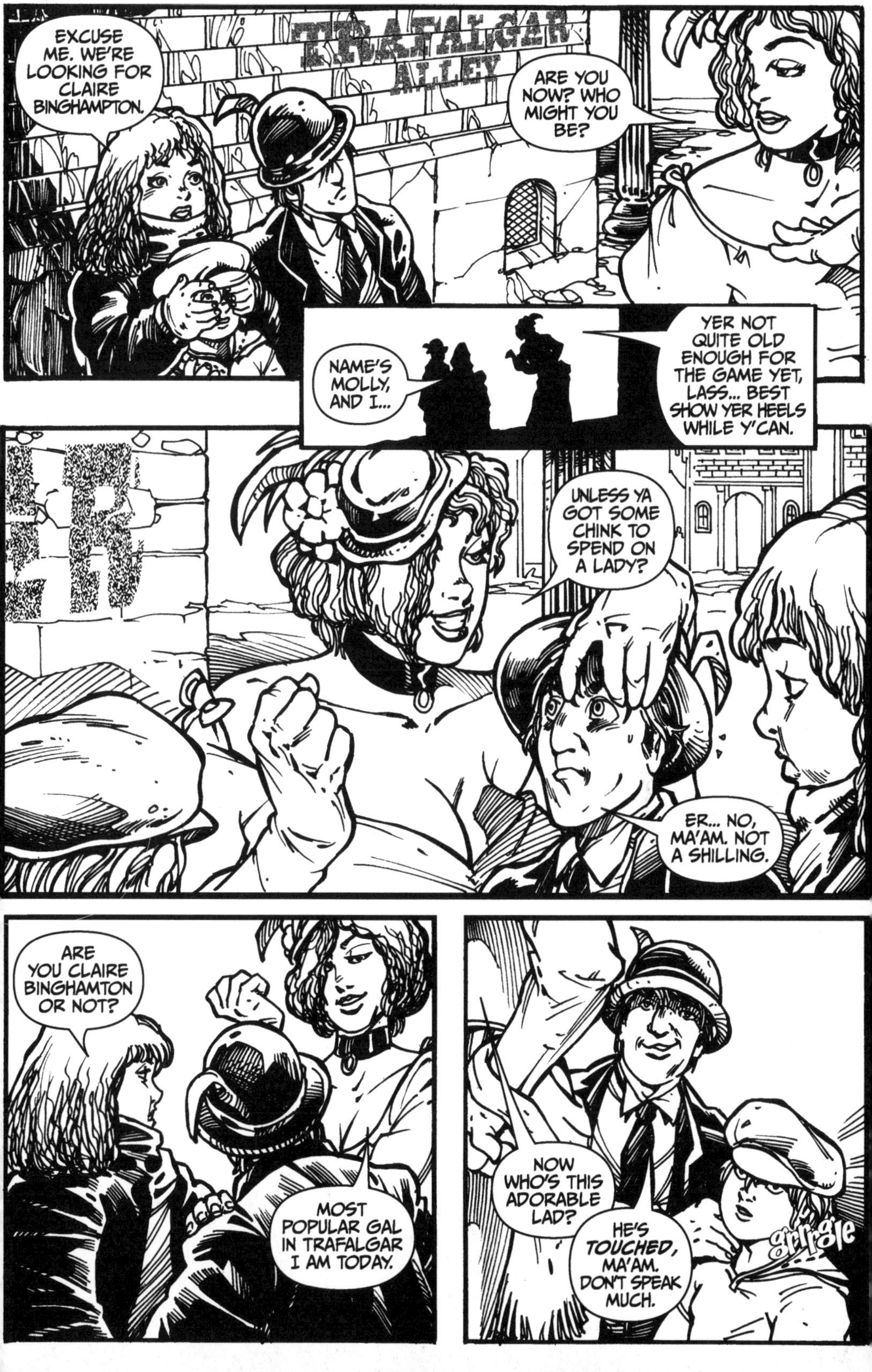
TRAFALGAR ALLEY
EXCUSE ME. WE'RE LOOKING FOR CLAIRE BINGHAMPTON.
ARE YOU NOW? WHO MIGHT YOU BE?
NAME'S MOLLY, AND I...
YER NOT QUITE OLD ENOUGH FOR THE GAME YET, LASS... BEST SHOW YER HEELS WHILE Y'CAN.
UNLESS YA GOT SOME CHINK TO SPEND ON A LADY?
ER... NO, MA'AM. NOT A SHILLING.
ARE YOU CLAIRE BINGHAMTON OR NOT?
MOST POPULAR GAL IN TRAFALGAR I AM TODAY.
NOW WHO'S THIS ADORABLE LAD?
HE'S *TOUCHED*, MA'AM. DON'T SPEAK MUCH.
grrrgle

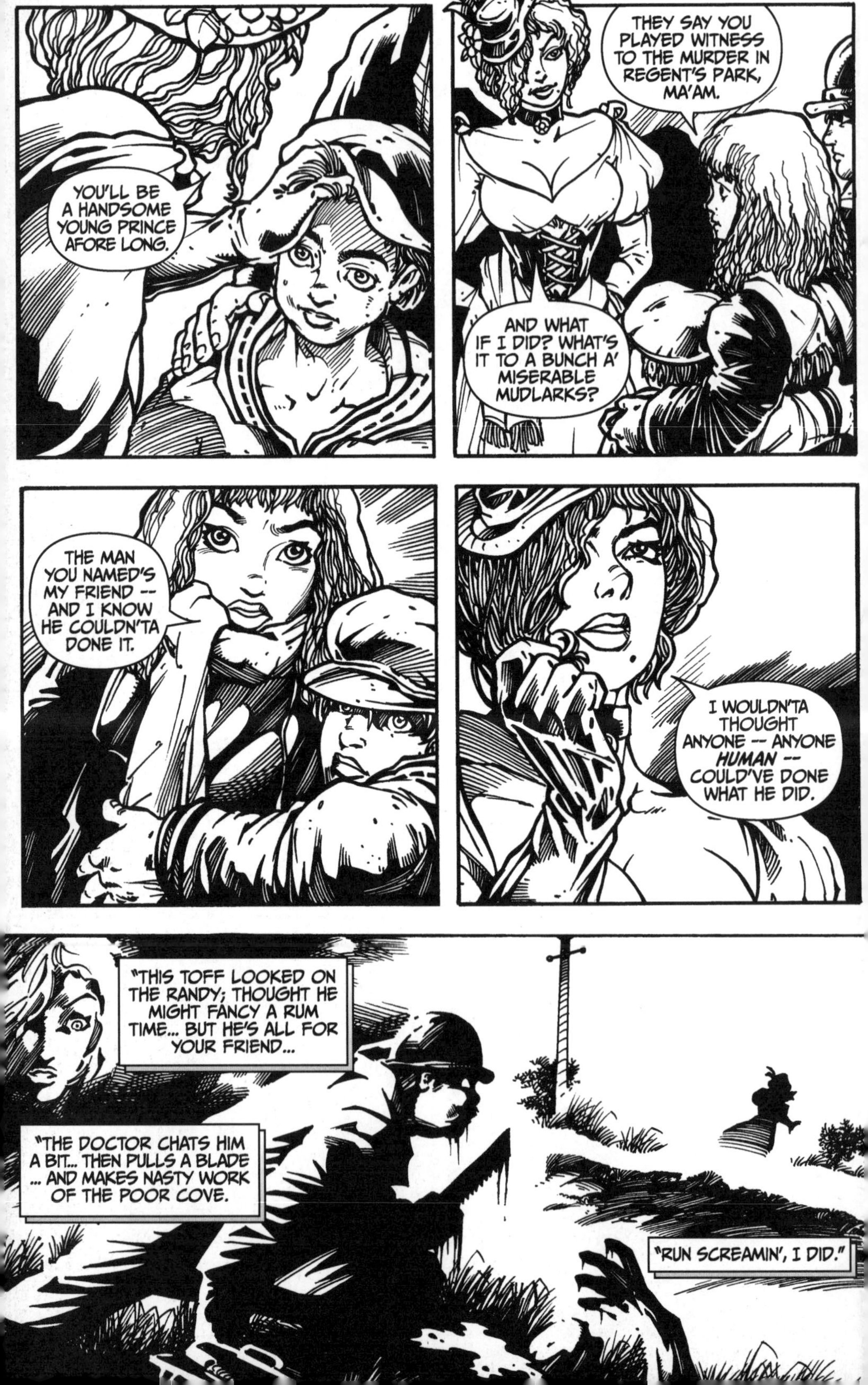
YOU'LL BE A HANDSOME YOUNG PRINCE AFORE LONG.
THEY SAY YOU PLAYED WITNESS TO THE MURDER IN REGENT'S PARK, MA'AM.
AND WHAT IF I DID? WHAT'S IT TO A BUNCH A' MISERABLE MUDLARKS?
THE MAN YOU NAMED'S MY FRIEND -- AND I KNOW HE COULDN'TA DONE IT.
I WOULDN'TA THOUGHT ANYONE -- ANYONE *HUMAN* -- COULD'VE DONE WHAT HE DID.
"THIS TOFF LOOKED ON THE RANDY; THOUGHT HE MIGHT FANCY A RUM TIME... BUT HE'S ALL FOR YOUR FRIEND...
"THE DOCTOR CHATS HIM A BIT... THEN PULLS A BLADE ... AND MAKES NASTY WORK OF THE POOR COVE.
"RUN SCREAMIN', I DID."

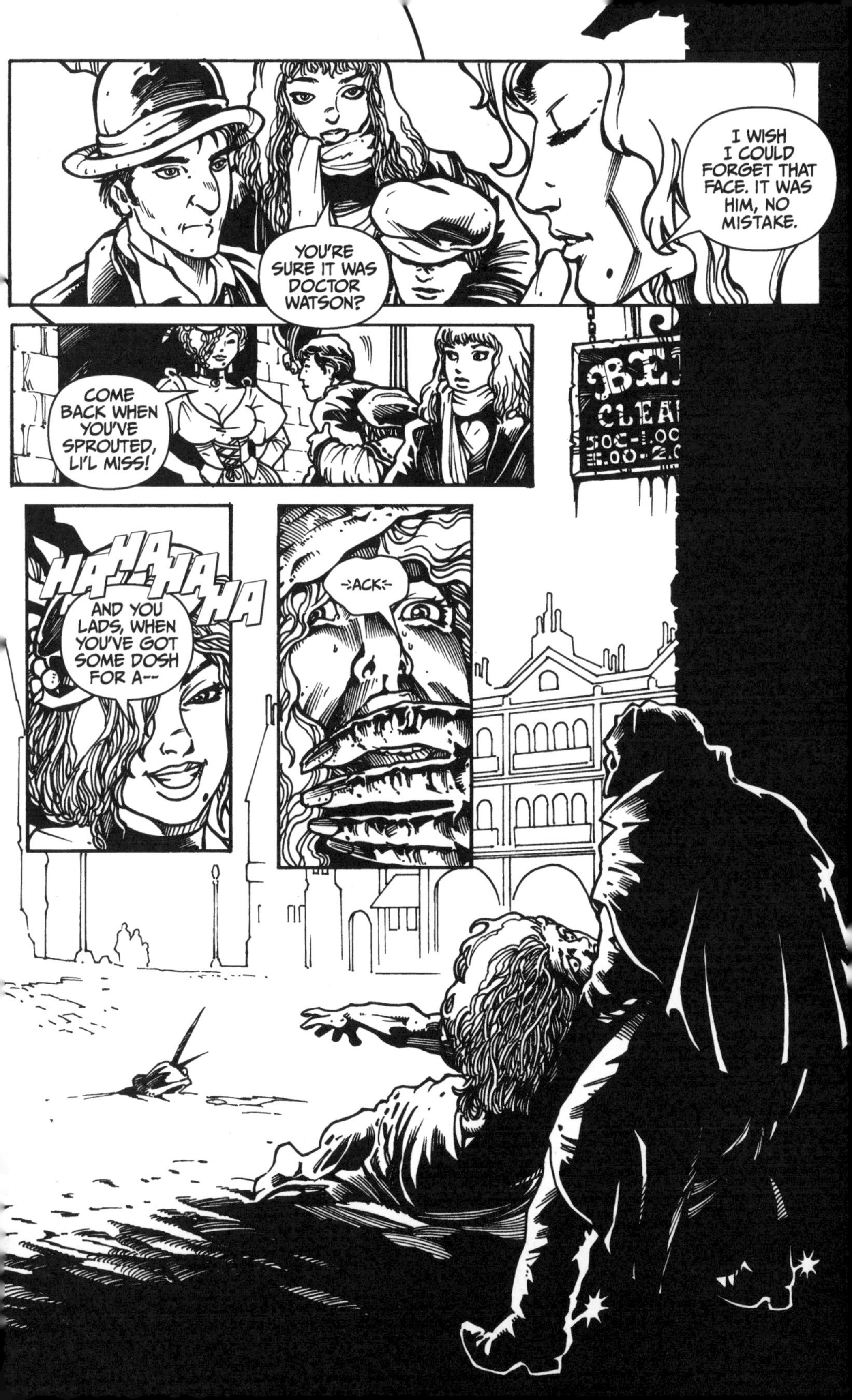
YOU'RE SURE IT WAS DOCTOR WATSON?
I WISH I COULD FORGET THAT FACE. IT WAS HIM, NO MISTAKE.
COME BACK WHEN YOU'VE SPROUTED, LI'L MISS!
HAHAHAHAHA
AND YOU LADS, WHEN YOU'VE GOT SOME DOSH FOR A--
-:ACK:-

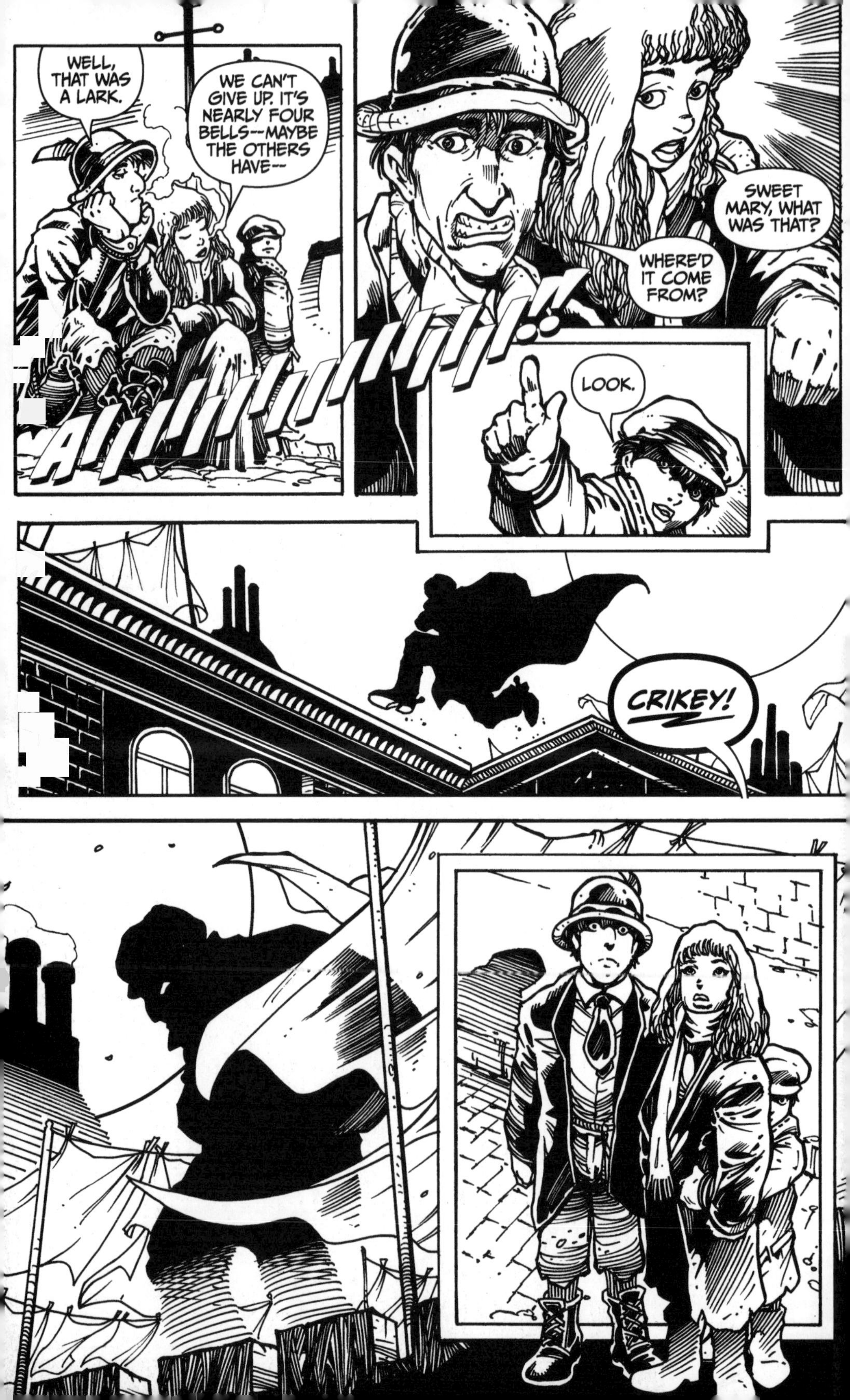

WELL, THAT WAS A LARK.
WE CAN'T GIVE UP. IT'S NEARLY FOUR BELLS--MAYBE THE OTHERS HAVE--
AIIIIIIIIIIIIIIIII!!
SWEET MARY, WHAT WAS THAT?
WHERE'D IT COME FROM?
LOOK.
CRIKEY!

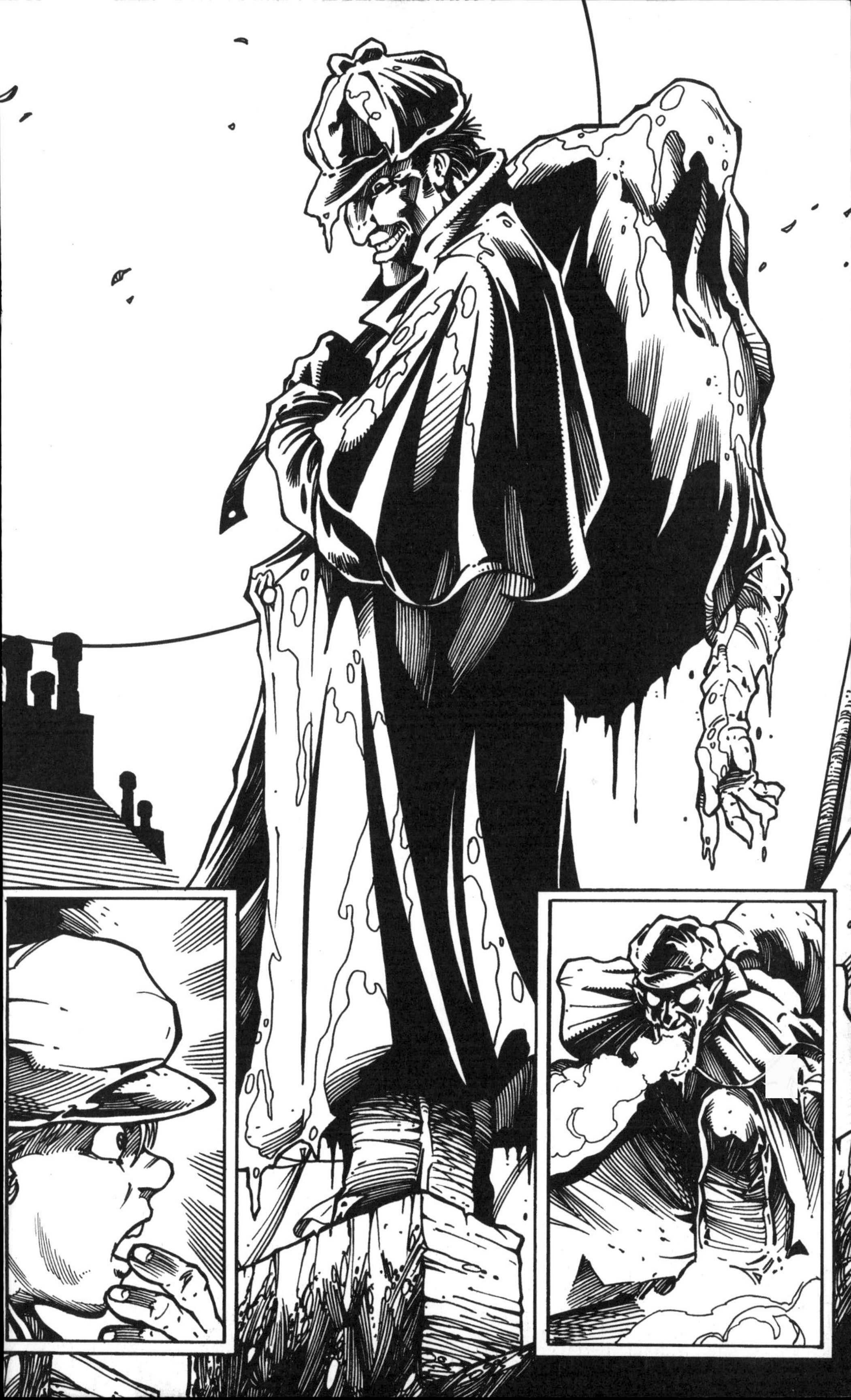

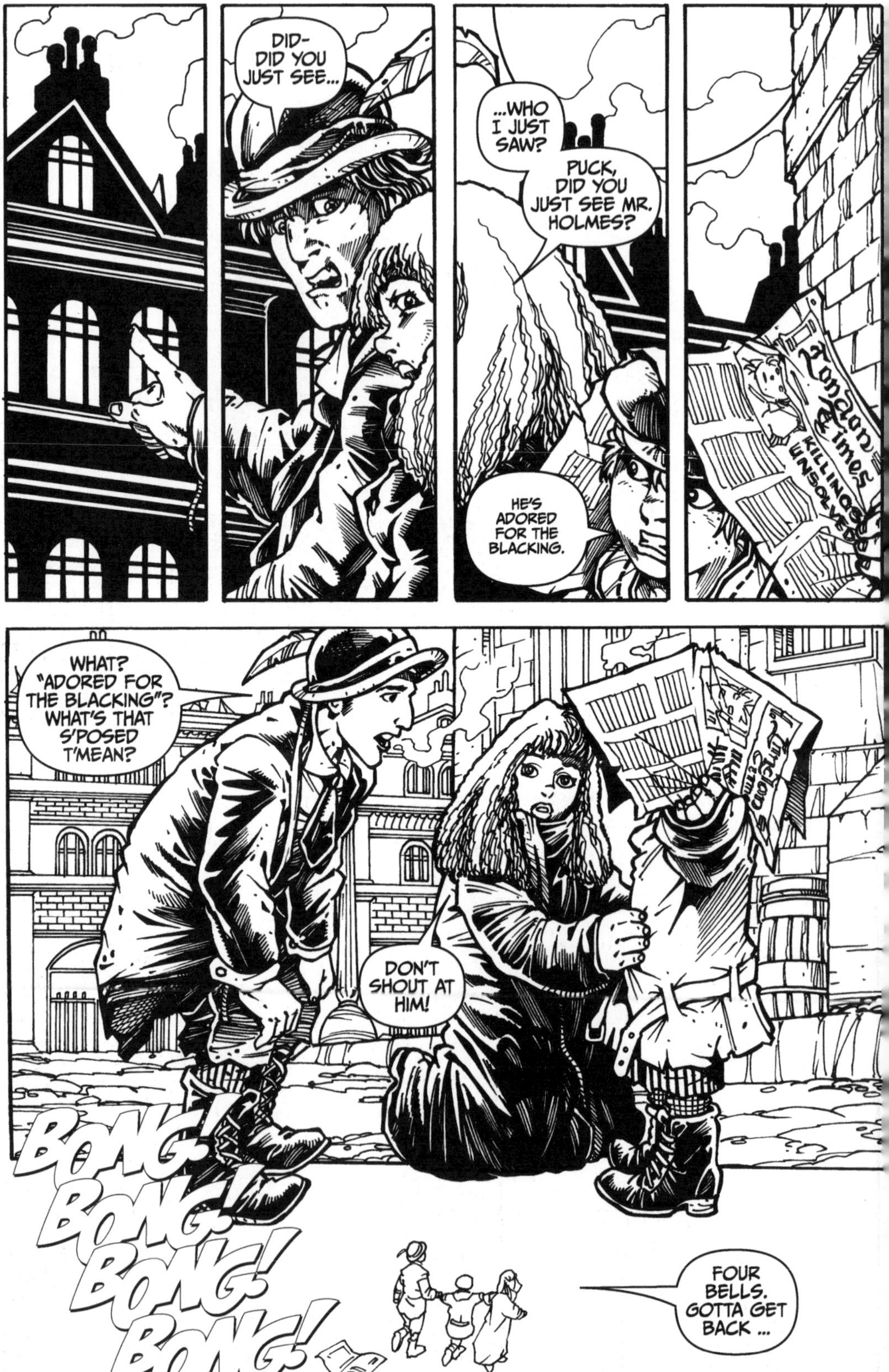
DID-
DID YOU JUST SEE...
...WHO I JUST SAW?
PUCK, DID YOU JUST SEE MR. HOLMES?
HE'S ADORED FOR THE BLACKING.
London Times
KILLINGS UNSOLVED
WHAT? "ADORED FOR THE BLACKING"? WHAT'S THAT S'POSED T'MEAN?
DON'T SHOUT AT HIM!
BONG! BONG! BONG! BONG!
FOUR BELLS. GOTTA GET BACK ...

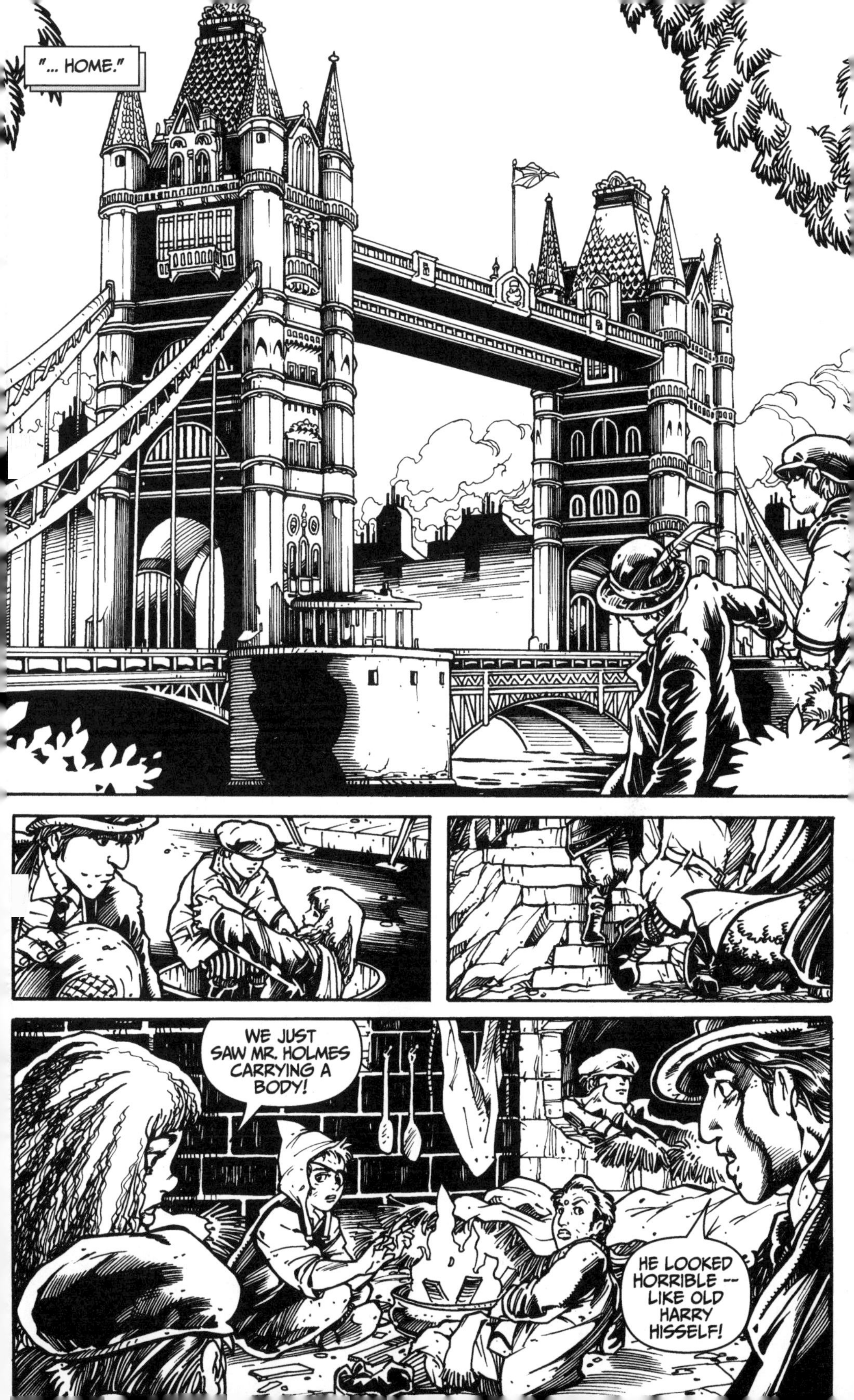
"... HOME."
WE JUST SAW MR. HOLMES CARRYING A BODY!
HE LOOKED HORRIBLE -- LIKE OLD HARRY HISSELF!

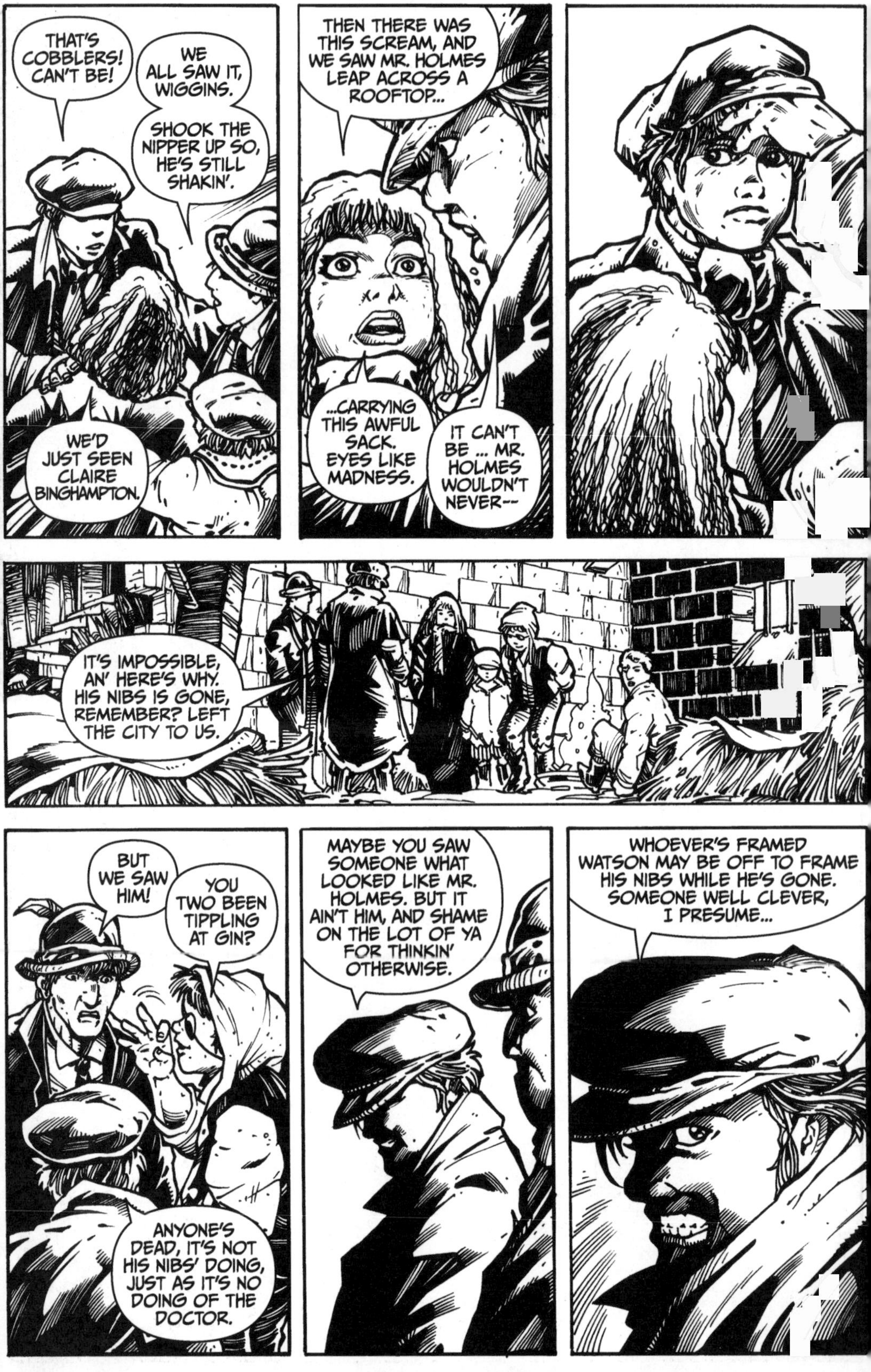
THAT'S COBBLERS! CAN'T BE!
WE ALL SAW IT, WIGGINS.
SHOOK THE NIPPER UP SO, HE'S STILL SHAKIN'.
WE'D JUST SEEN CLAIRE BINGHAMPTON.
THEN THERE WAS THIS SCREAM, AND WE SAW MR. HOLMES LEAP ACROSS A ROOFTOP...
...CARRYING THIS AWFUL SACK. EYES LIKE MADNESS.
IT CAN'T BE ... MR. HOLMES WOULDN'T NEVER--
IT'S IMPOSSIBLE, AN' HERE'S WHY. HIS NIBS IS GONE, REMEMBER? LEFT THE CITY TO US.
BUT WE SAW HIM!
YOU TWO BEEN TIPPLING AT GIN?
ANYONE'S DEAD, IT'S NOT HIS NIBS' DOING, JUST AS IT'S NO DOING OF THE DOCTOR.
MAYBE YOU SAW SOMEONE WHAT LOOKED LIKE MR. HOLMES. BUT IT AIN'T HIM, AND SHAME ON THE LOT OF YA FOR THINKIN' OTHERWISE.
WHOEVER'S FRAMED WATSON MAY BE OFF TO FRAME HIS NIBS WHILE HE'S GONE. SOMEONE WELL CLEVER, I PRESUME...

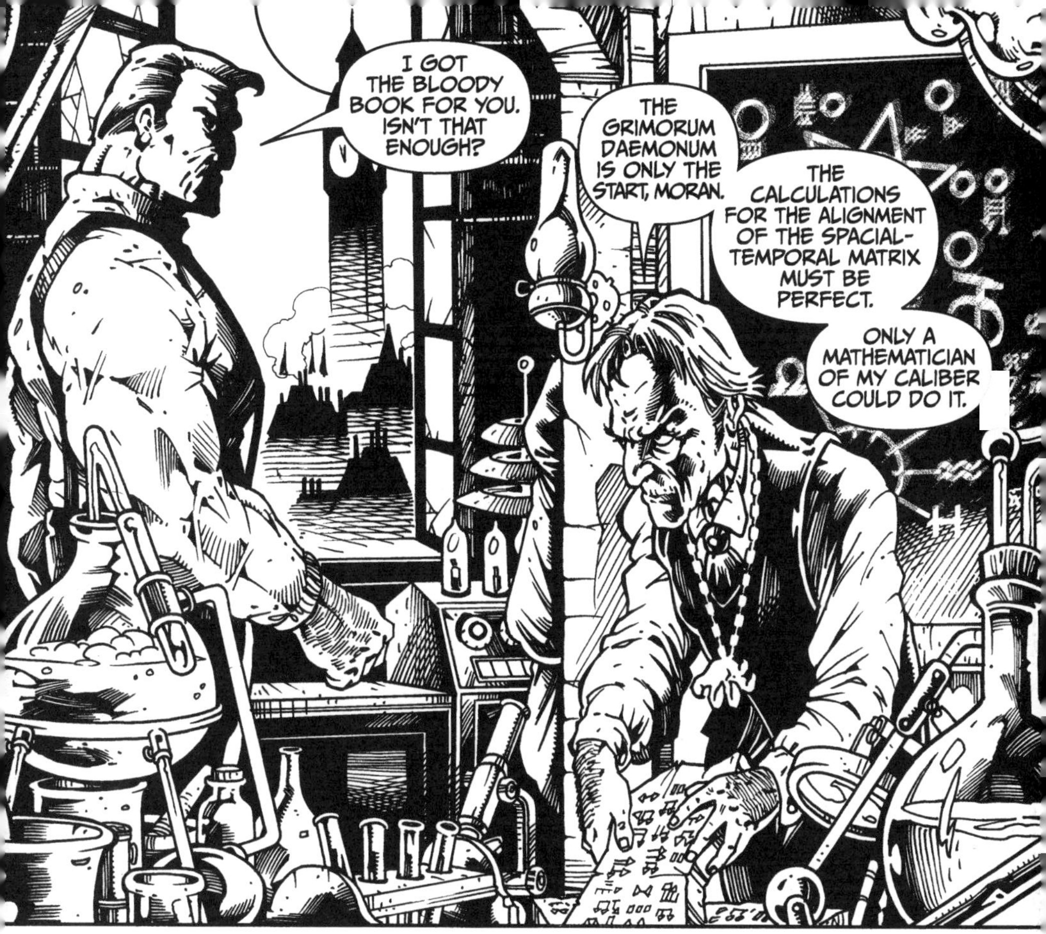
I GOT THE BLOODY BOOK FOR YOU. ISN'T THAT ENOUGH?
THE GRIMORUM DAEMONUM IS ONLY THE START, MORAN.
THE CALCULATIONS FOR THE ALIGNMENT OF THE SPACIAL-TEMPORAL MATRIX MUST BE PERFECT.
ONLY A MATHEMATICIAN OF MY CALIBER COULD DO IT.

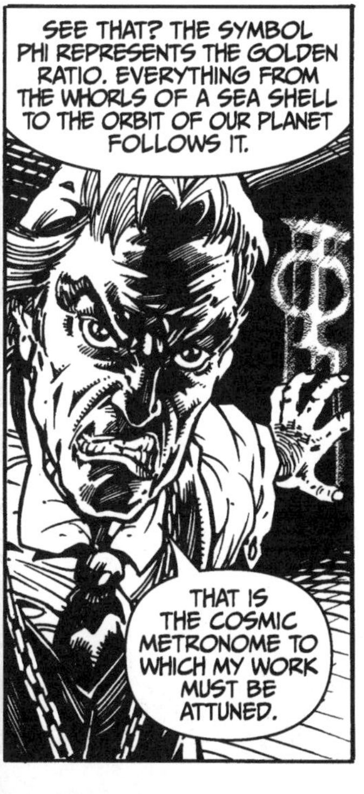
SEE THAT? THE SYMBOL PHI REPRESENTS THE GOLDEN RATIO. EVERYTHING FROM THE WHORLS OF A SEA SHELL TO THE ORBIT OF OUR PLANET FOLLOWS IT.
THAT IS THE COSMIC METRONOME TO WHICH MY WORK MUST BE ATTUNED.

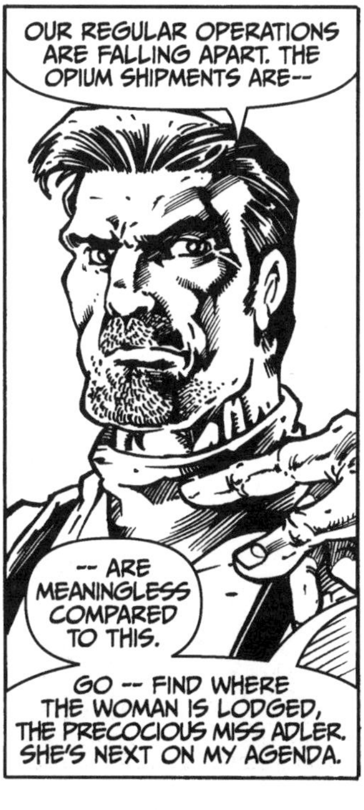
OUR REGULAR OPERATIONS ARE FALLING APART. THE OPIUM SHIPMENTS ARE--
-- ARE MEANINGLESS COMPARED TO THIS.
GO -- FIND WHERE THE WOMAN IS LODGED, THE PRECOCIOUS MISS ADLER. SHE'S NEXT ON MY AGENDA.

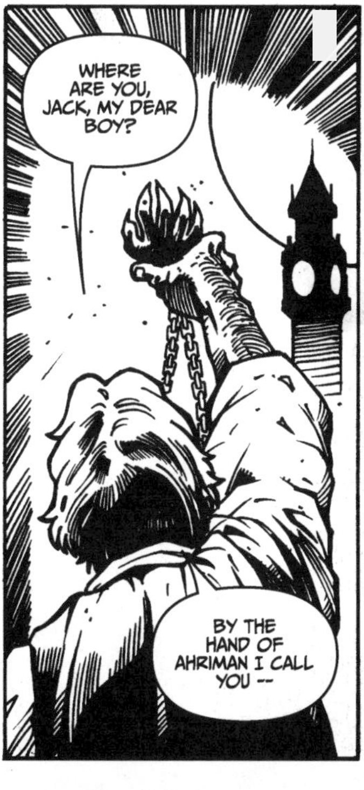
WHERE ARE YOU, JACK, MY DEAR BOY?
BY THE HAND OF AHRIMAN I CALL YOU --

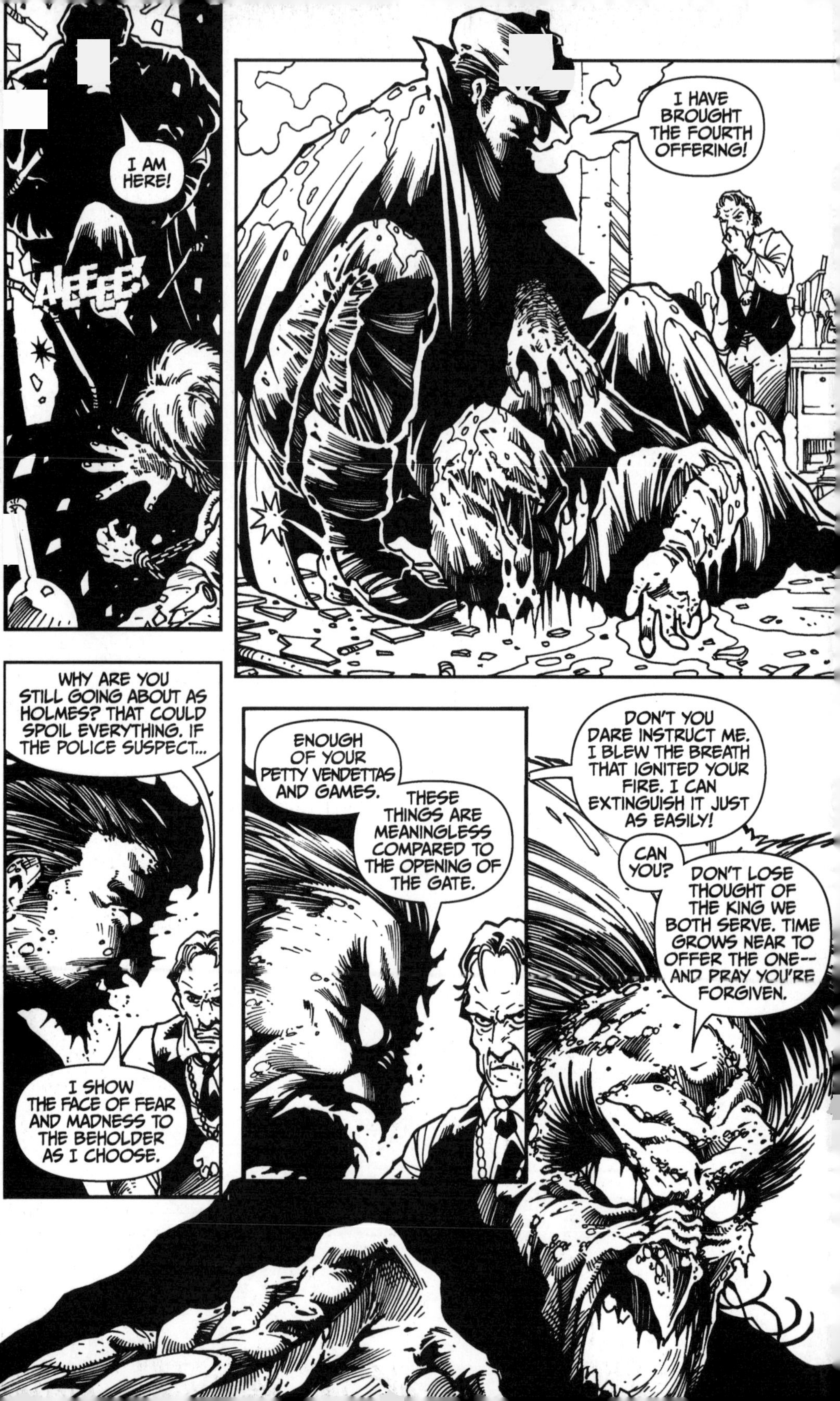
I AM HERE!
AIEEEEE!
I HAVE BROUGHT THE FOURTH OFFERING!
WHY ARE YOU STILL GOING ABOUT AS HOLMES? THAT COULD SPOIL EVERYTHING. IF THE POLICE SUSPECT...
I SHOW THE FACE OF FEAR AND MADNESS TO THE BEHOLDER AS I CHOOSE.
ENOUGH OF YOUR PETTY VENDETTAS AND GAMES.
THESE THINGS ARE MEANINGLESS COMPARED TO THE OPENING OF THE GATE.
DON'T YOU DARE INSTRUCT ME. I BLEW THE BREATH THAT IGNITED YOUR FIRE. I CAN EXTINGUISH IT JUST AS EASILY!
CAN YOU?
DON'T LOSE THOUGHT OF THE KING WE BOTH SERVE. TIME GROWS NEAR TO OFFER THE ONE-- AND PRAY YOU'RE FORGIVEN.

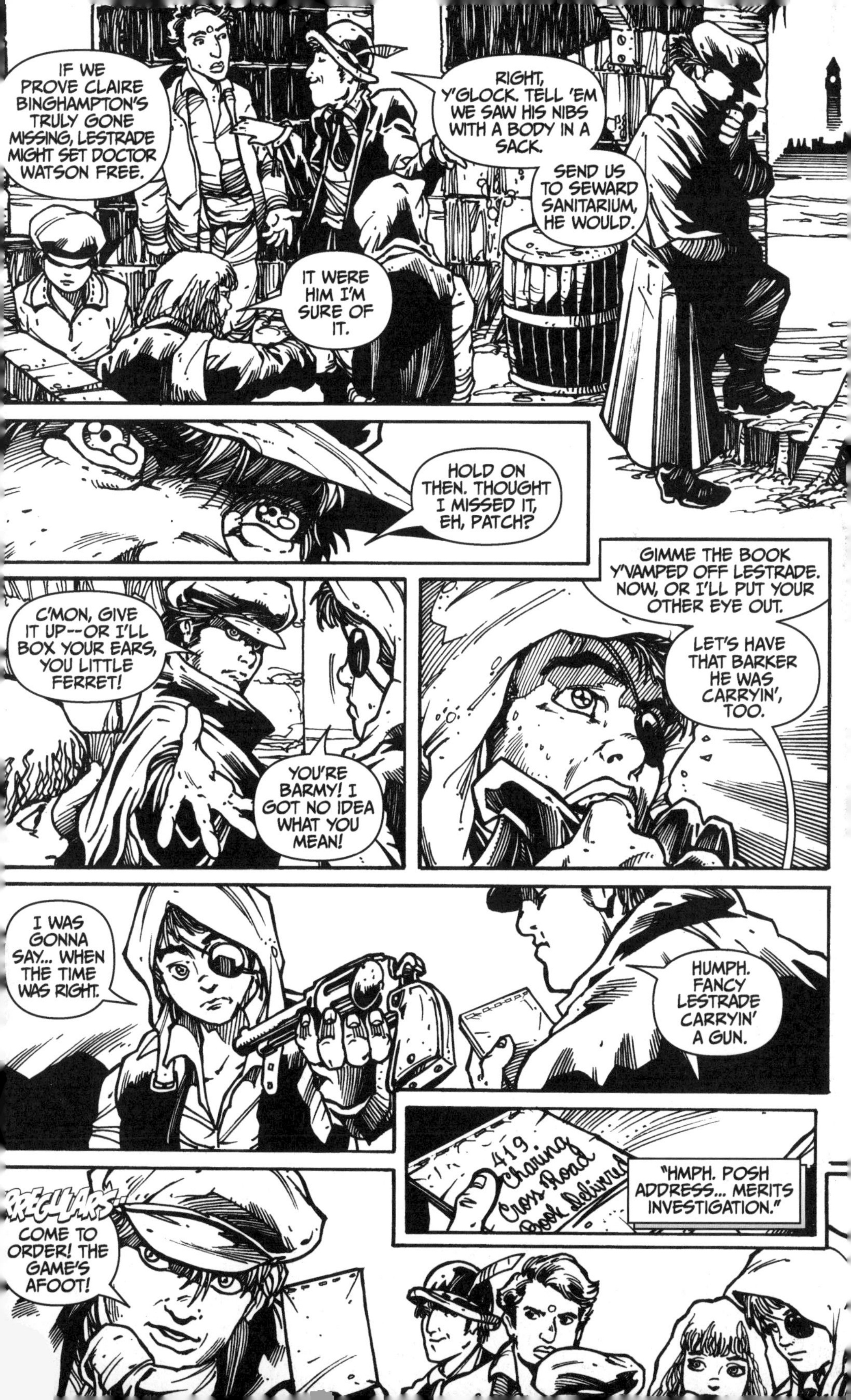
IF WE PROVE CLAIRE BINGHAMPTON'S TRULY GONE MISSING, LESTRADE MIGHT SET DOCTOR WATSON FREE.
RIGHT, Y'GLOCK. TELL 'EM WE SAW HIS NIBS WITH A BODY IN A SACK.
SEND US TO SEWARD SANITARIUM, HE WOULD.
IT WERE HIM I'M SURE OF IT.
HOLD ON THEN. THOUGHT I MISSED IT, EH, PATCH?
C'MON, GIVE IT UP--OR I'LL BOX YOUR EARS, YOU LITTLE FERRET!
YOU'RE BARMY! I GOT NO IDEA WHAT YOU MEAN!
GIMME THE BOOK Y'VAMPED OFF LESTRADE. NOW, OR I'LL PUT YOUR OTHER EYE OUT.
LET'S HAVE THAT BARKER HE WAS CARRYIN', TOO.
I WAS GONNA SAY... WHEN THE TIME WAS RIGHT.
HUMPH. FANCY LESTRADE CARRYIN' A GUN.
419 Charing Cross Road Book Delivered
"HMPH. POSH ADDRESS... MERITS INVESTIGATION."
RREGULARS...
COME TO ORDER! THE GAME'S AFOOT!

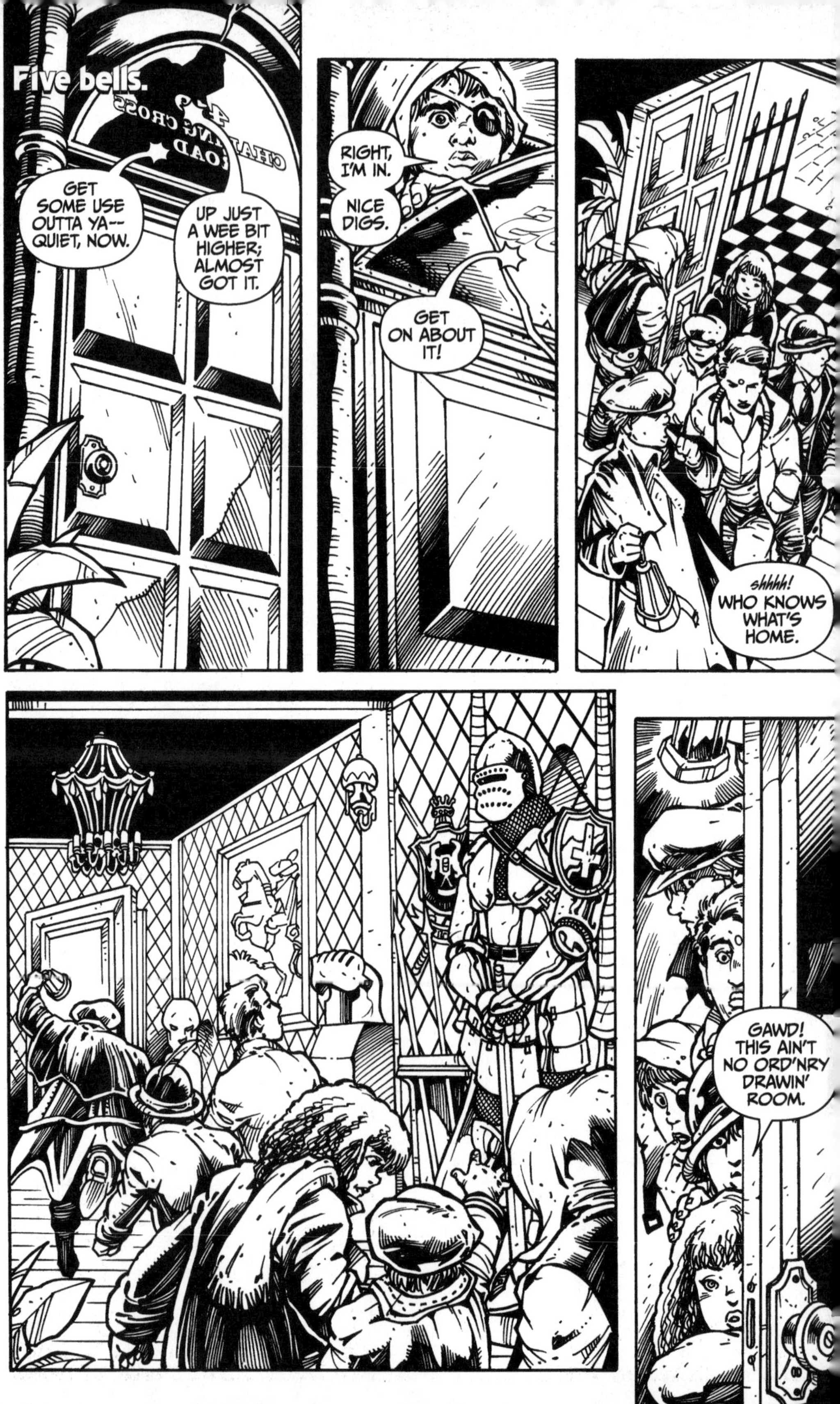
Five bells.
GET SOME USE OUTTA YA-- QUIET, NOW.
UP JUST A WEE BIT HIGHER; ALMOST GOT IT.
RIGHT, I'M IN.
NICE DIGS.
GET ON ABOUT IT!
shhhh! WHO KNOWS WHAT'S HOME.
GAWD! THIS AIN'T NO ORD'NRY DRAWIN' ROOM.

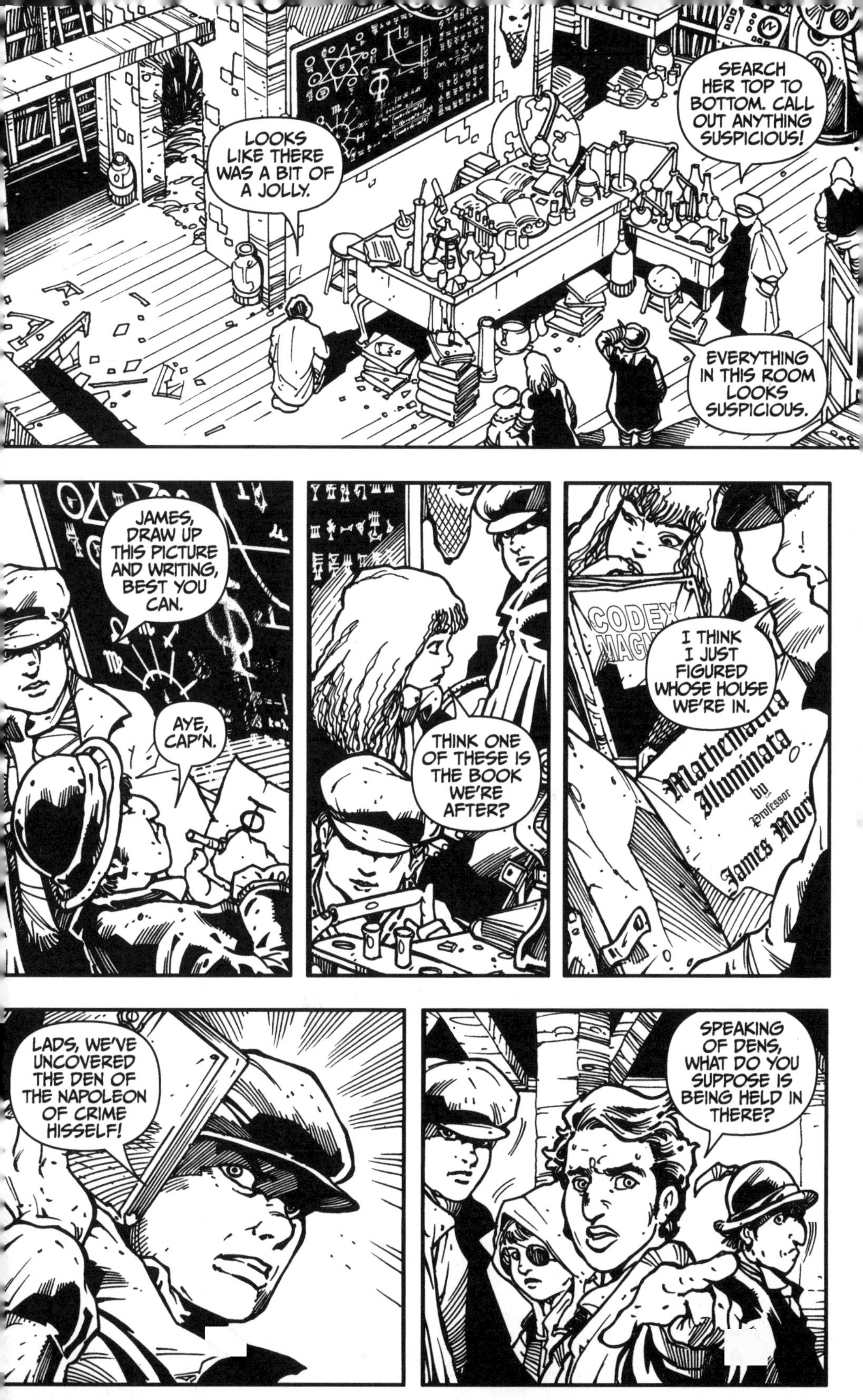
LOOKS LIKE THERE WAS A BIT OF A JOLLY.
SEARCH HER TOP TO BOTTOM. CALL OUT ANYTHING SUSPICIOUS!
EVERYTHING IN THIS ROOM LOOKS SUSPICIOUS.
JAMES, DRAW UP THIS PICTURE AND WRITING, BEST YOU CAN.
AYE, CAP'N.
THINK ONE OF THESE IS THE BOOK WE'RE AFTER?
CODEX
I THINK I JUST FIGURED WHOSE HOUSE WE'RE IN.
Mathematica Illuminata by Professor
LADS, WE'VE UNCOVERED THE DEN OF THE NAPOLEON OF CRIME HISSELF!
SPEAKING OF DENS, WHAT DO YOU SUPPOSE IS BEING HELD IN THERE?

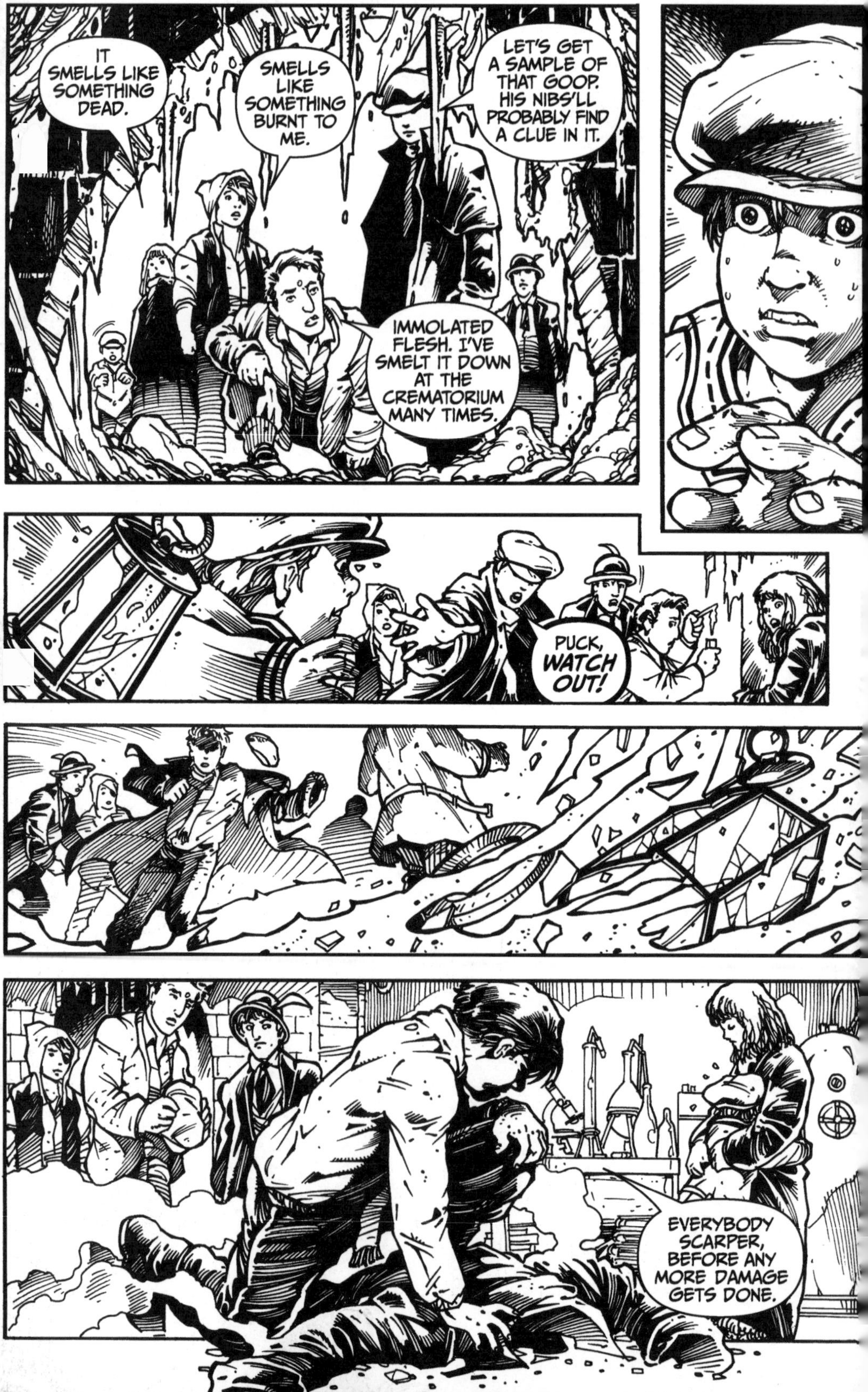
IT SMELLS LIKE SOMETHING DEAD.
SMELLS LIKE SOMETHING BURNT TO ME.
LET'S GET A SAMPLE OF THAT GOOP. HIS NIBS'LL PROBABLY FIND A CLUE IN IT.
IMMOLATED FLESH. I'VE SMELT IT DOWN AT THE CREMATORIUM MANY TIMES.
PUCK, WATCH OUT!
EVERYBODY SCARPER, BEFORE ANY MORE DAMAGE GETS DONE.

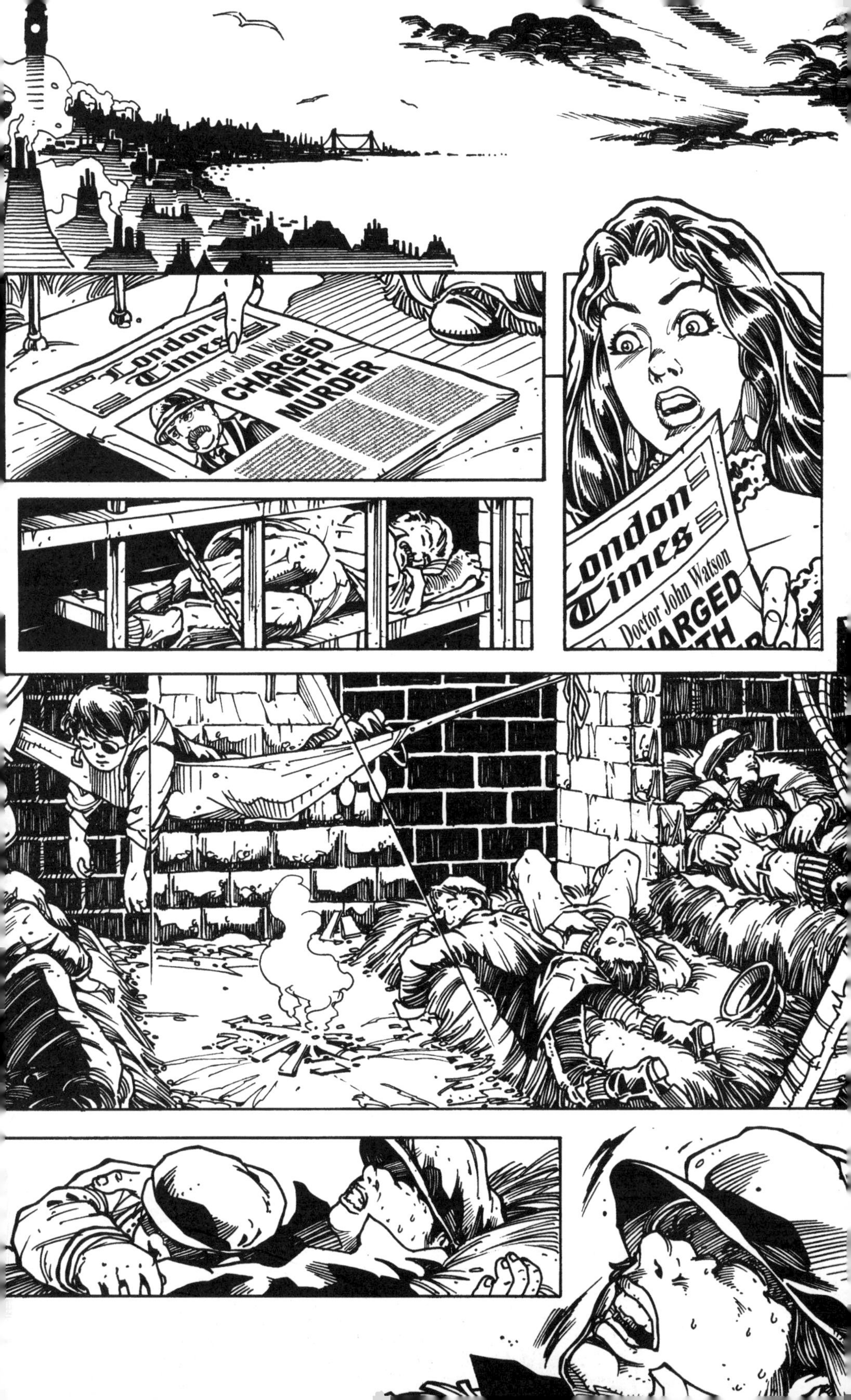

London Times
Doctor John Watson
CHARGED WITH MURDER

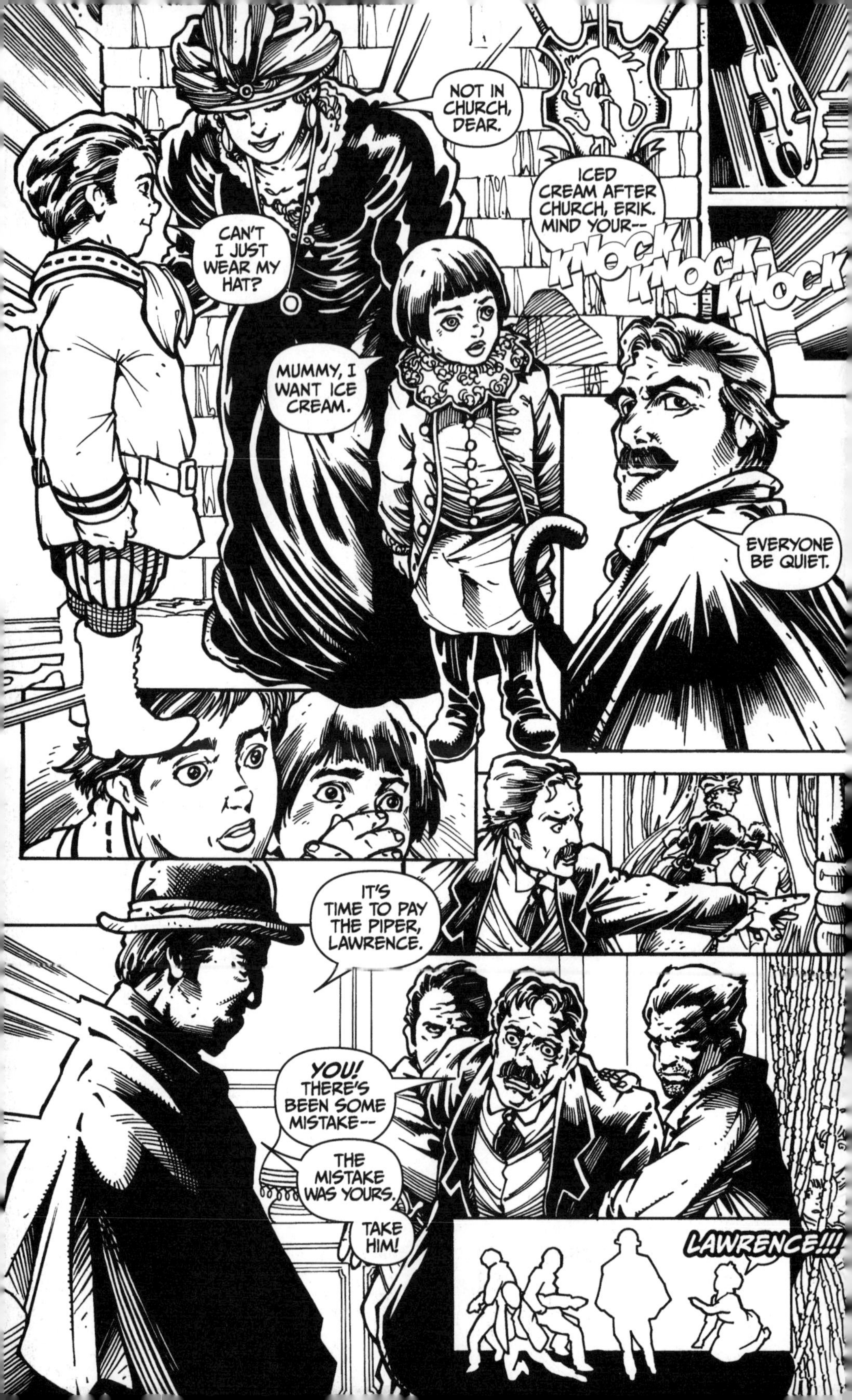
NOT IN CHURCH, DEAR.
CAN'T I JUST WEAR MY HAT?
ICED CREAM AFTER CHURCH, ERIK. MIND YOUR--
KNOCK KNOCK KNOCK
MUMMY, I WANT ICE CREAM.
EVERYONE BE QUIET.
IT'S TIME TO PAY THE PIPER, LAWRENCE.
YOU! THERE'S BEEN SOME MISTAKE--
THE MISTAKE WAS YOURS.
TAKE HIM!
LAWRENCE!!!

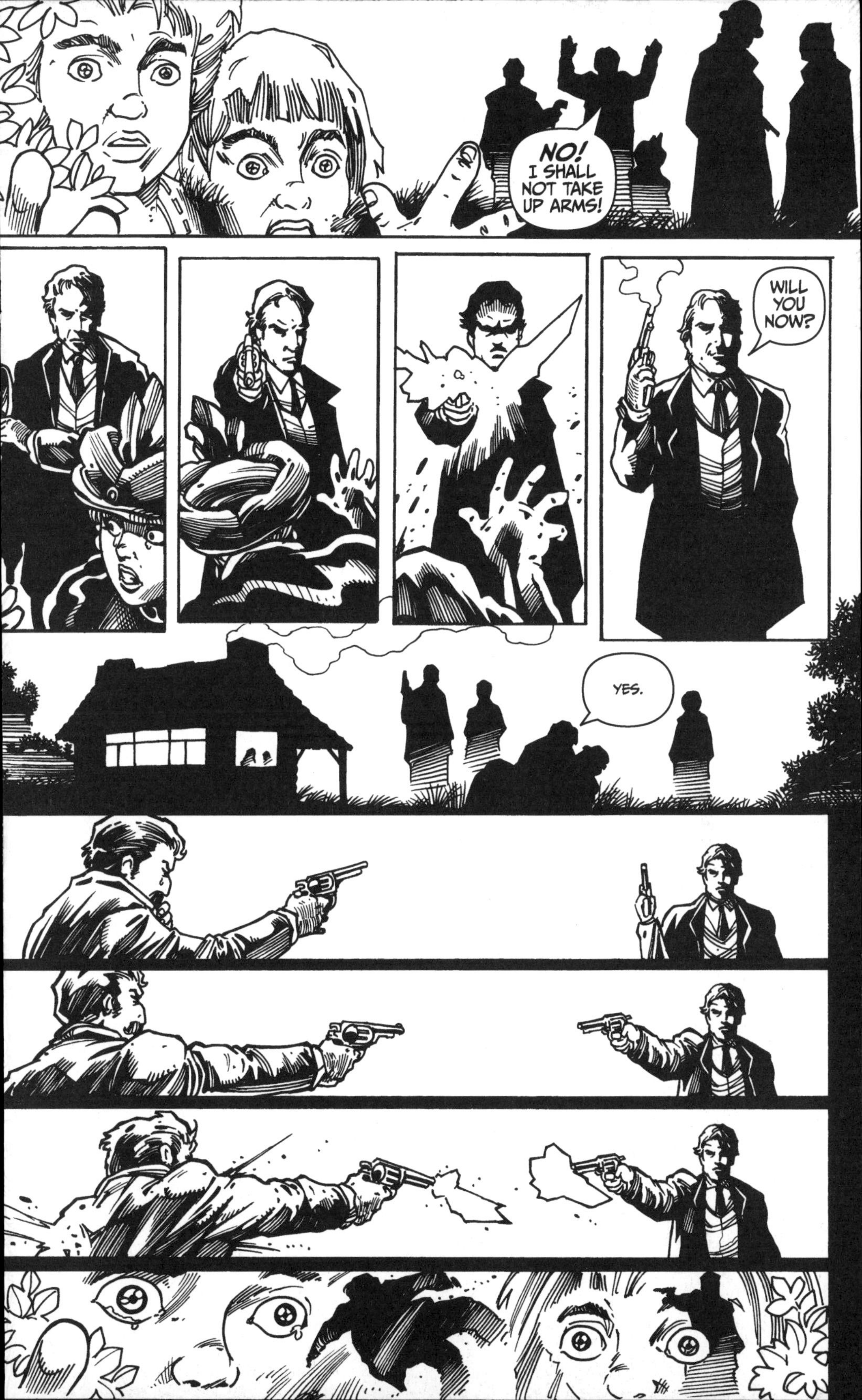
NO! I SHALL NOT TAKE UP ARMS!
WILL YOU NOW?
YES.

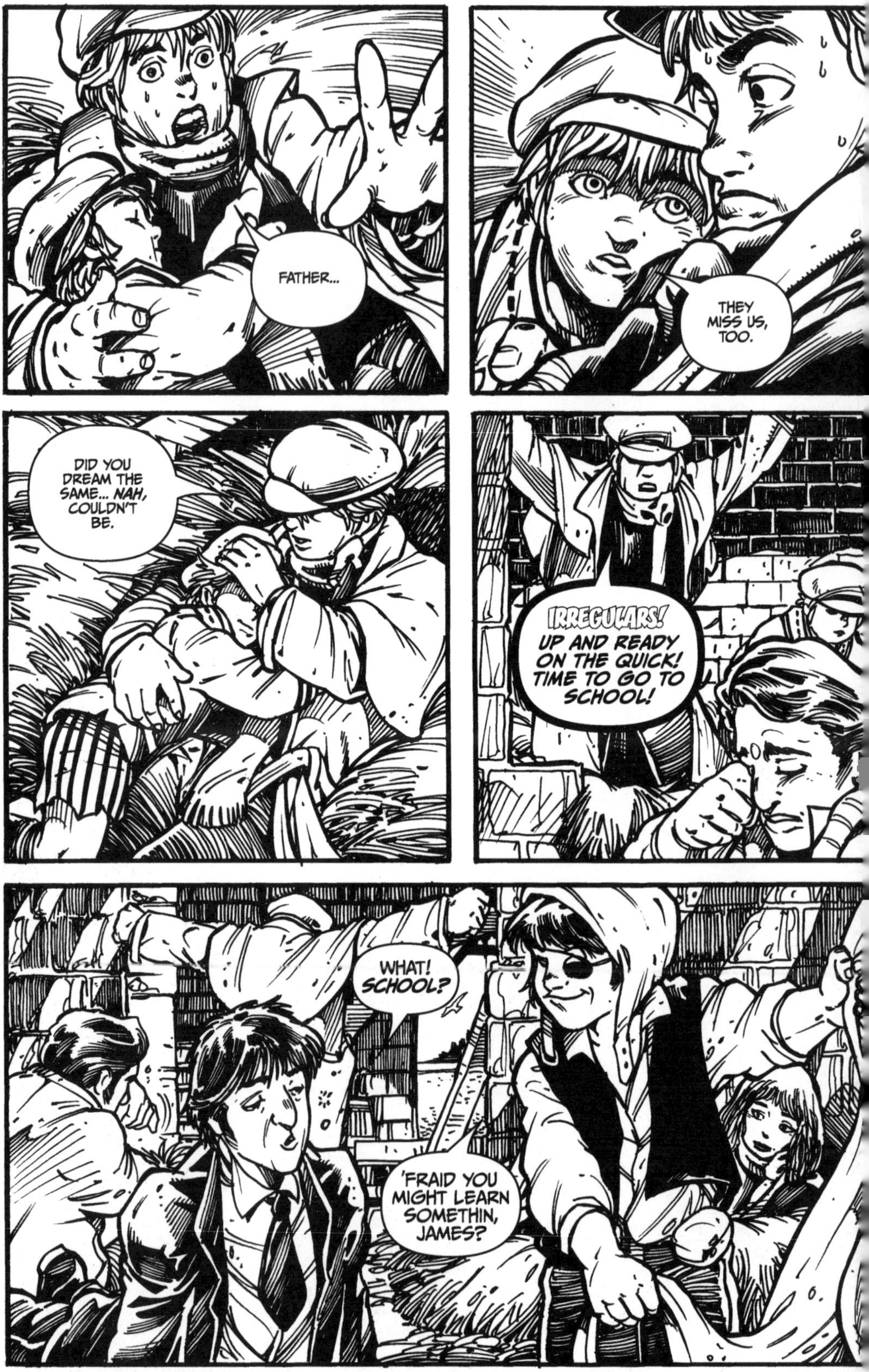
FATHER...
THEY MISS US, TOO.
DID YOU DREAM THE SAME... *NAH,* COULDN'T BE.
IRREGULARS!
UP AND READY ON THE QUICK! TIME TO GO TO SCHOOL!
WHAT! SCHOOL?
'FRAID YOU MIGHT LEARN SOMETHIN, JAMES?

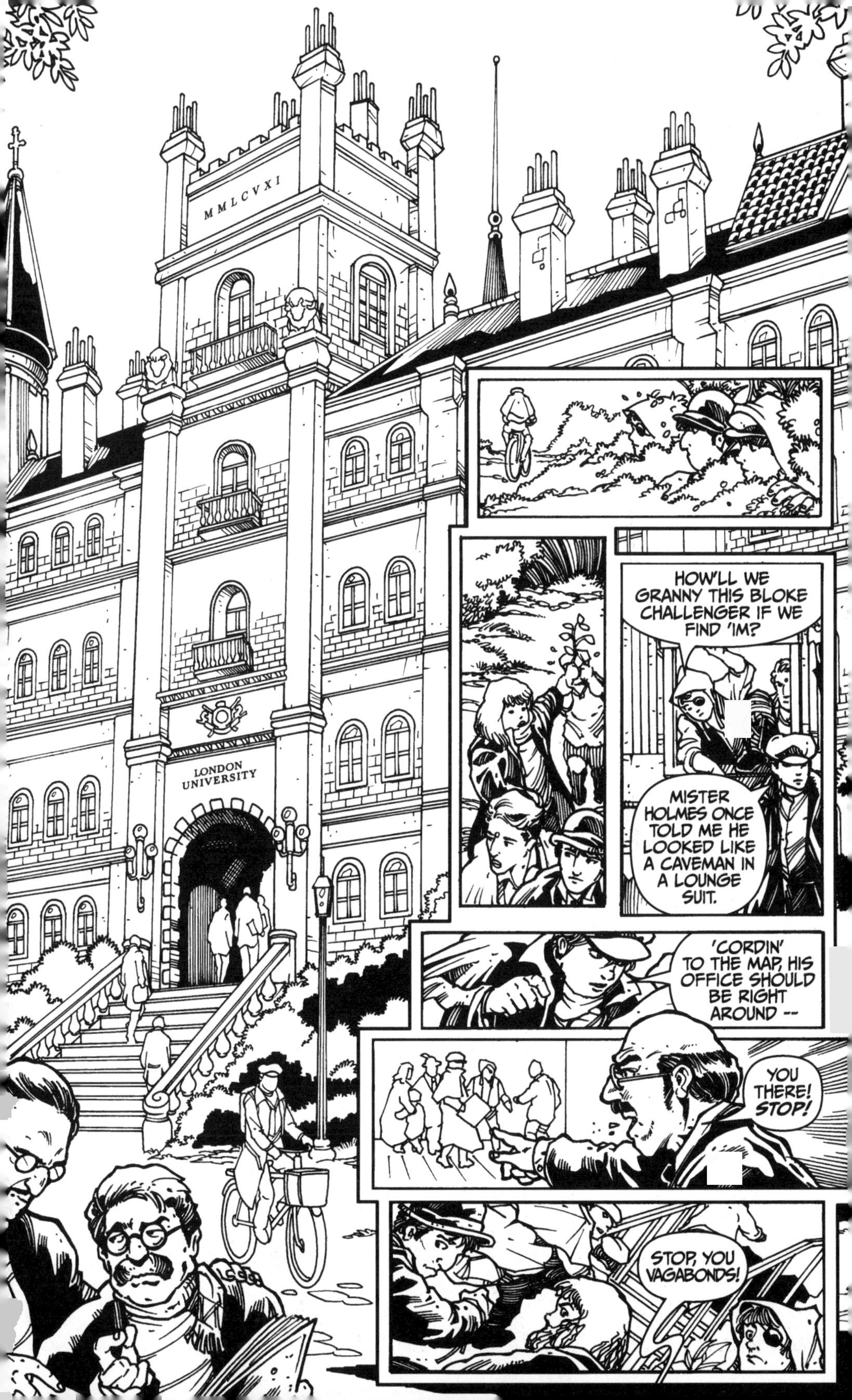

MMLCVXI
LONDON UNIVERSITY
HOW'LL WE GRANNY THIS BLOKE CHALLENGER IF WE FIND 'IM?
MISTER HOLMES ONCE TOLD ME HE LOOKED LIKE A CAVEMAN IN A LOUNGE SUIT.
'CORDIN' TO THE MAP, HIS OFFICE SHOULD BE RIGHT AROUND --
YOU THERE! STOP!
STOP, YOU VAGABONDS!

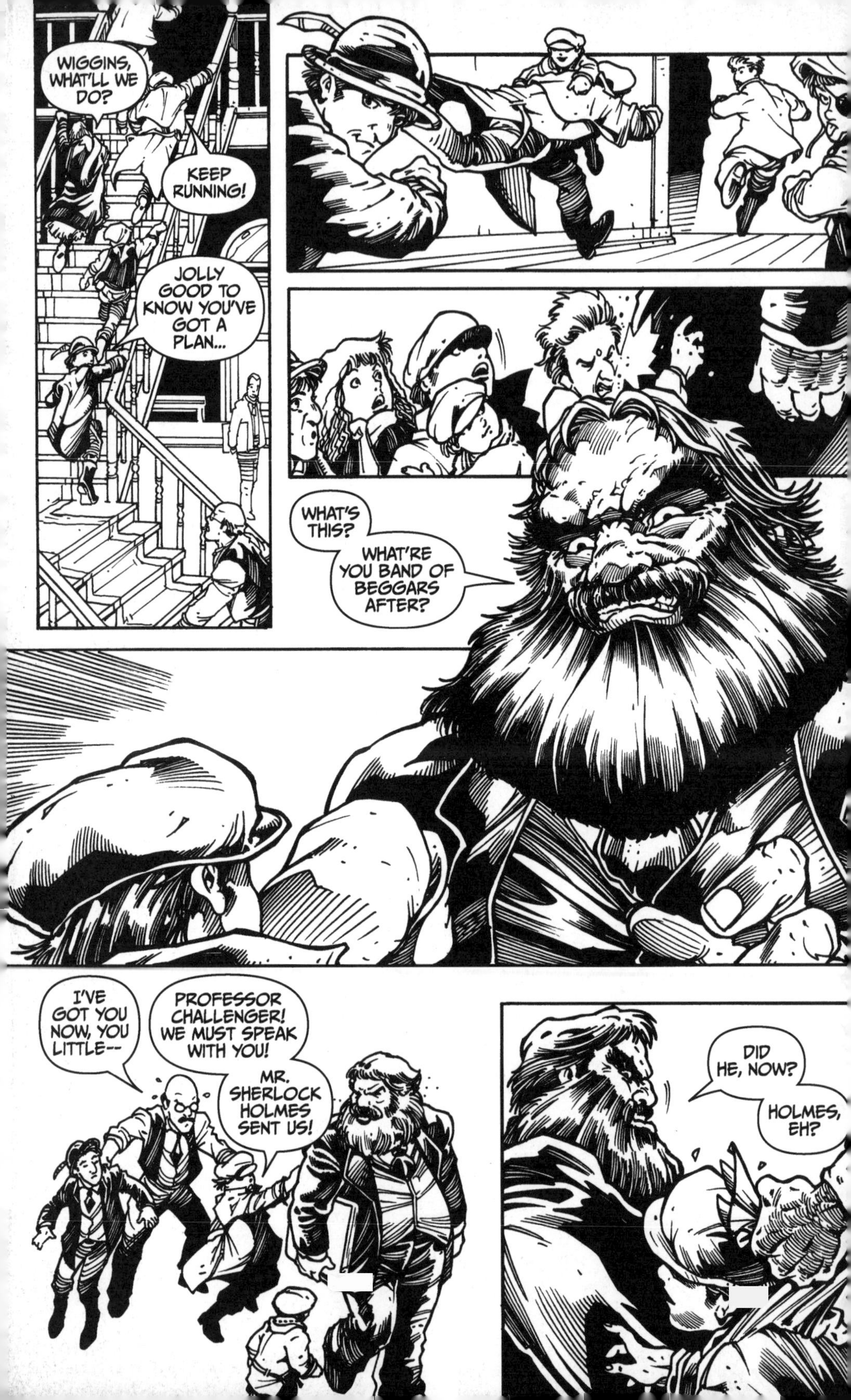
WIGGINS, WHAT'LL WE DO?
KEEP RUNNING!
JOLLY GOOD TO KNOW YOU'VE GOT A PLAN...
WHAT'S THIS?
WHAT'RE YOU BAND OF BEGGARS AFTER?
I'VE GOT YOU NOW, YOU LITTLE--
PROFESSOR CHALLENGER! WE MUST SPEAK WITH YOU!
MR. SHERLOCK HOLMES SENT US!
DID HE, NOW?
HOLMES, EH?

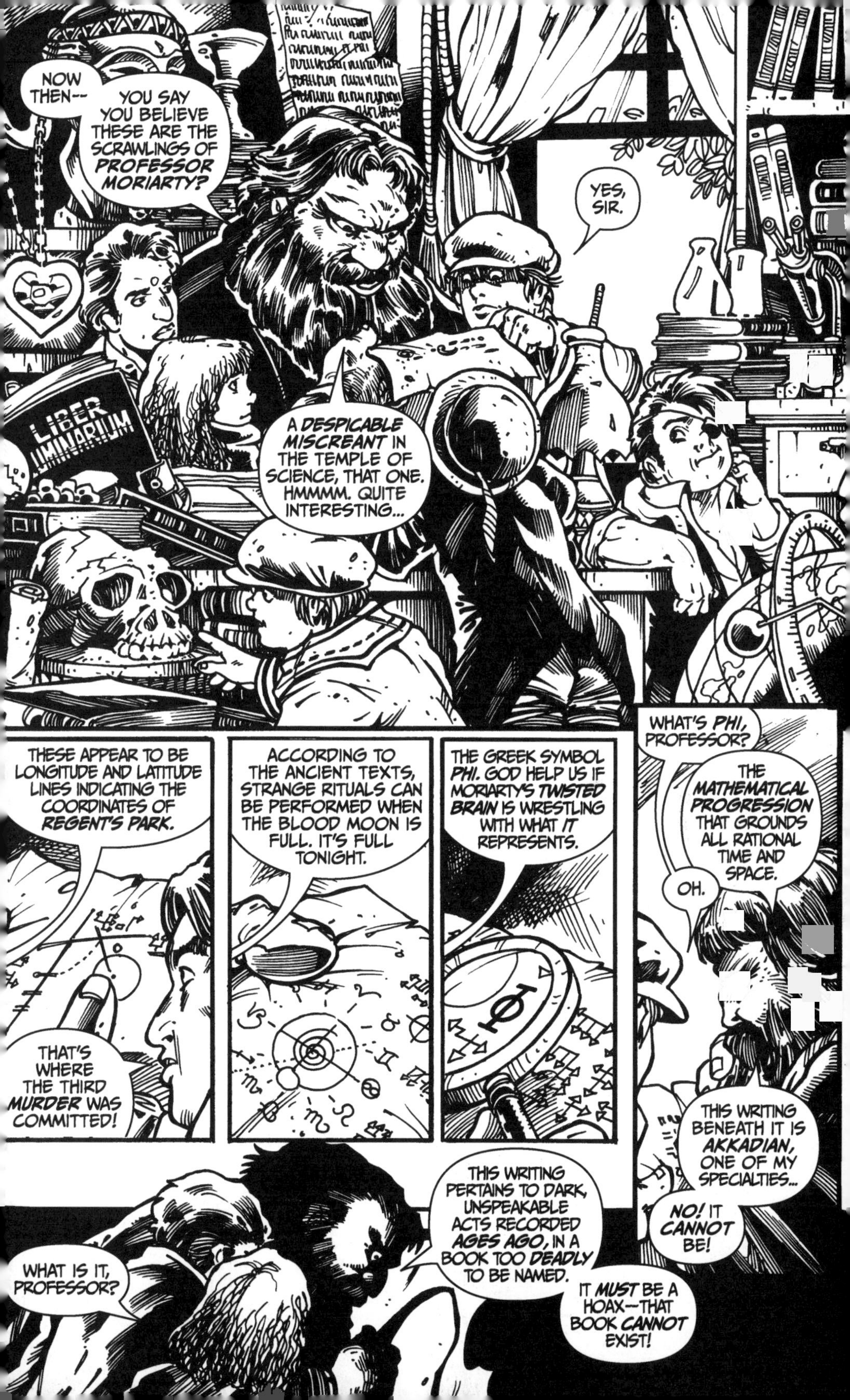
NOW THEN--
YOU SAY YOU BELIEVE THESE ARE THE SCRAWLINGS OF PROFESSOR MORIARTY?
YES, SIR.
LIBER LUMINARIUM
A DESPICABLE MISCREANT IN THE TEMPLE OF SCIENCE, THAT ONE. HMMMM. QUITE INTERESTING...
THESE APPEAR TO BE LONGITUDE AND LATITUDE LINES INDICATING THE COORDINATES OF REGENT'S PARK.
THAT'S WHERE THE THIRD MURDER WAS COMMITTED!
ACCORDING TO THE ANCIENT TEXTS, STRANGE RITUALS CAN BE PERFORMED WHEN THE BLOOD MOON IS FULL. IT'S FULL TONIGHT.
THE GREEK SYMBOL PHI. GOD HELP US IF MORIARTY'S TWISTED BRAIN IS WRESTLING WITH WHAT IT REPRESENTS.
WHAT'S PHI, PROFESSOR?
THE MATHEMATICAL PROGRESSION THAT GROUNDS ALL RATIONAL TIME AND SPACE.
OH.
THIS WRITING BENEATH IT IS AKKADIAN, ONE OF MY SPECIALTIES...
NO! IT CANNOT BE!
WHAT IS IT, PROFESSOR?
THIS WRITING PERTAINS TO DARK, UNSPEAKABLE ACTS RECORDED AGES AGO, IN A BOOK TOO DEADLY TO BE NAMED.
IT MUST BE A HOAX--THAT BOOK CANNOT EXIST!

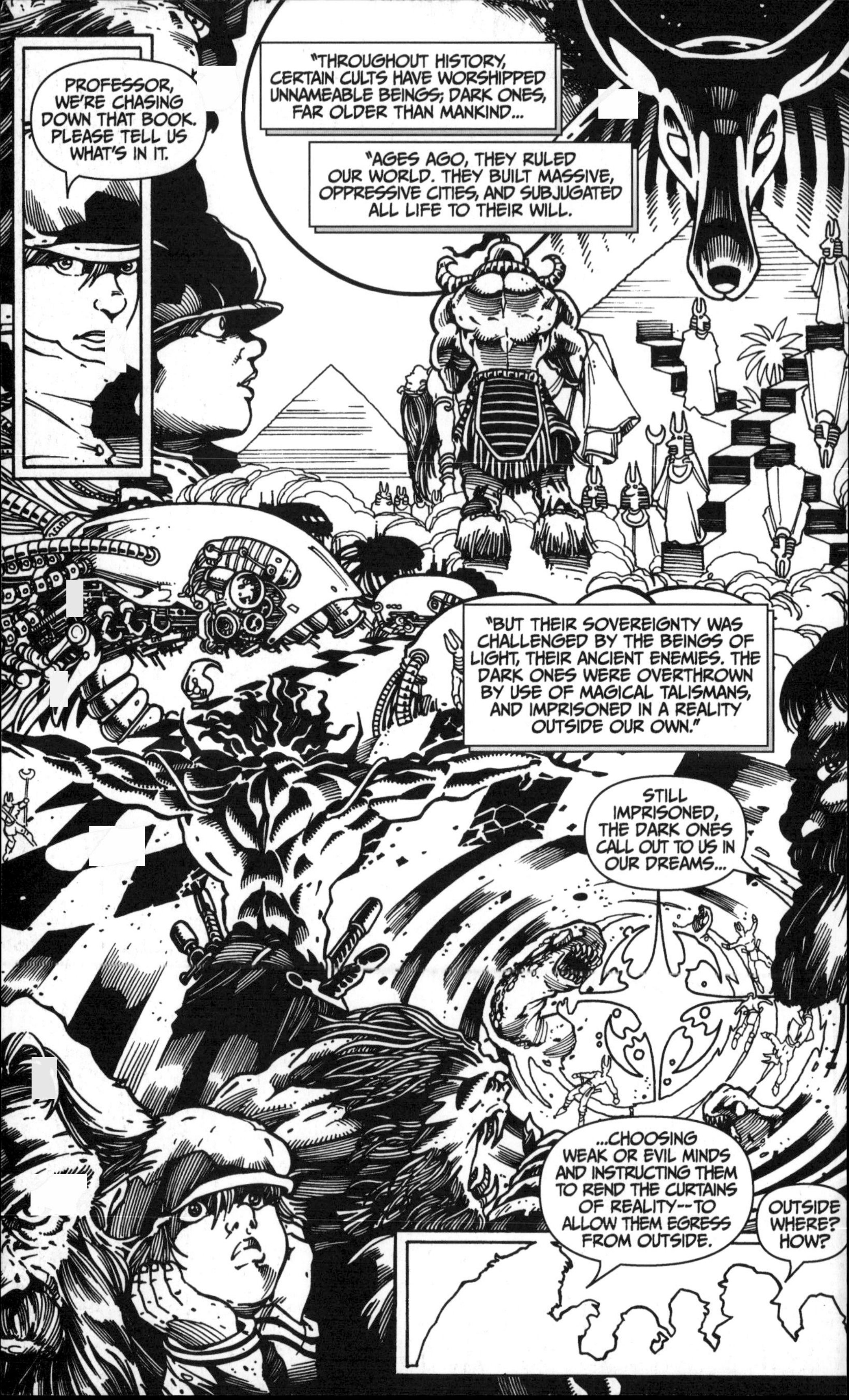
PROFESSOR, WE'RE CHASING DOWN THAT BOOK. PLEASE TELL US WHAT'S IN IT.
"THROUGHOUT HISTORY, CERTAIN CULTS HAVE WORSHIPPED UNNAMEABLE BEINGS; DARK ONES, FAR OLDER THAN MANKIND...
"AGES AGO, THEY RULED OUR WORLD. THEY BUILT MASSIVE, OPPRESSIVE CITIES, AND SUBJUGATED ALL LIFE TO THEIR WILL.
"BUT THEIR SOVEREIGNTY WAS CHALLENGED BY THE BEINGS OF LIGHT, THEIR ANCIENT ENEMIES. THE DARK ONES WERE OVERTHROWN BY USE OF MAGICAL TALISMANS, AND IMPRISONED IN A REALITY OUTSIDE OUR OWN."
STILL IMPRISONED, THE DARK ONES CALL OUT TO US IN OUR DREAMS...
...CHOOSING WEAK OR EVIL MINDS AND INSTRUCTING THEM TO REND THE CURTAINS OF REALITY--TO ALLOW THEM EGRESS FROM OUTSIDE.
OUTSIDE WHERE? HOW?

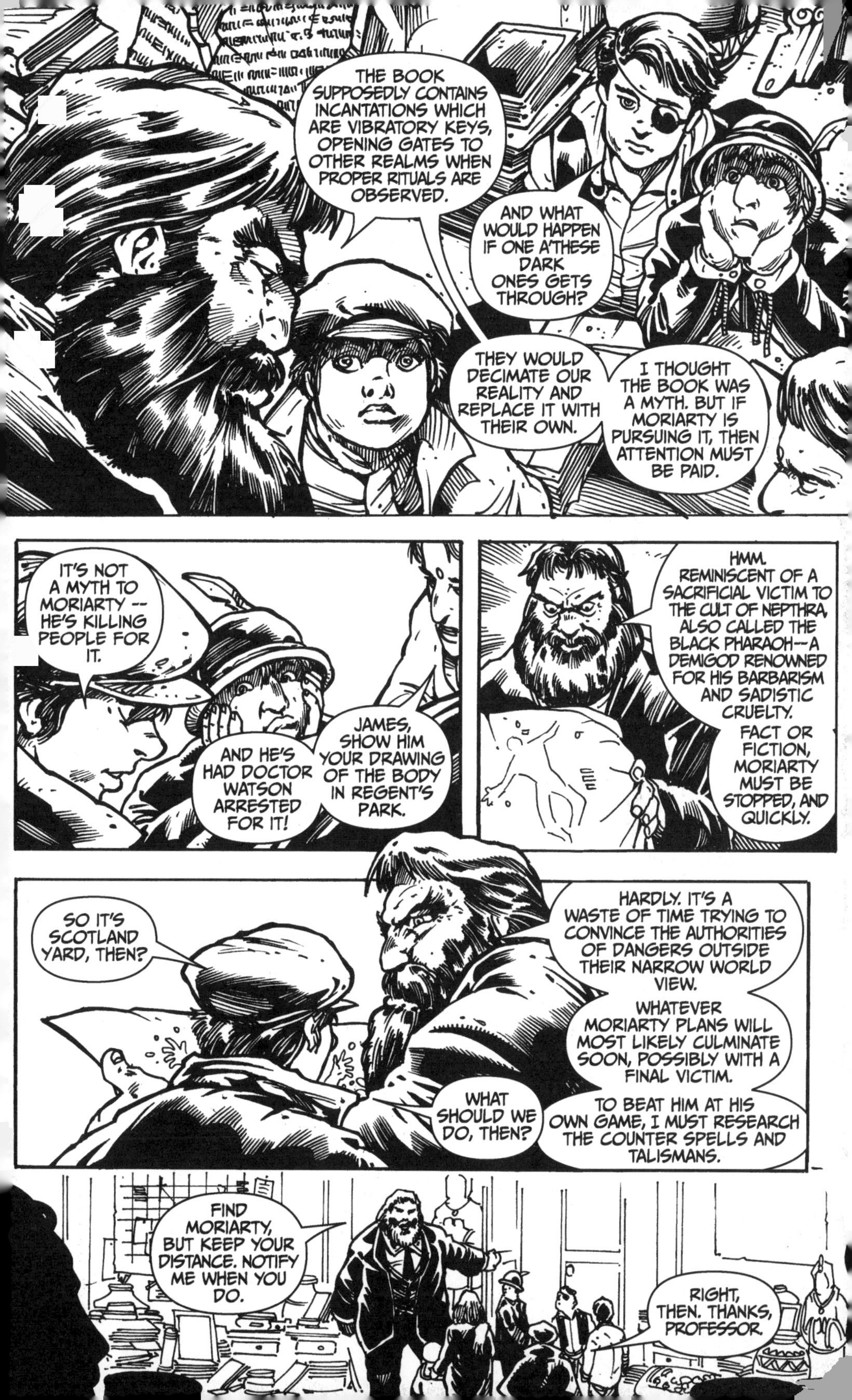
THE BOOK SUPPOSEDLY CONTAINS INCANTATIONS WHICH ARE VIBRATORY KEYS, OPENING GATES TO OTHER REALMS WHEN PROPER RITUALS ARE OBSERVED.
AND WHAT WOULD HAPPEN IF ONE A'THESE DARK ONES GETS THROUGH?
THEY WOULD DECIMATE OUR REALITY AND REPLACE IT WITH THEIR OWN.
I THOUGHT THE BOOK WAS A MYTH. BUT IF MORIARTY IS PURSUING IT, THEN ATTENTION MUST BE PAID.
IT'S NOT A MYTH TO MORIARTY -- HE'S KILLING PEOPLE FOR IT.
AND HE'S HAD DOCTOR WATSON ARRESTED FOR IT!
JAMES, SHOW HIM YOUR DRAWING OF THE BODY IN REGENT'S PARK.
HMM. REMINISCENT OF A SACRIFICIAL VICTIM TO THE CULT OF NEPTHRA, ALSO CALLED THE BLACK PHARAOH--A DEMIGOD RENOWNED FOR HIS BARBARISM AND SADISTIC CRUELTY.
FACT OR FICTION, MORIARTY MUST BE STOPPED, AND QUICKLY.
SO IT'S SCOTLAND YARD, THEN?
HARDLY. IT'S A WASTE OF TIME TRYING TO CONVINCE THE AUTHORITIES OF DANGERS OUTSIDE THEIR NARROW WORLD VIEW.
WHATEVER MORIARTY PLANS WILL MOST LIKELY CULMINATE SOON, POSSIBLY WITH A FINAL VICTIM.
WHAT SHOULD WE DO, THEN?
TO BEAT HIM AT HIS OWN GAME, I MUST RESEARCH THE COUNTER SPELLS AND TALISMANS.
FIND MORIARTY, BUT KEEP YOUR DISTANCE. NOTIFY ME WHEN YOU DO.
RIGHT, THEN. THANKS, PROFESSOR.

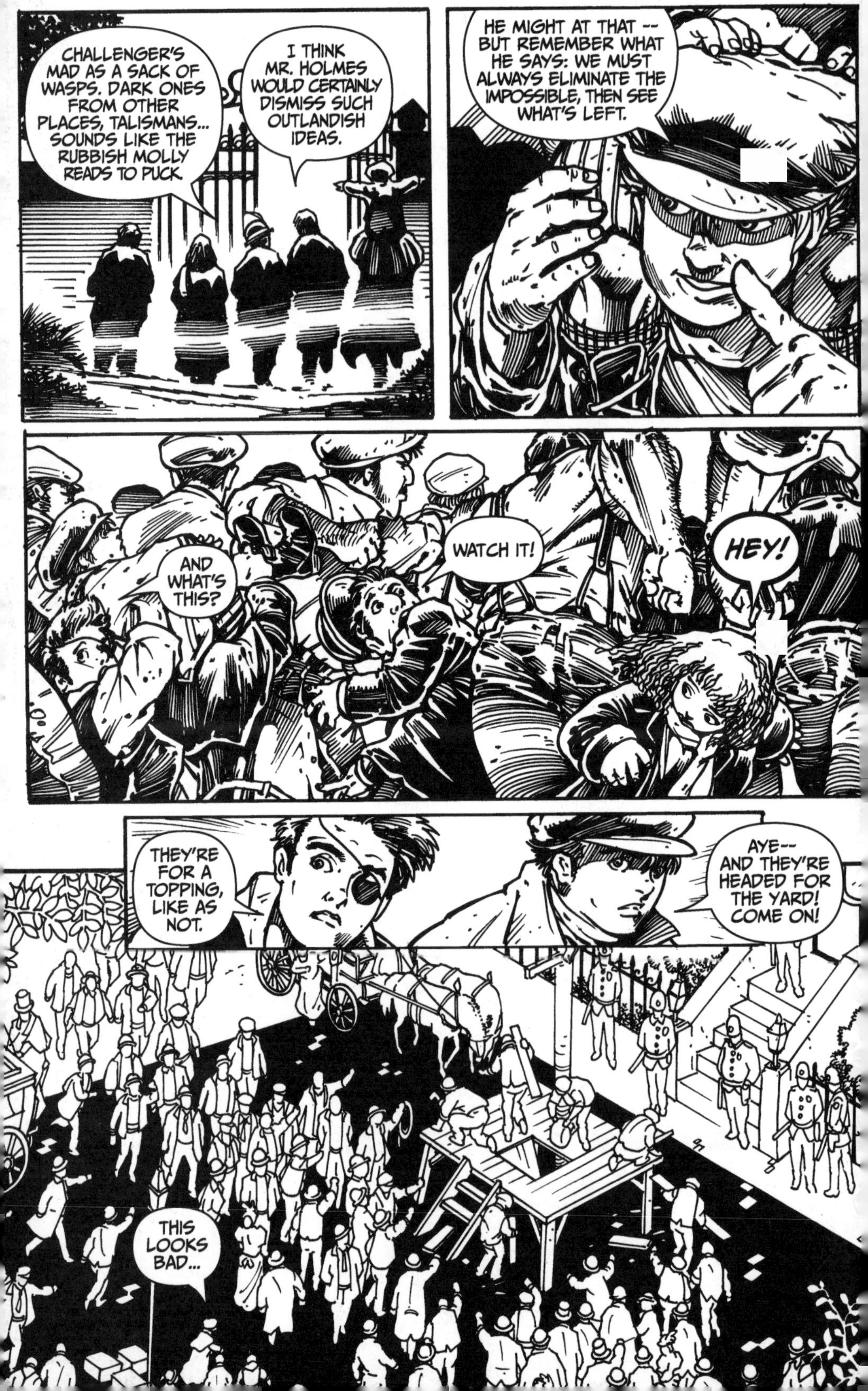
CHALLENGER'S MAD AS A SACK OF WASPS. DARK ONES FROM OTHER PLACES, TALISMANS... SOUNDS LIKE THE RUBBISH MOLLY READS TO PUCK.
I THINK MR. HOLMES WOULD CERTAINLY DISMISS SUCH OUTLANDISH IDEAS.
HE MIGHT AT THAT -- BUT REMEMBER WHAT HE SAYS: WE MUST ALWAYS ELIMINATE THE IMPOSSIBLE, THEN SEE WHAT'S LEFT.
AND WHAT'S THIS?
WATCH IT!
HEY!
THEY'RE FOR A TOPPING, LIKE AS NOT.
AYE-- AND THEY'RE HEADED FOR THE YARD! COME ON!
THIS LOOKS BAD...

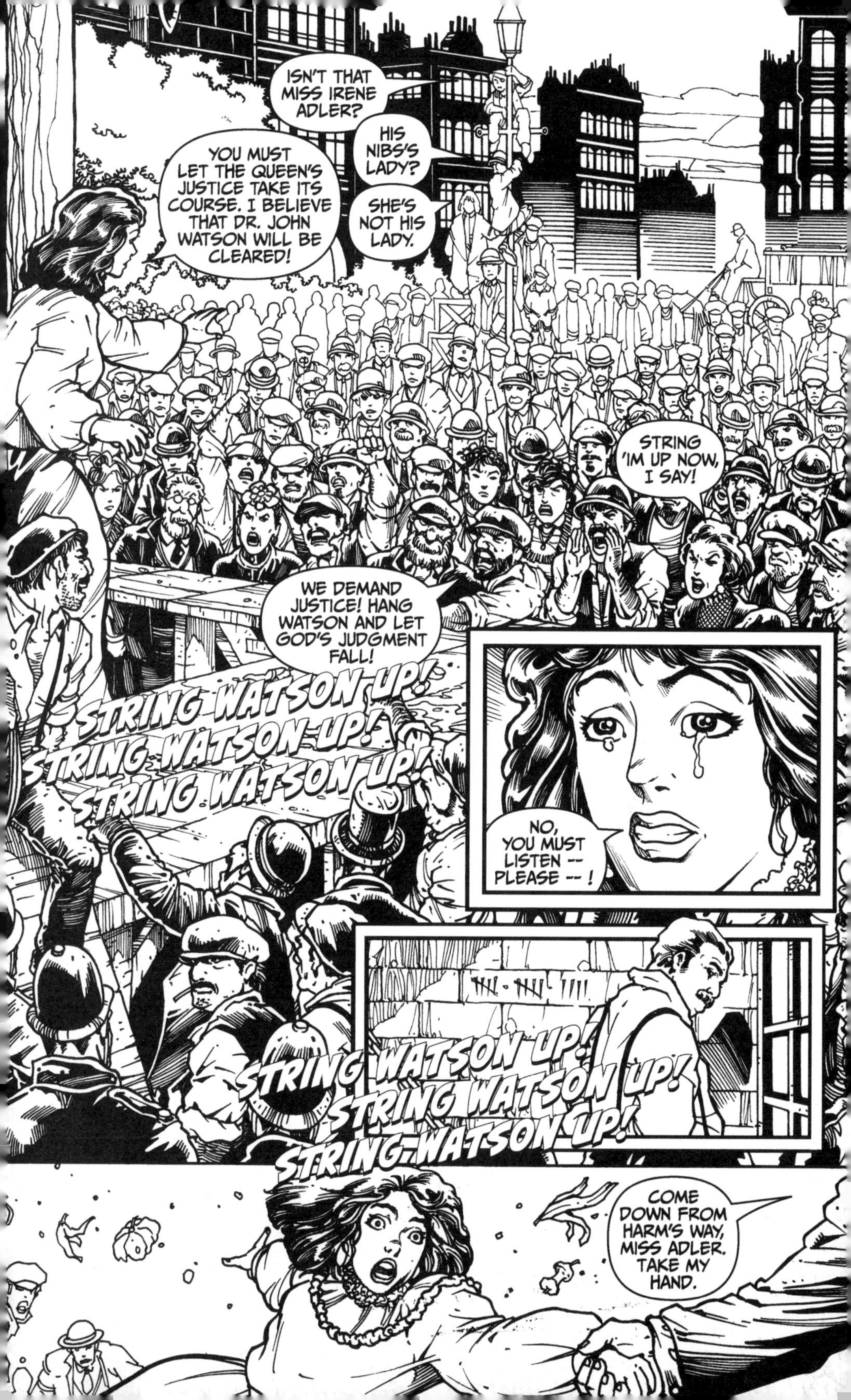
ISN'T THAT MISS IRENE ADLER?
HIS NIBS'S LADY?
SHE'S NOT HIS LADY.
YOU MUST LET THE QUEEN'S JUSTICE TAKE ITS COURSE. I BELIEVE THAT DR. JOHN WATSON WILL BE CLEARED!
STRING 'IM UP NOW, I SAY!
WE DEMAND JUSTICE! HANG WATSON AND LET GOD'S JUDGMENT FALL!
STRING WATSON UP! STRING WATSON UP! STRING WATSON UP!
NO, YOU MUST LISTEN -- PLEASE -- !
STRING WATSON UP! STRING WATSON UP! STRING WATSON UP!
COME DOWN FROM HARM'S WAY, MISS ADLER. TAKE MY HAND.

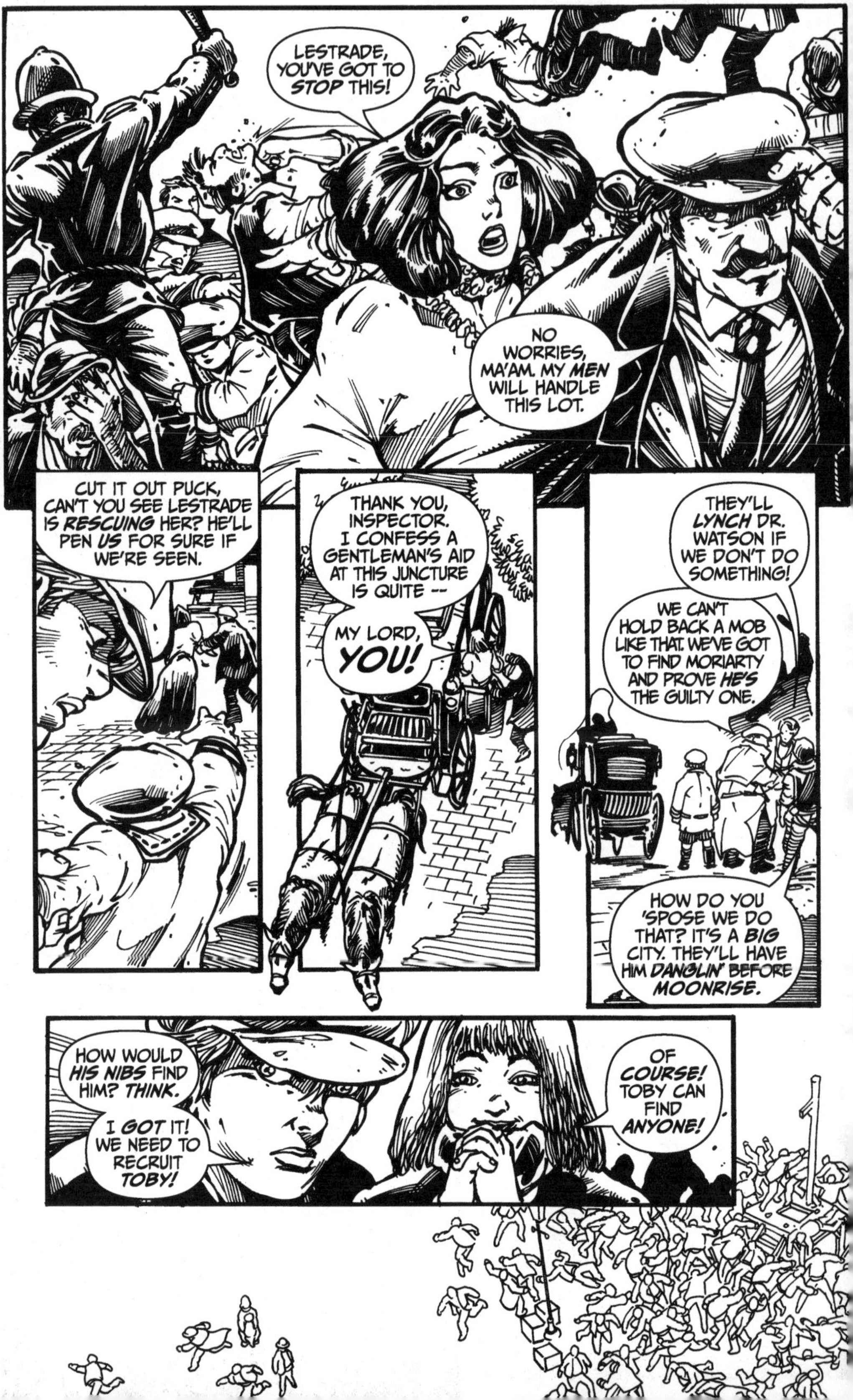
LESTRADE, YOU'VE GOT TO STOP THIS!
NO WORRIES, MA'AM. MY MEN WILL HANDLE THIS LOT.
CUT IT OUT PUCK, CAN'T YOU SEE LESTRADE IS RESCUING HER? HE'LL PEN US FOR SURE IF WE'RE SEEN.
THANK YOU, INSPECTOR. I CONFESS A GENTLEMAN'S AID AT THIS JUNCTURE IS QUITE --
MY LORD, YOU!
THEY'LL LYNCH DR. WATSON IF WE DON'T DO SOMETHING!
WE CAN'T HOLD BACK A MOB LIKE THAT. WE'VE GOT TO FIND MORIARTY AND PROVE HE'S THE GUILTY ONE.
HOW DO YOU 'SPOSE WE DO THAT? IT'S A BIG CITY. THEY'LL HAVE HIM DANGLIN' BEFORE MOONRISE.
HOW WOULD HIS NIBS FIND HIM? THINK.
I GOT IT! WE NEED TO RECRUIT TOBY!
OF COURSE! TOBY CAN FIND ANYONE!

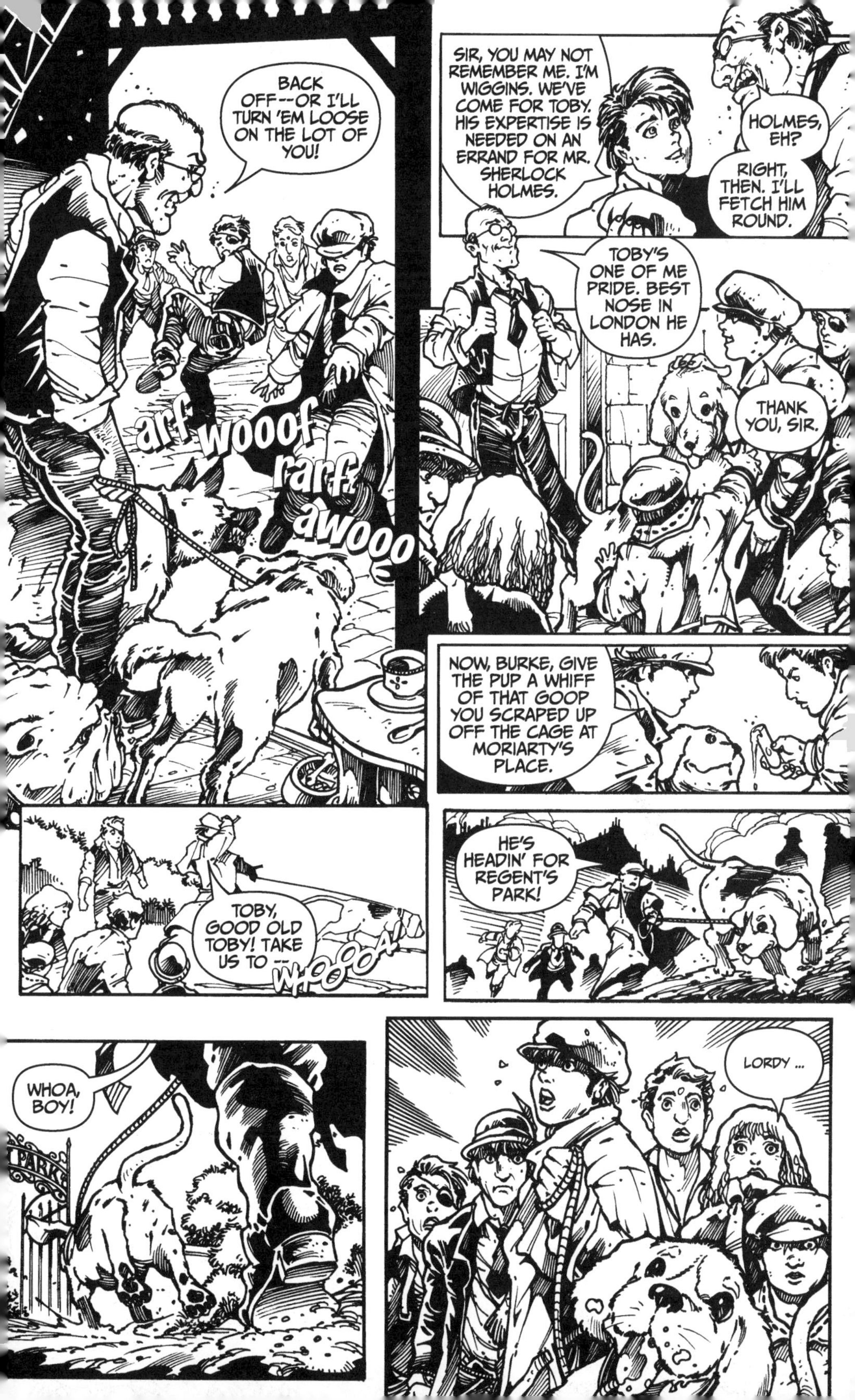
BACK OFF--OR I'LL TURN 'EM LOOSE ON THE LOT OF YOU!
arf wooof rarf awooo
SIR, YOU MAY NOT REMEMBER ME. I'M WIGGINS. WE'VE COME FOR TOBY. HIS EXPERTISE IS NEEDED ON AN ERRAND FOR MR. SHERLOCK HOLMES.
HOLMES, EH?
RIGHT, THEN. I'LL FETCH HIM ROUND.
TOBY'S ONE OF ME PRIDE. BEST NOSE IN LONDON HE HAS.
THANK YOU, SIR.
NOW, BURKE, GIVE THE PUP A WHIFF OF THAT GOOP YOU SCRAPED UP OFF THE CAGE AT MORIARTY'S PLACE.
TOBY, GOOD OLD TOBY! TAKE US TO --
WHOOOOA!
HE'S HEADIN' FOR REGENT'S PARK!
WHOA, BOY!
PARK
LORDY ...

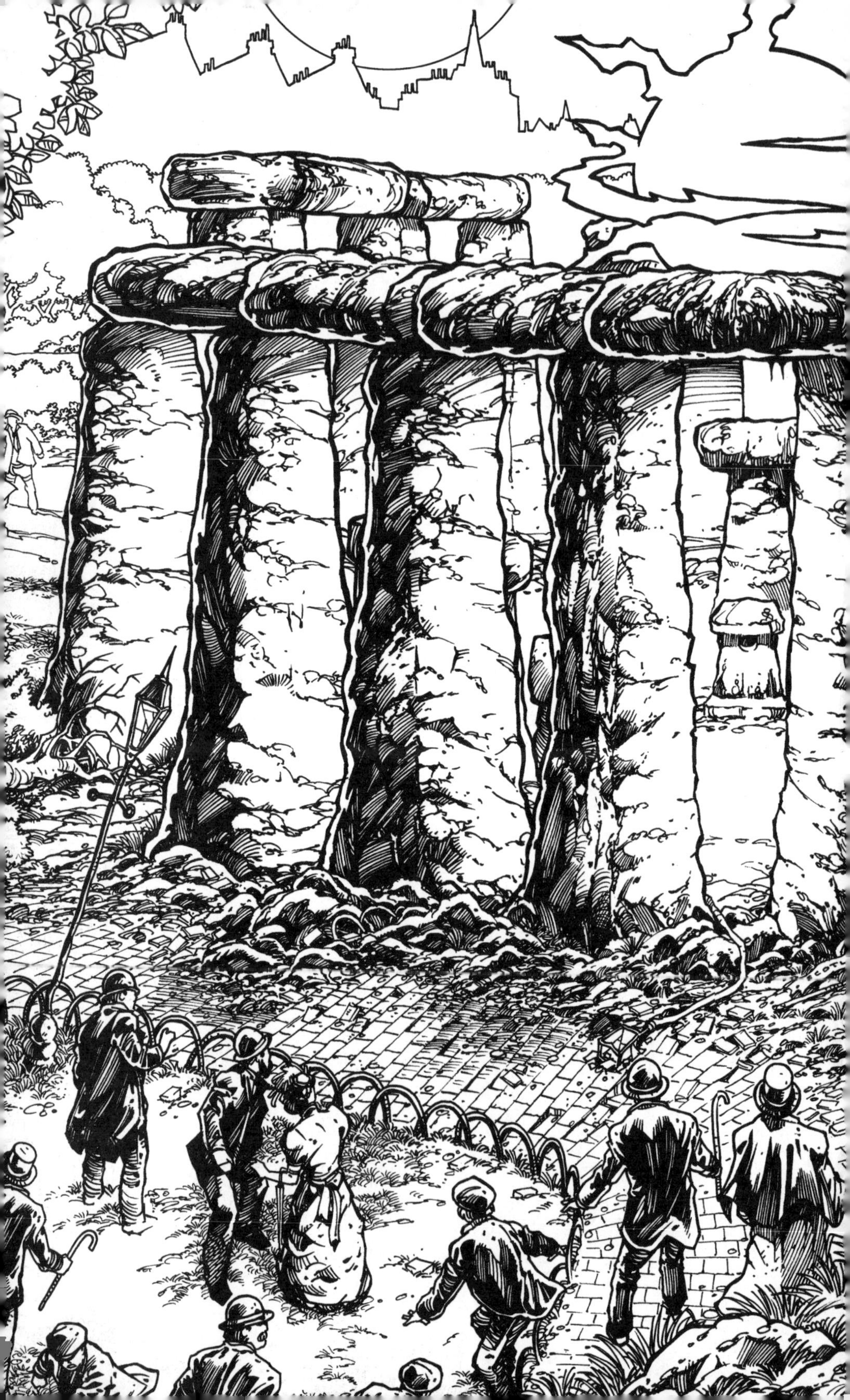

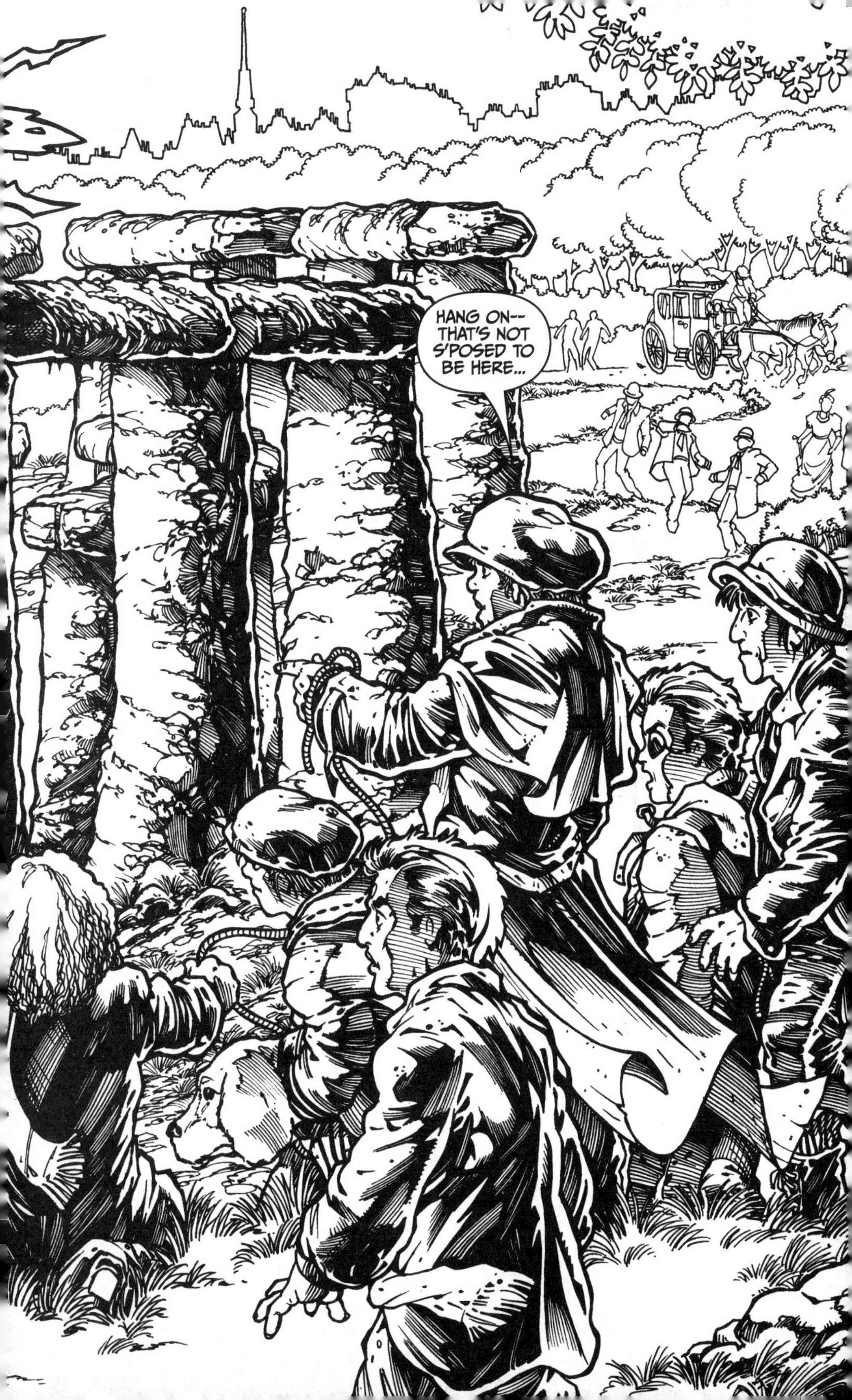
HANG ON--
THAT'S NOT
S'POSED TO
BE HERE...

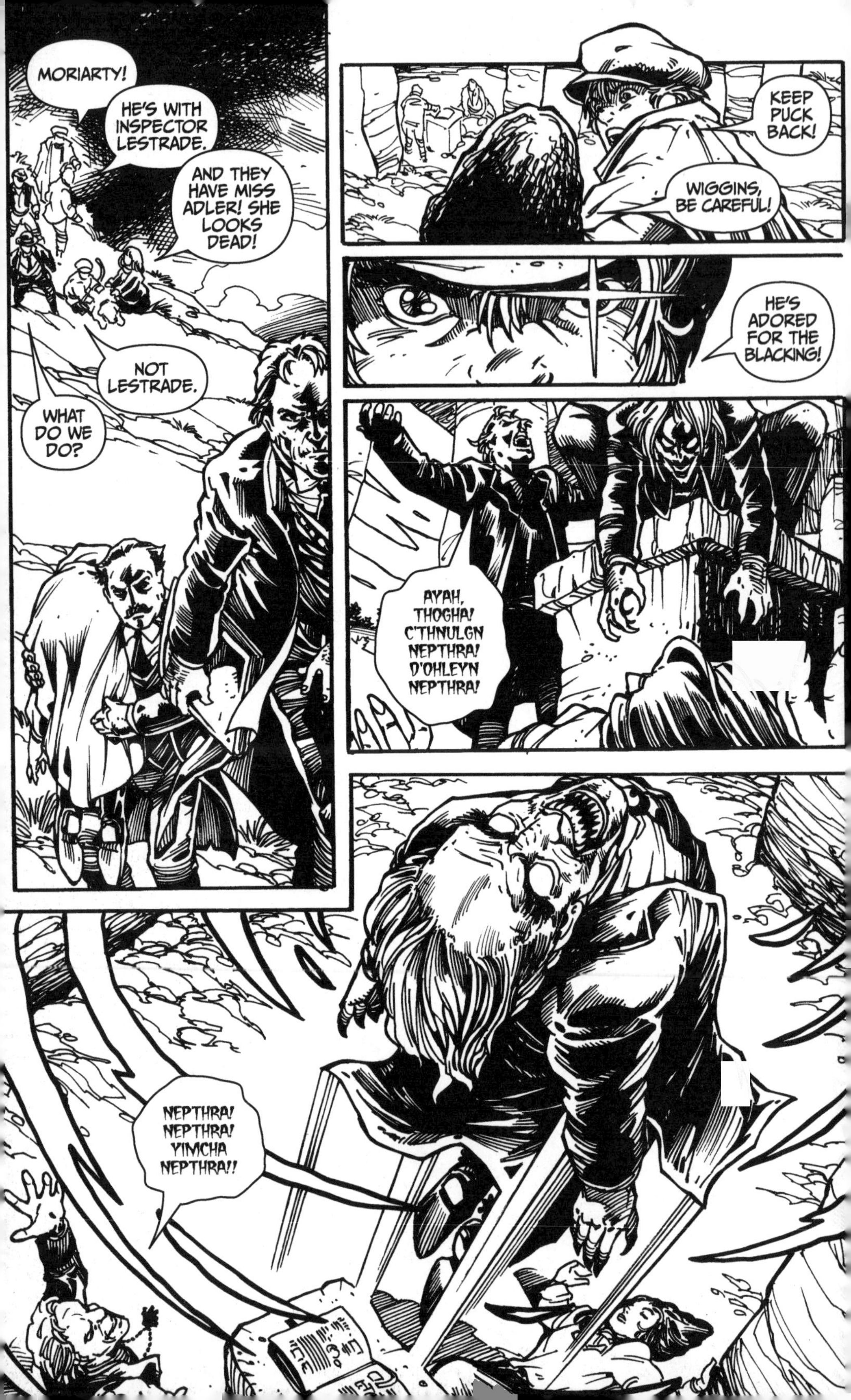
MORIARTY!
HE'S WITH INSPECTOR LESTRADE.
AND THEY HAVE MISS ADLER! SHE LOOKS DEAD!
NOT LESTRADE.
WHAT DO WE DO?
KEEP PUCK BACK!
WIGGINS, BE CAREFUL!
HE'S ADORED FOR THE BLACKING!
AYAH, THOGHA! C'THNULGN NEPTHRA! D'OHLEYN NEPTHRA!
NEPTHRA! NEPTHRA! YIMCHA NEPTHRA!!

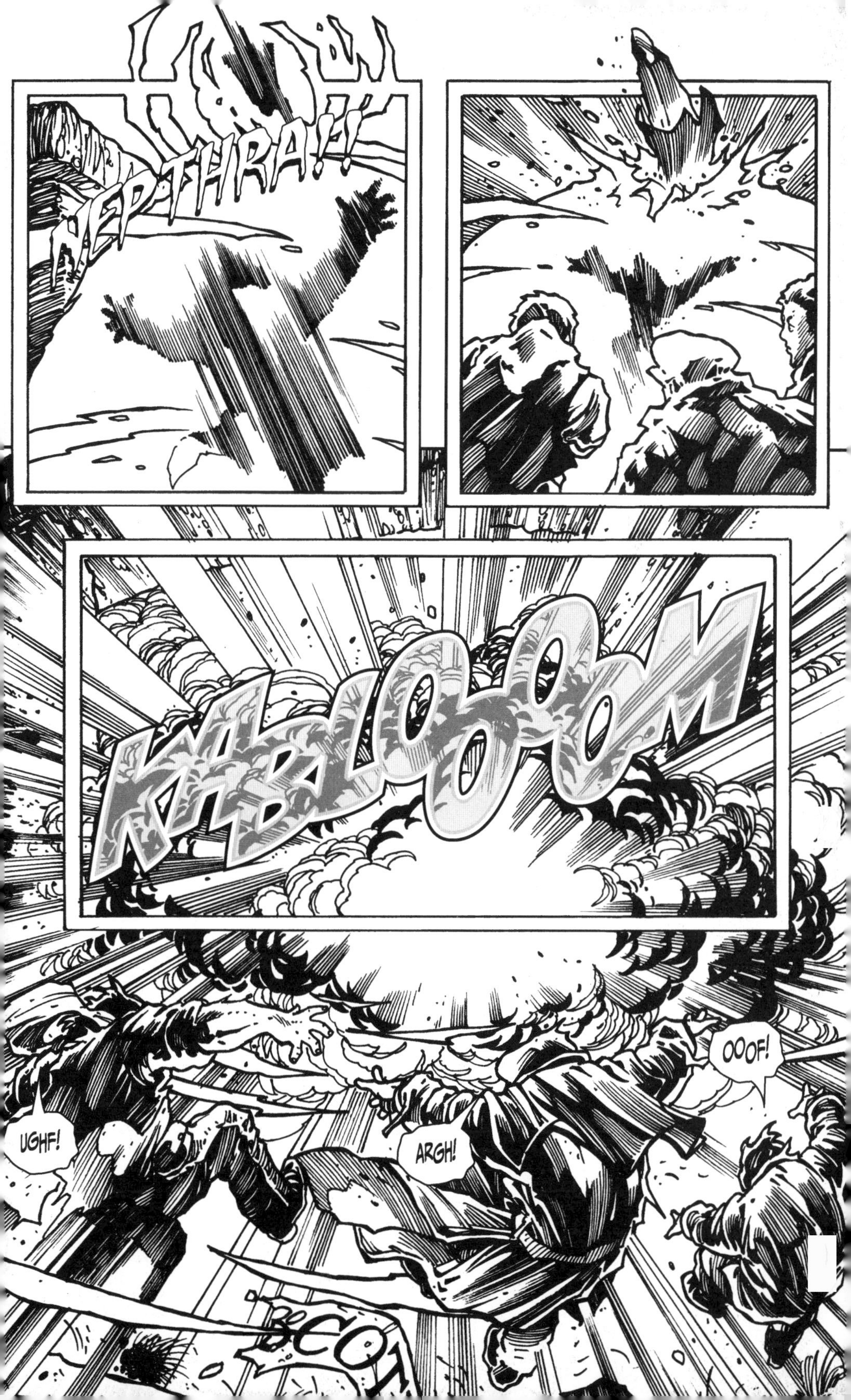
NEPTHRA!!
KABLOOOOM
OOOF!
UGHF!
ARGH!

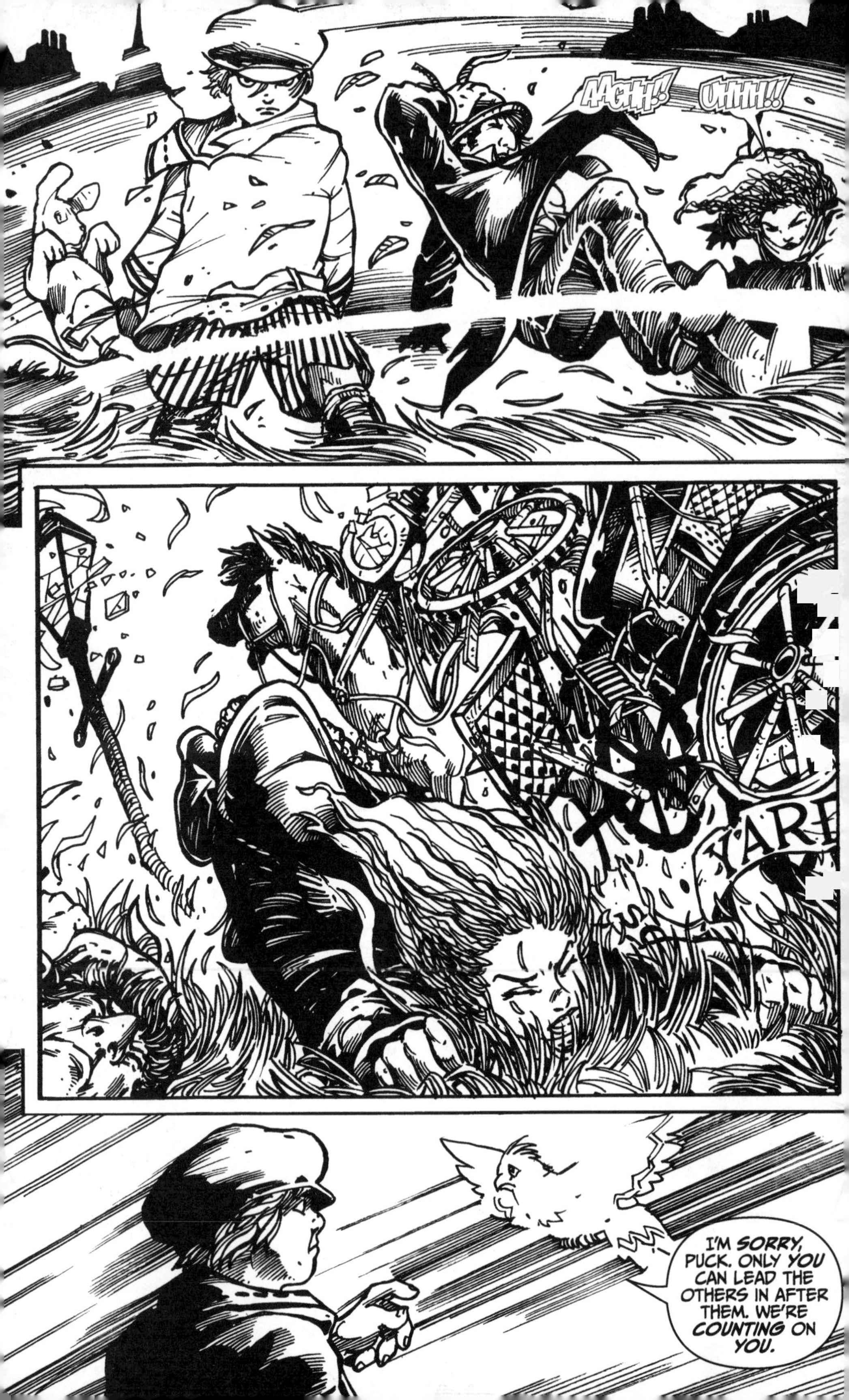
AAGHH!!
UHHH!!
YARD
I'M SORRY, PUCK. ONLY YOU CAN LEAD THE OTHERS IN AFTER THEM. WE'RE COUNTING ON YOU.

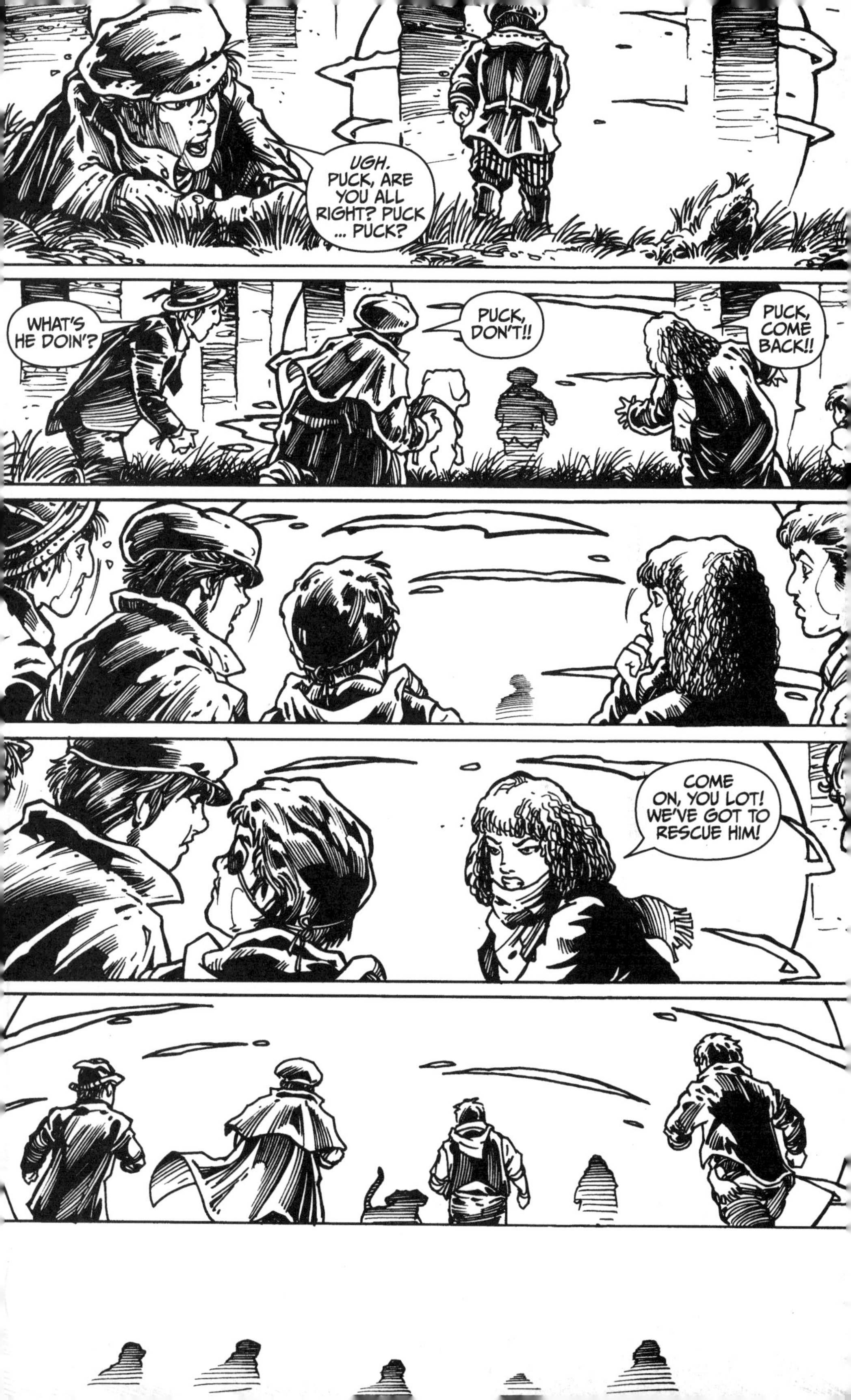
UGH. PUCK, ARE YOU ALL RIGHT? PUCK ... PUCK?
WHAT'S HE DOIN'?
PUCK, DON'T!!
PUCK, COME BACK!!
COME ON, YOU LOT! WE'VE GOT TO RESCUE HIM!

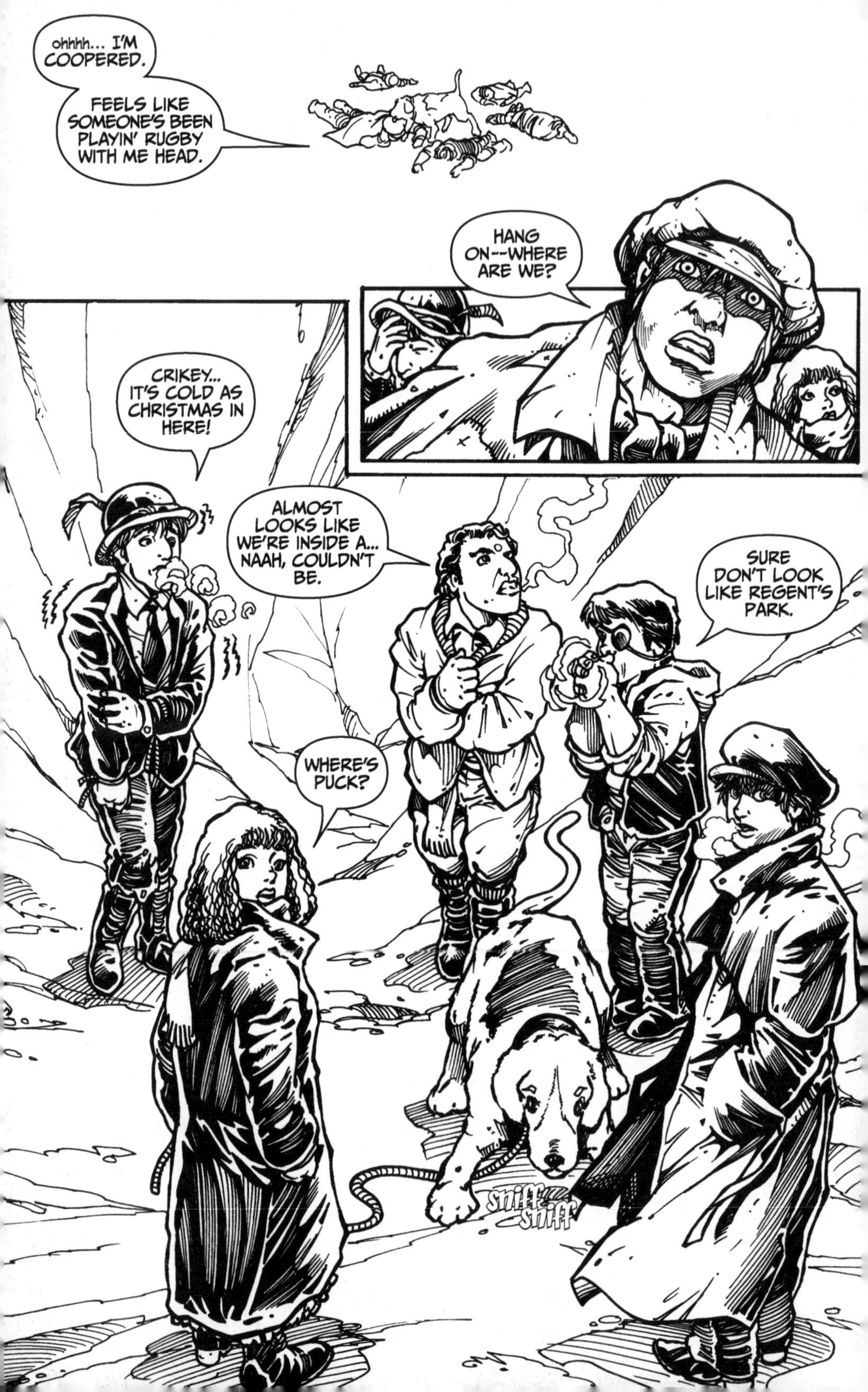
ohhhh... I'M COOPERED.
FEELS LIKE SOMEONE'S BEEN PLAYIN' RUGBY WITH ME HEAD.
HANG ON--WHERE ARE WE?
CRIKEY... IT'S COLD AS CHRISTMAS IN HERE!
ALMOST LOOKS LIKE WE'RE INSIDE A... NAAH, COULDN'T BE.
SURE DON'T LOOK LIKE REGENT'S PARK.
WHERE'S PUCK?
SNIFF SNIFF

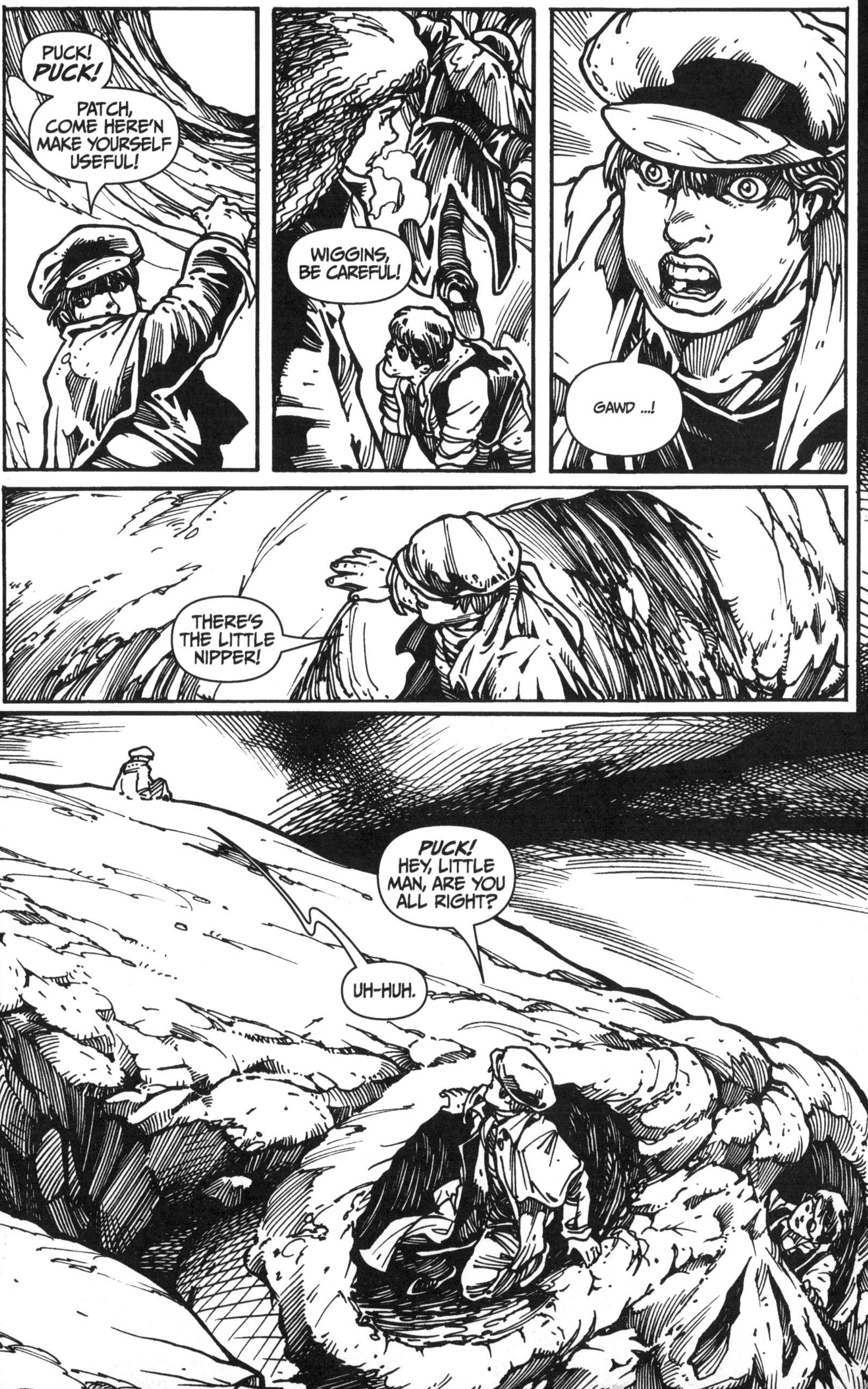
PUCK! *PUCK!*
PATCH, COME HERE'N MAKE YOURSELF USEFUL!
WIGGINS, BE CAREFUL!
GAWD ...!
THERE'S THE LITTLE NIPPER!
PUCK! HEY, LITTLE MAN, ARE YOU ALL RIGHT?
UH-HUH.

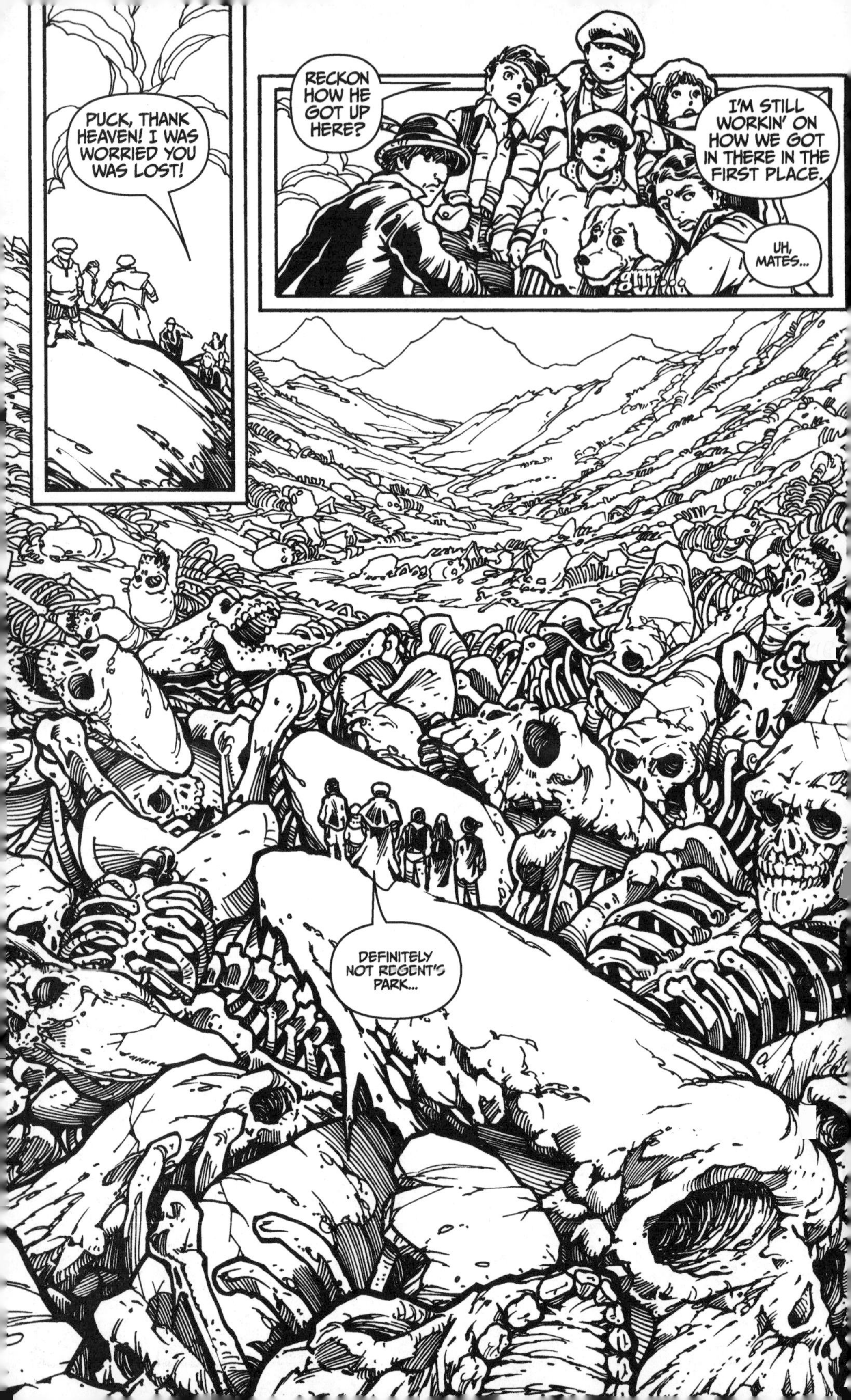
PUCK, THANK HEAVEN! I WAS WORRIED YOU WAS LOST!
RECKON HOW HE GOT UP HERE?
I'M STILL WORKIN' ON HOW WE GOT IN THERE IN THE FIRST PLACE.
UH, MATES...
grrr...
DEFINITELY NOT REGENT'S PARK...

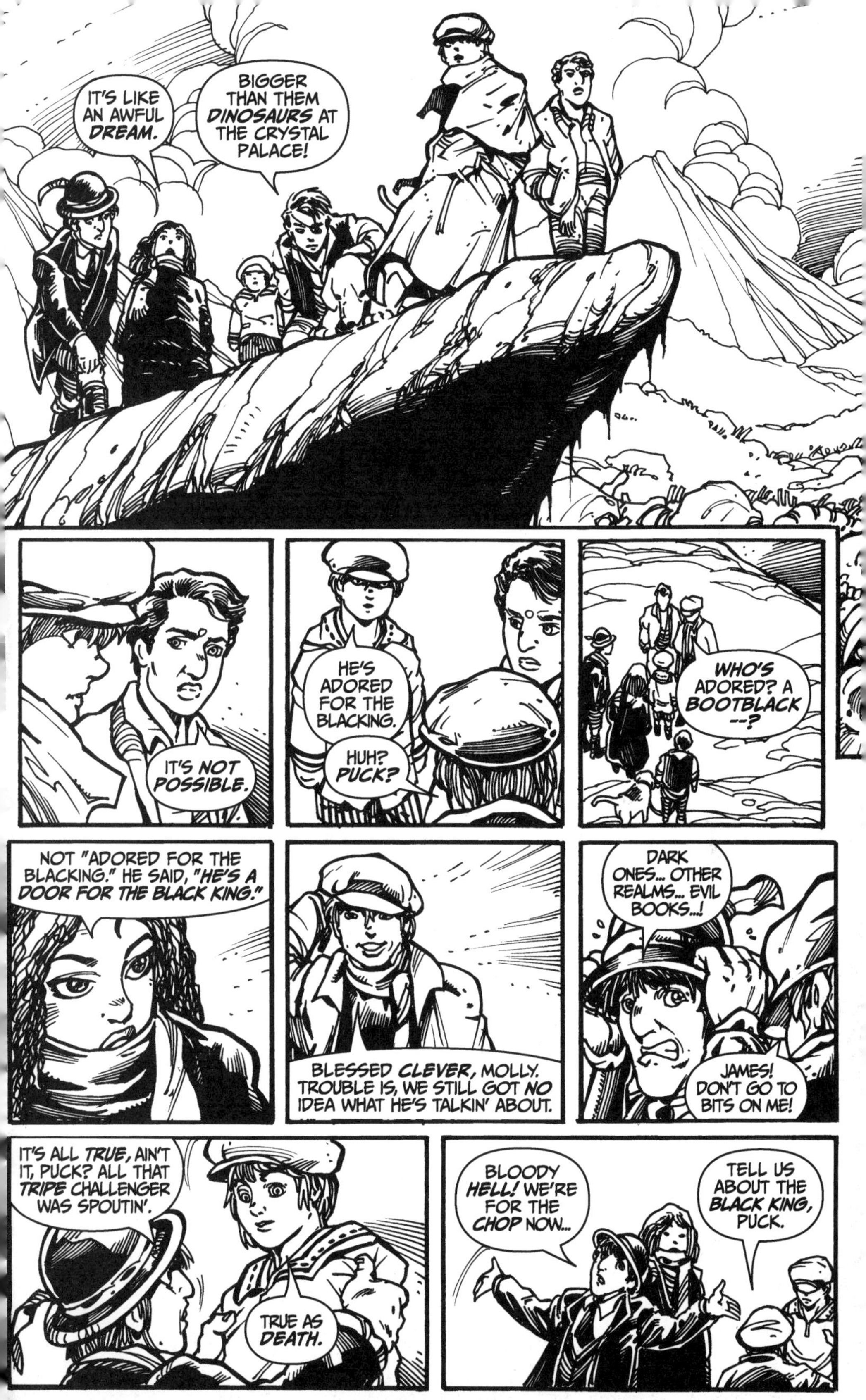
IT'S LIKE AN AWFUL *DREAM.*
BIGGER THAN THEM *DINOSAURS* AT THE CRYSTAL PALACE!
IT'S *NOT POSSIBLE.*
HE'S ADORED FOR THE BLACKING.
HUH? *PUCK?*
WHO'S ADORED? A *BOOTBLACK* --?
NOT "ADORED FOR THE BLACKING." HE SAID, "*HE'S A DOOR FOR THE BLACK KING.*"
BLESSED *CLEVER,* MOLLY. TROUBLE IS, WE STILL GOT *NO* IDEA WHAT HE'S TALKIN' ABOUT.
DARK ONES... OTHER REALMS... EVIL BOOKS...!
JAMES! DON'T GO TO BITS ON ME!
IT'S ALL *TRUE,* AIN'T IT, PUCK? ALL THAT *TRIPE* CHALLENGER WAS SPOUTIN'.
TRUE AS *DEATH.*
BLOODY *HELL!* WE'RE FOR THE *CHOP* NOW...
TELL US ABOUT THE *BLACK KING,* PUCK.

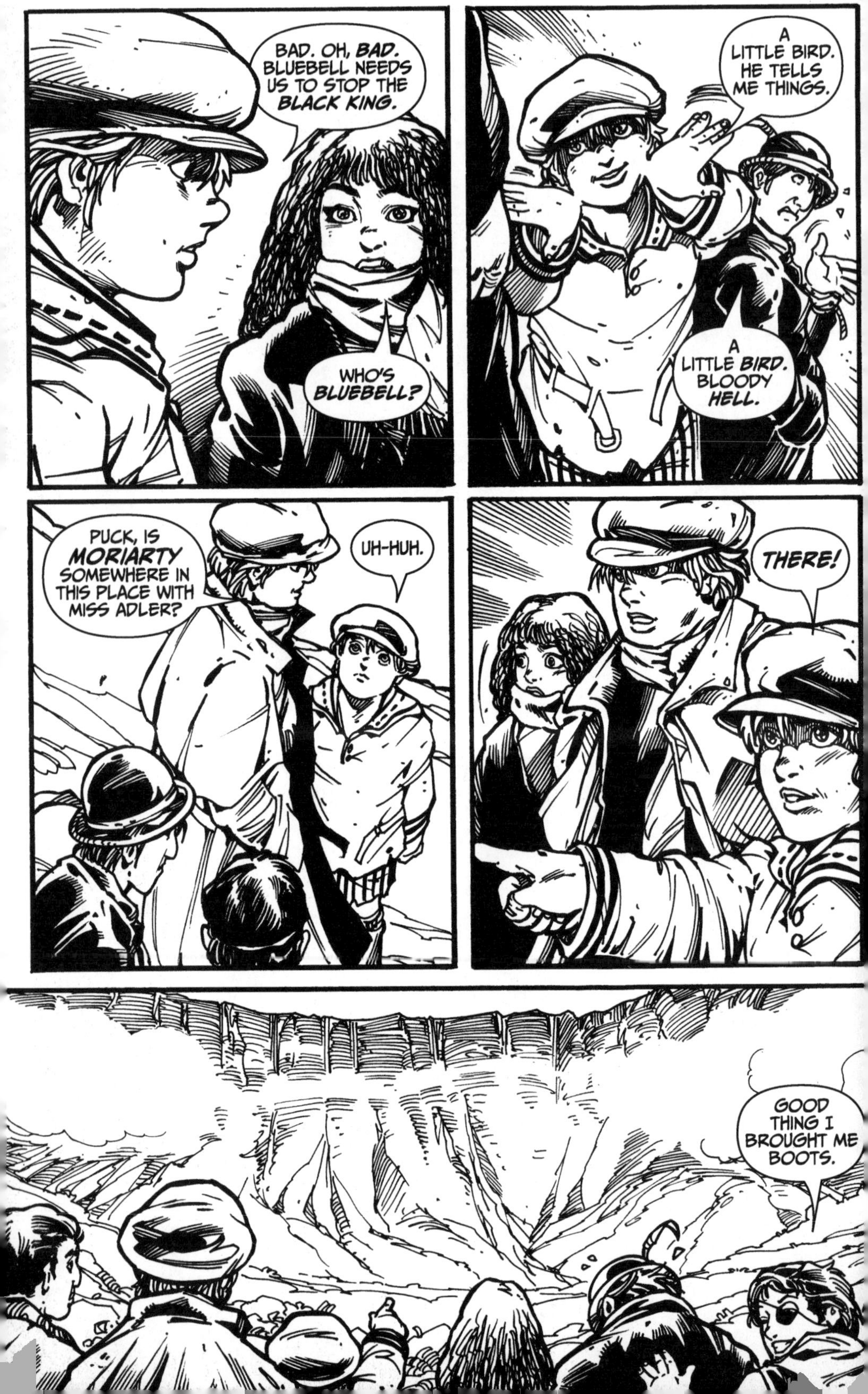
BAD. OH, BAD. BLUEBELL NEEDS US TO STOP THE BLACK KING.
WHO'S BLUEBELL?
A LITTLE BIRD. HE TELLS ME THINGS.
A LITTLE BIRD. BLOODY HELL.
PUCK, IS MORIARTY SOMEWHERE IN THIS PLACE WITH MISS ADLER?
UH-HUH.
THERE!
GOOD THING I BROUGHT ME BOOTS.

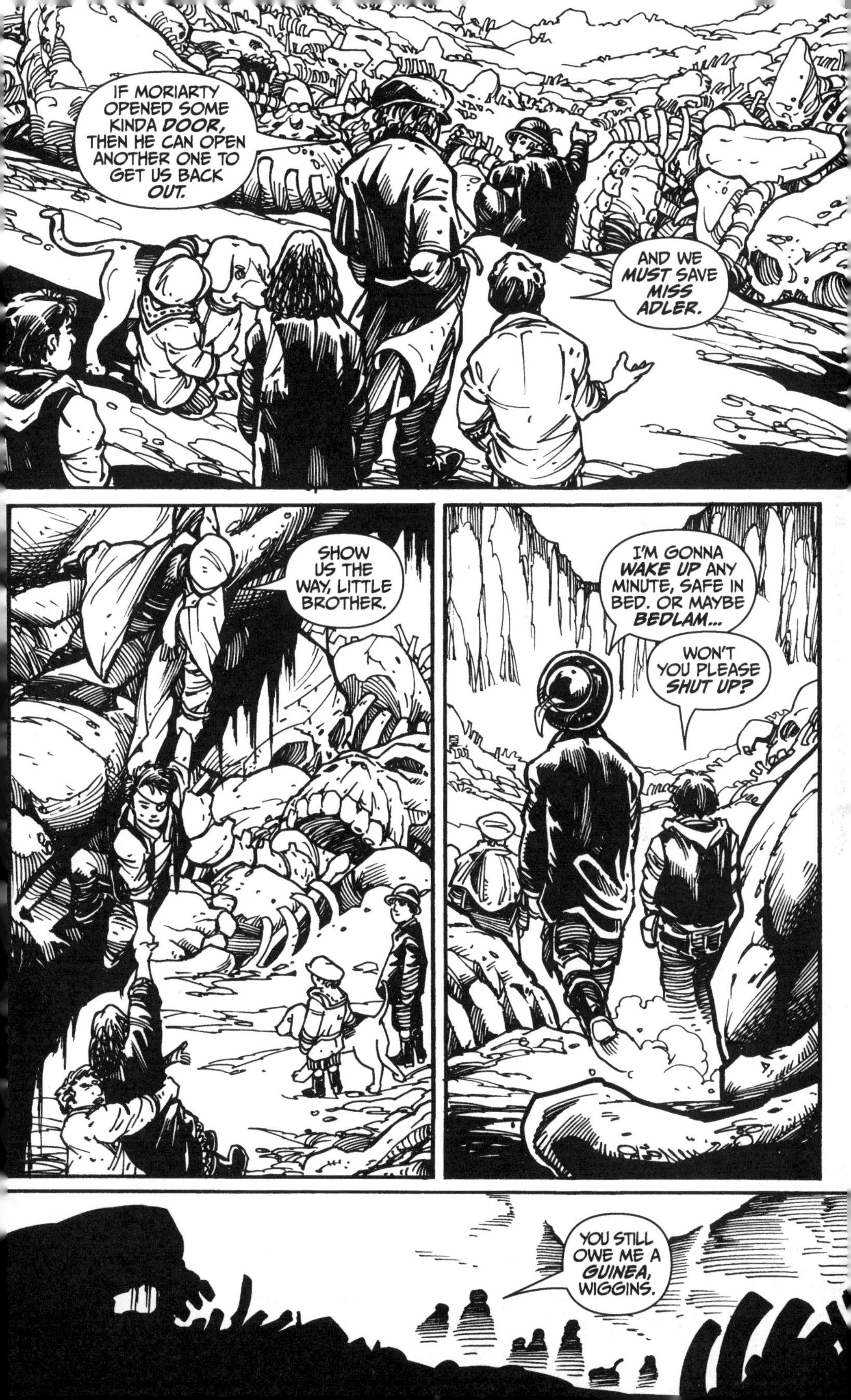
IF MORIARTY OPENED SOME KINDA *DOOR,* THEN HE CAN OPEN ANOTHER ONE TO GET US BACK *OUT.*
AND WE *MUST* SAVE *MISS* ADLER.
SHOW US THE WAY, LITTLE BROTHER.
I'M GONNA *WAKE UP* ANY MINUTE, SAFE IN BED. OR MAYBE *BEDLAM...*
WON'T YOU PLEASE *SHUT UP?*
YOU STILL OWE ME A *GUINEA,* WIGGINS.

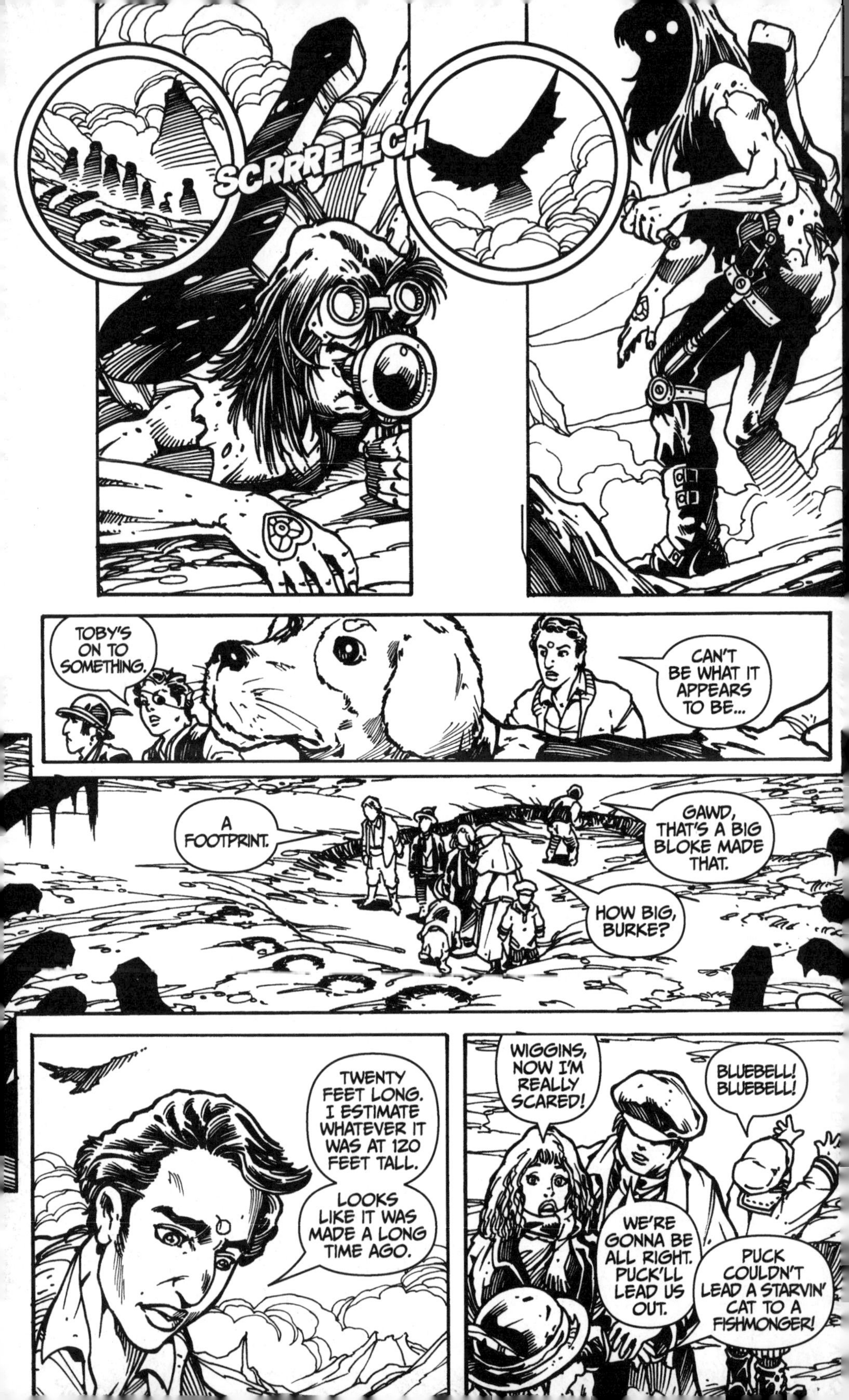
SCRRREEECH
TOBY'S ON TO SOMETHING.
CAN'T BE WHAT IT APPEARS TO BE...
A FOOTPRINT.
GAWD, THAT'S A BIG BLOKE MADE THAT.
HOW BIG, BURKE?
TWENTY FEET LONG. I ESTIMATE WHATEVER IT WAS AT 120 FEET TALL.
LOOKS LIKE IT WAS MADE A LONG TIME AGO.
WIGGINS, NOW I'M REALLY SCARED!
BLUEBELL! BLUEBELL!
WE'RE GONNA BE ALL RIGHT. PUCK'LL LEAD US OUT.
PUCK COULDN'T LEAD A STARVIN' CAT TO A FISHMONGER!

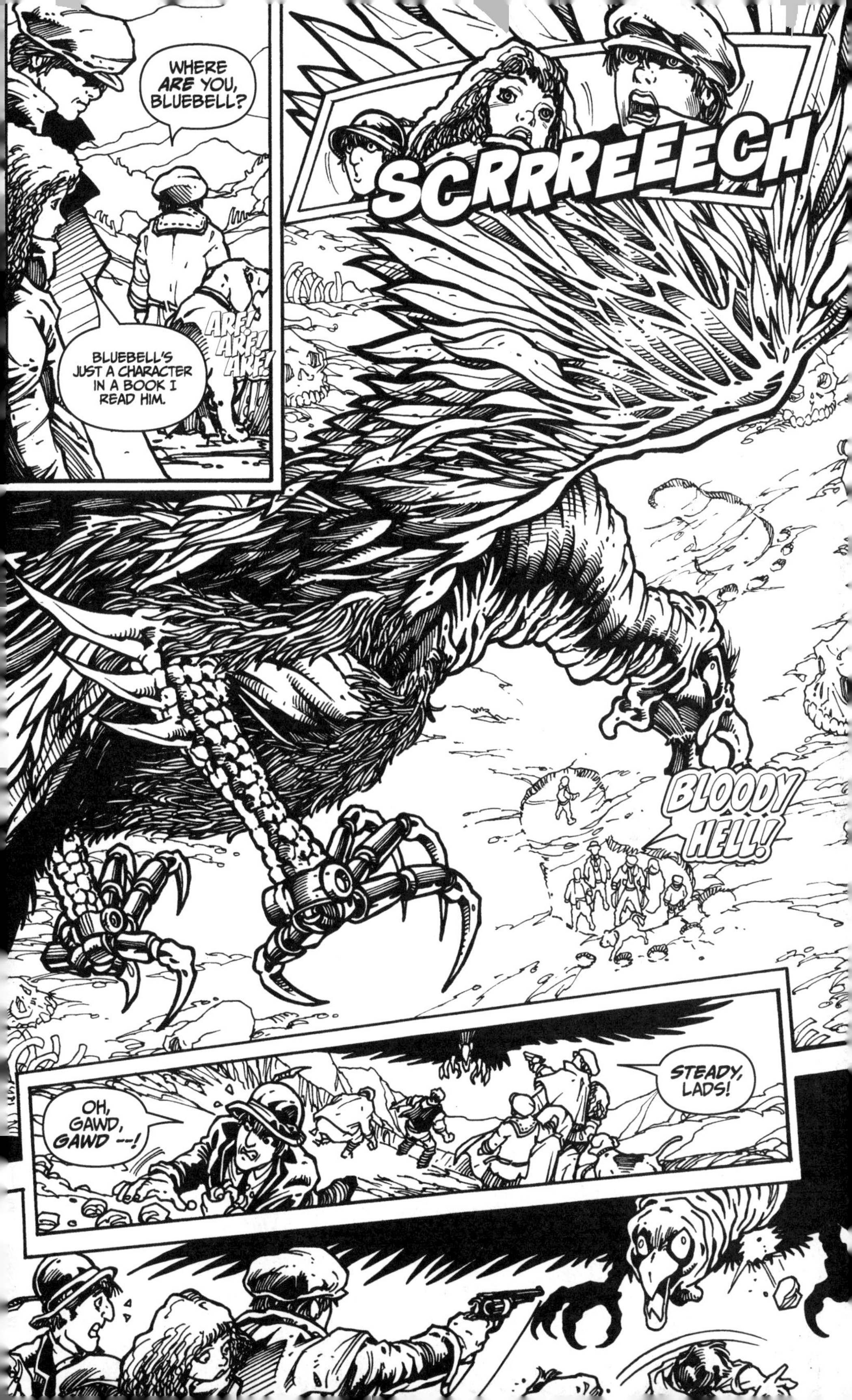
WHERE *ARE* YOU, BLUEBELL?
BLUEBELL'S JUST A CHARACTER IN A BOOK I READ HIM.
ARF! ARF! ARF!
SCRRRREEEECH
BLOODY HELL!
STEADY, LADS!
OH, GAWD, GAWD --!

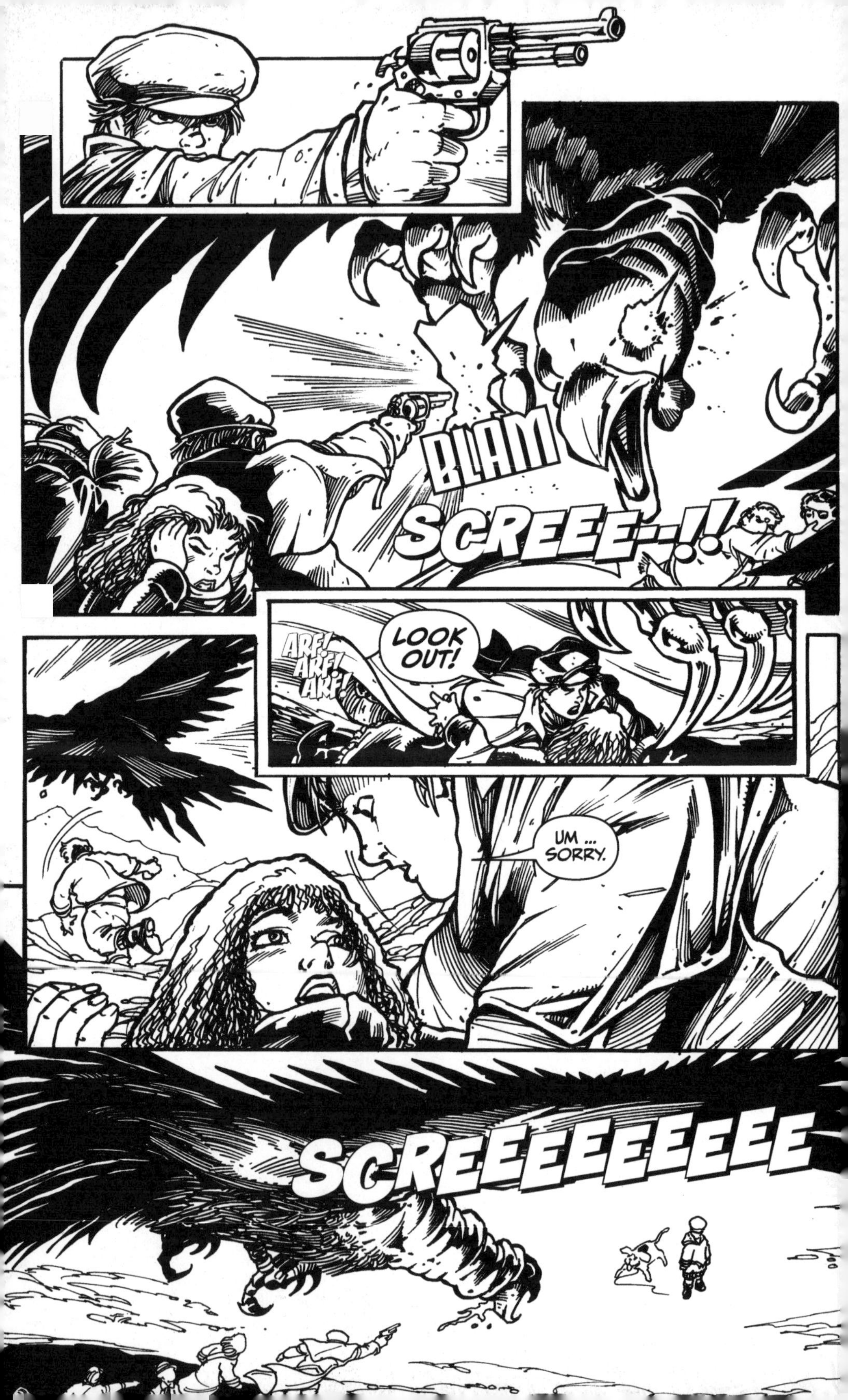
BLAM
SCREEE--!!
ARF! ARF! ARF!
LOOK OUT!
UM ... SORRY.
SCREEEEEEEEEE

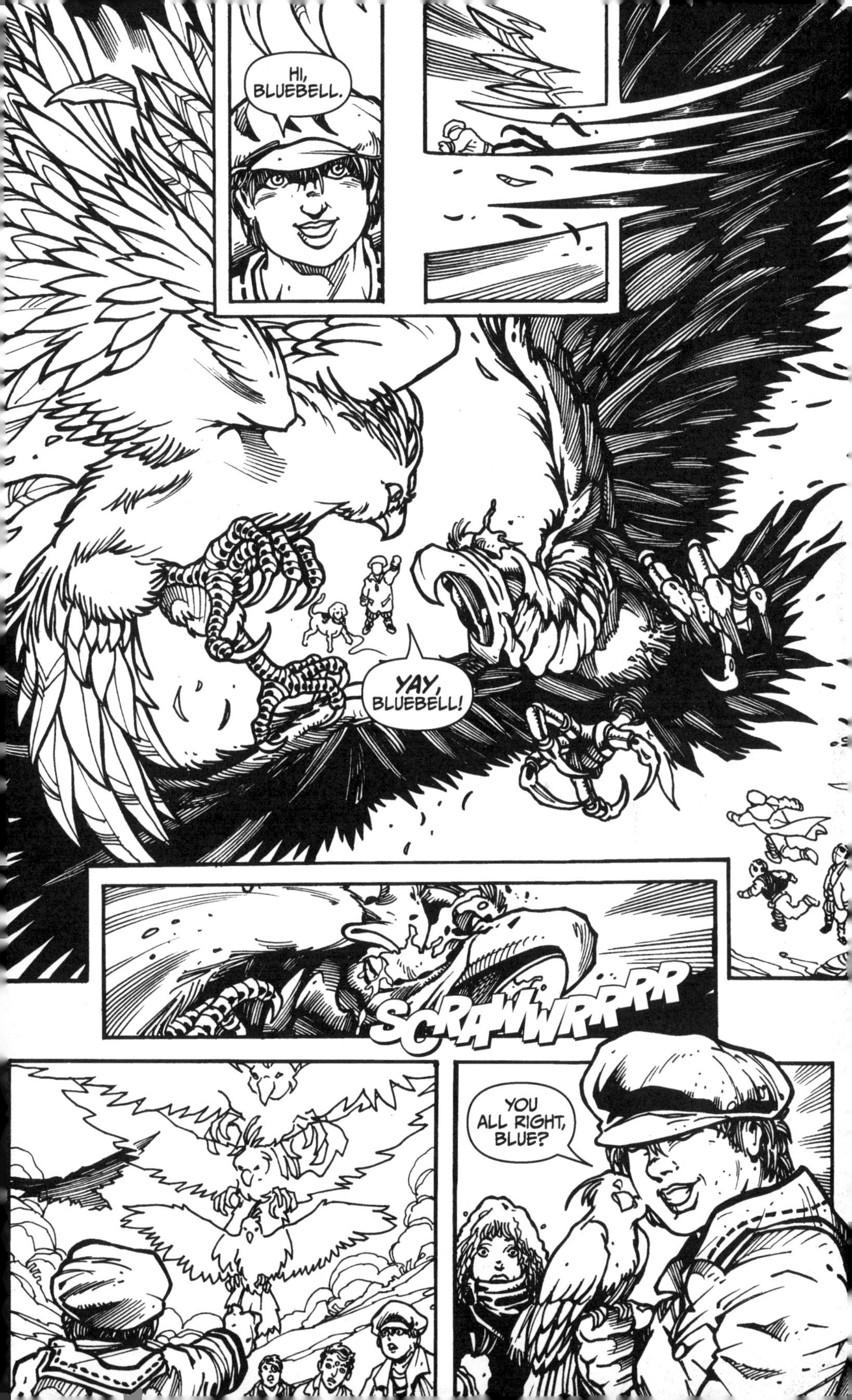

HI, BLUEBELL.
YAY, BLUEBELL!
SCRAWWRRRR
YOU ALL RIGHT, BLUE?

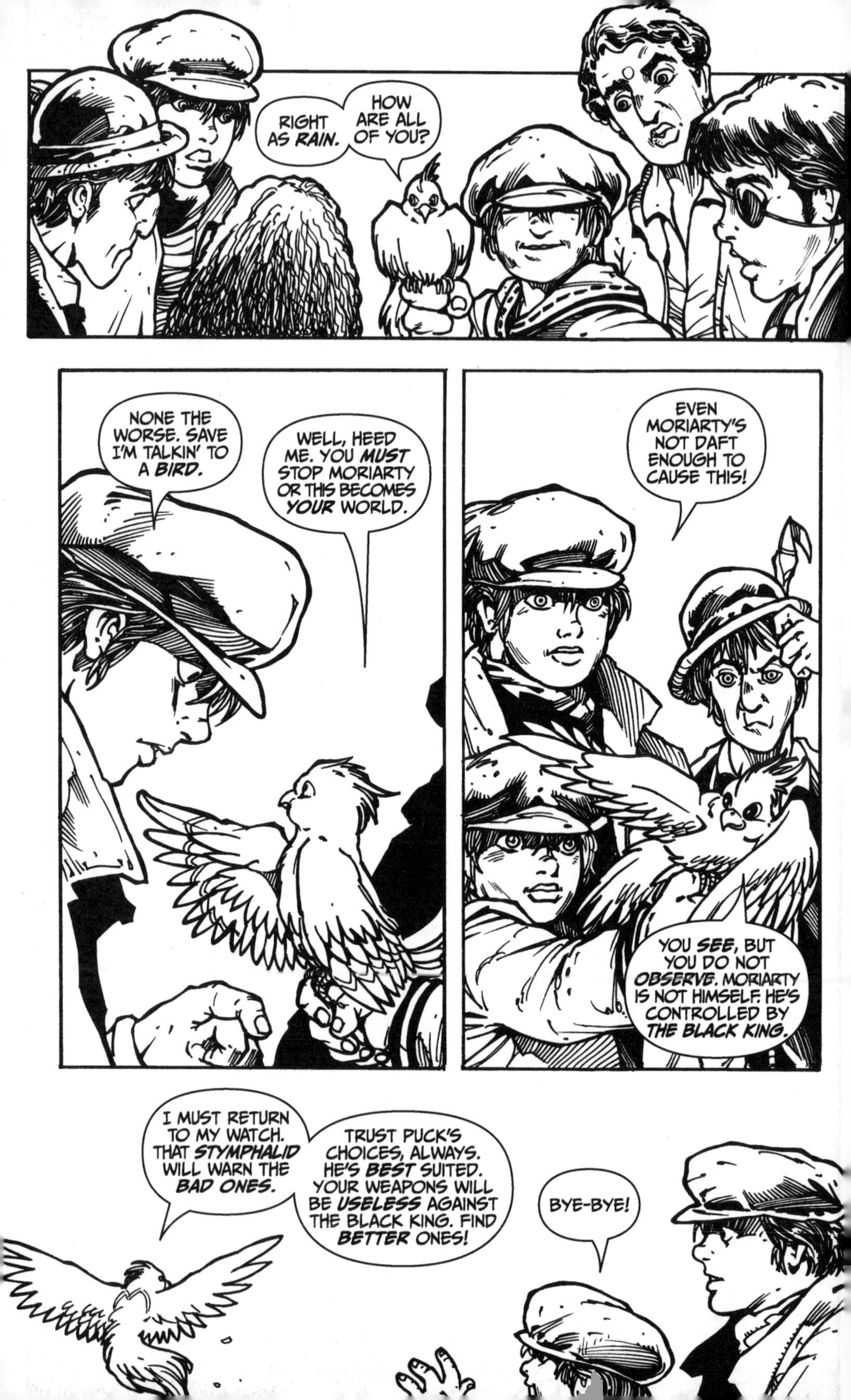

RIGHT AS RAIN.
HOW ARE ALL OF YOU?
NONE THE WORSE. SAVE I'M TALKIN' TO A BIRD.
WELL, HEED ME. YOU MUST STOP MORIARTY OR THIS BECOMES YOUR WORLD.
EVEN MORIARTY'S NOT DAFT ENOUGH TO CAUSE THIS!
YOU SEE, BUT YOU DO NOT OBSERVE. MORIARTY IS NOT HIMSELF. HE'S CONTROLLED BY THE BLACK KING.
I MUST RETURN TO MY WATCH. THAT STYMPHALID WILL WARN THE BAD ONES.
TRUST PUCK'S CHOICES, ALWAYS. HE'S BEST SUITED. YOUR WEAPONS WILL BE USELESS AGAINST THE BLACK KING. FIND BETTER ONES!
BYE-BYE!

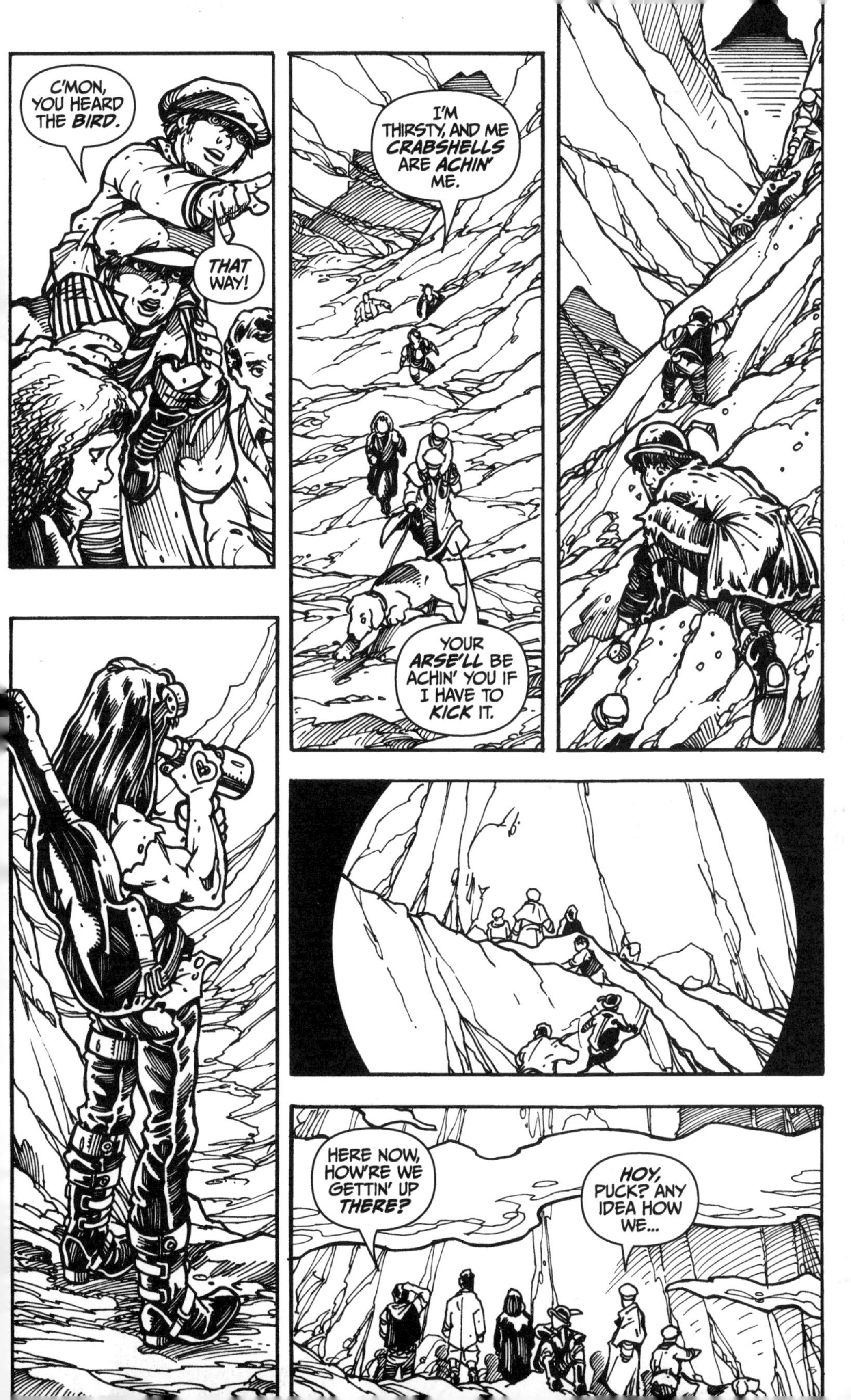
C'MON, YOU HEARD THE *BIRD*.
THAT WAY!
I'M THIRSTY, AND ME *CRABSHELLS* ARE *ACHIN'* ME.
YOUR *ARSE'LL* BE ACHIN' YOU IF I HAVE TO *KICK* IT.
HERE NOW, HOW'RE WE GETTIN' UP *THERE?*
HOY, PUCK? ANY IDEA HOW WE...

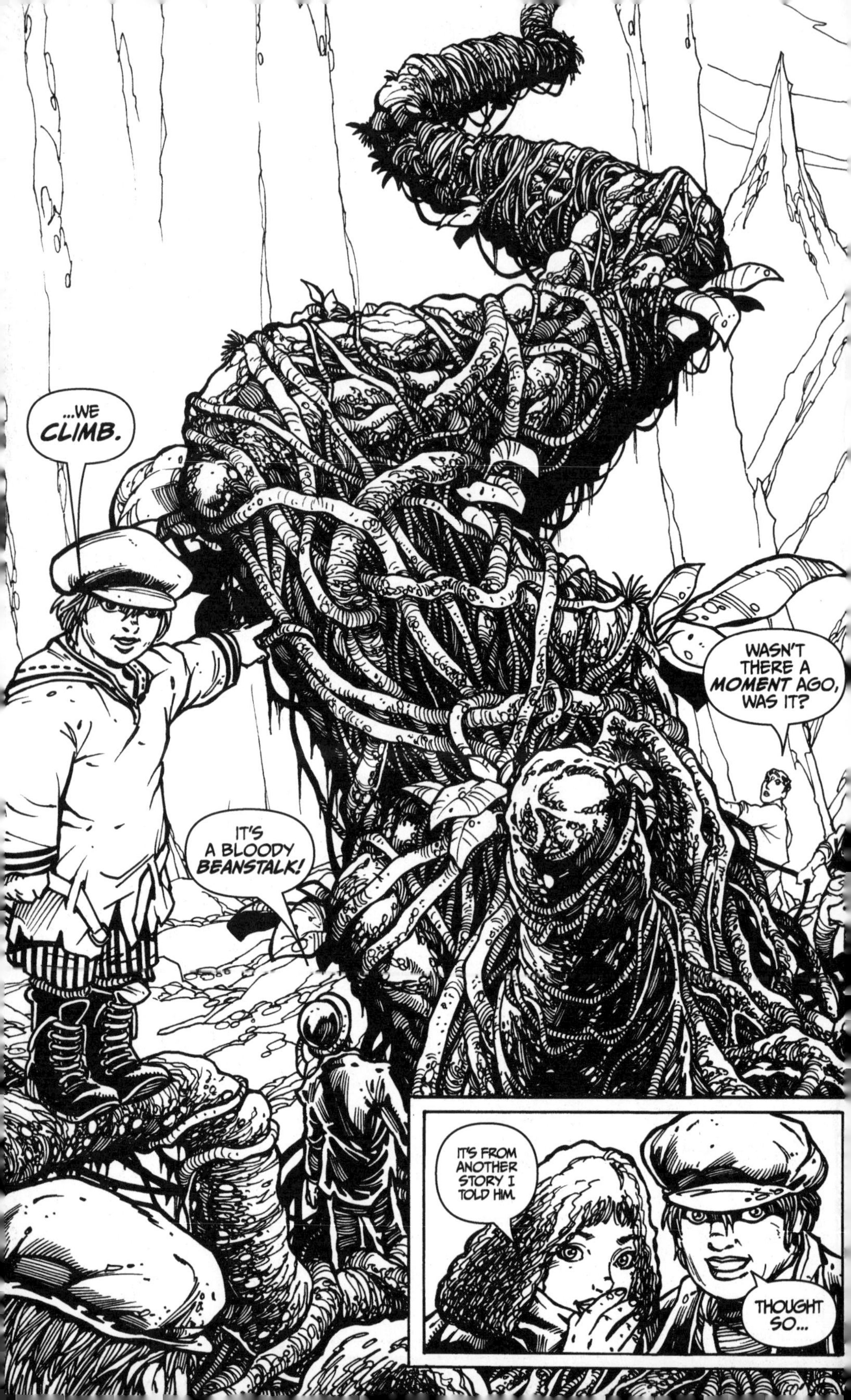
...WE CLIMB.
WASN'T THERE A MOMENT AGO, WAS IT?
IT'S A BLOODY BEANSTALK!
IT'S FROM ANOTHER STORY I TOLD HIM.
THOUGHT SO...

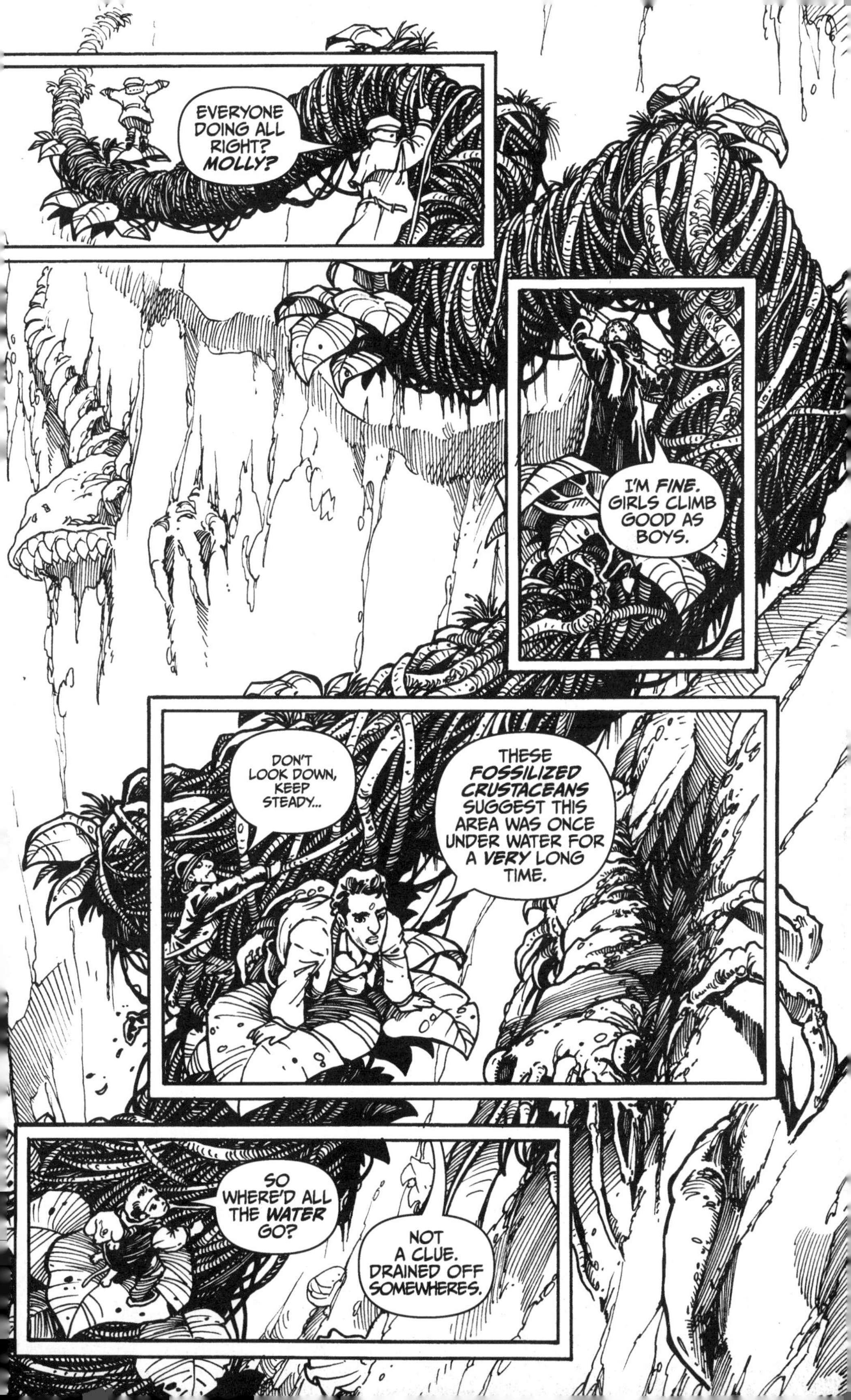
EVERYONE DOING ALL RIGHT? MOLLY?
I'M FINE. GIRLS CLIMB GOOD AS BOYS.
DON'T LOOK DOWN, KEEP STEADY...
THESE FOSSILIZED CRUSTACEANS SUGGEST THIS AREA WAS ONCE UNDER WATER FOR A VERY LONG TIME.
SO WHERE'D ALL THE WATER GO?
NOT A CLUE. DRAINED OFF SOMEWHERES.

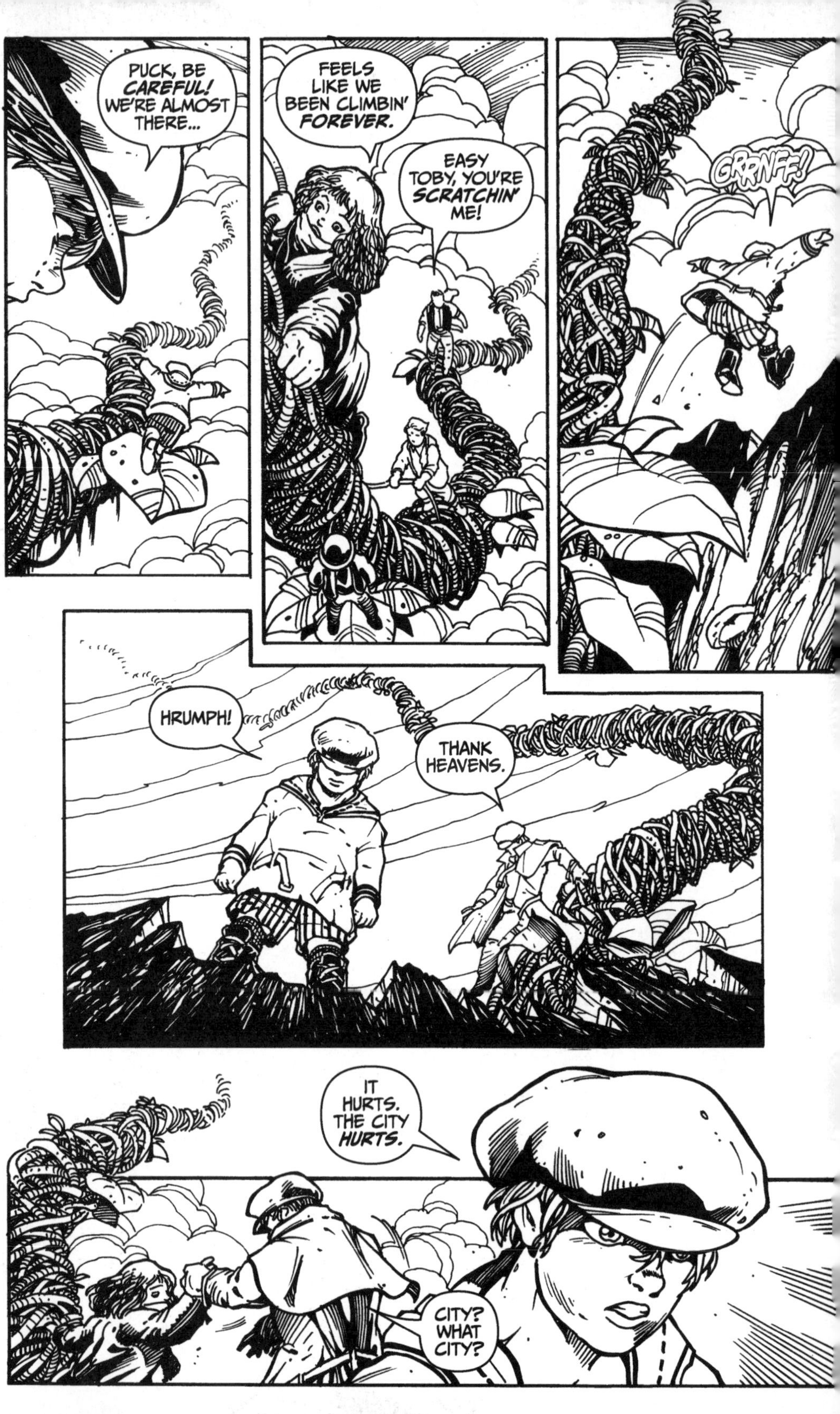
PUCK, BE CAREFUL! WE'RE ALMOST THERE...
FEELS LIKE WE BEEN CLIMBIN' FOREVER.
EASY TOBY, YOU'RE SCRATCHIN' ME!
GRRNFF!
HRUMPH!
THANK HEAVENS.
IT HURTS. THE CITY HURTS.
CITY? WHAT CITY?

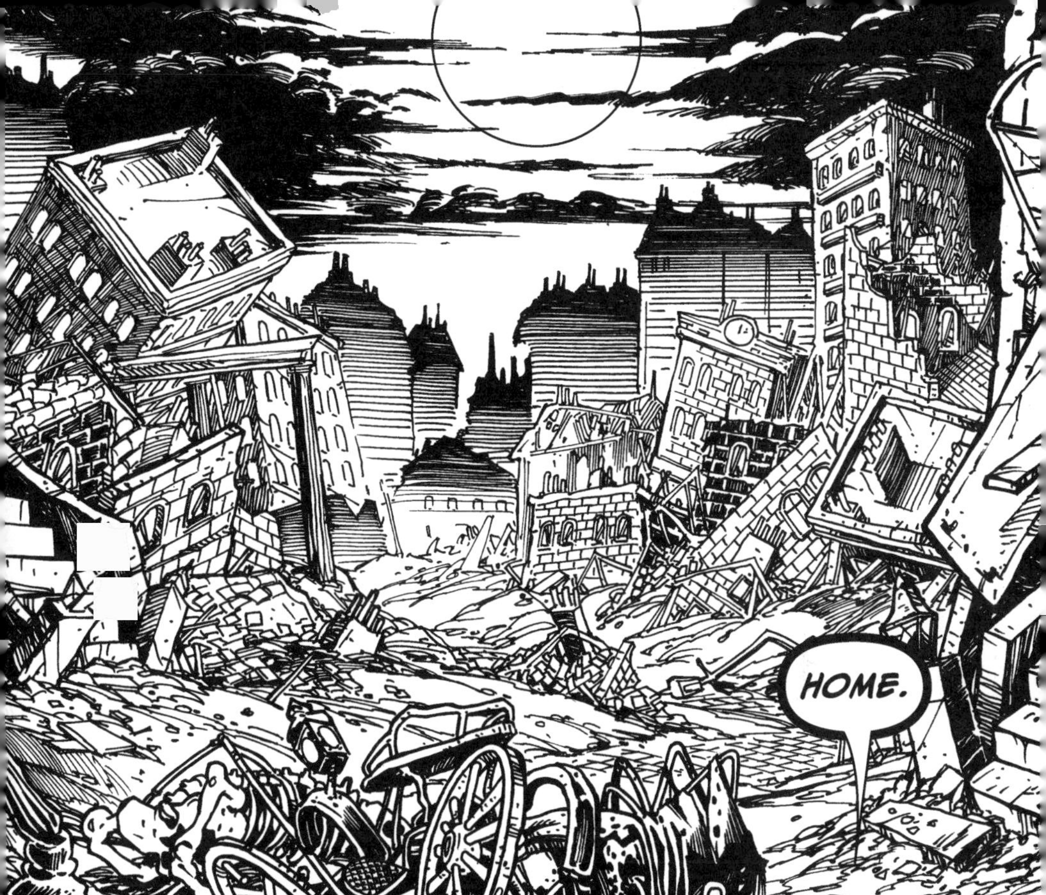
HOME.

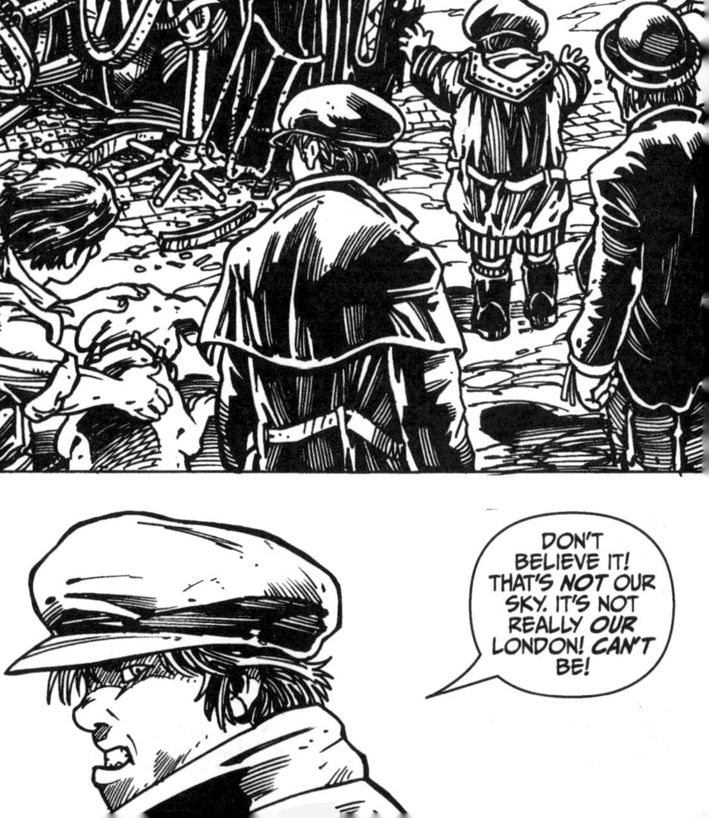
DON'T BELIEVE IT! THAT'S NOT OUR SKY. IT'S NOT REALLY OUR LONDON! CAN'T BE!

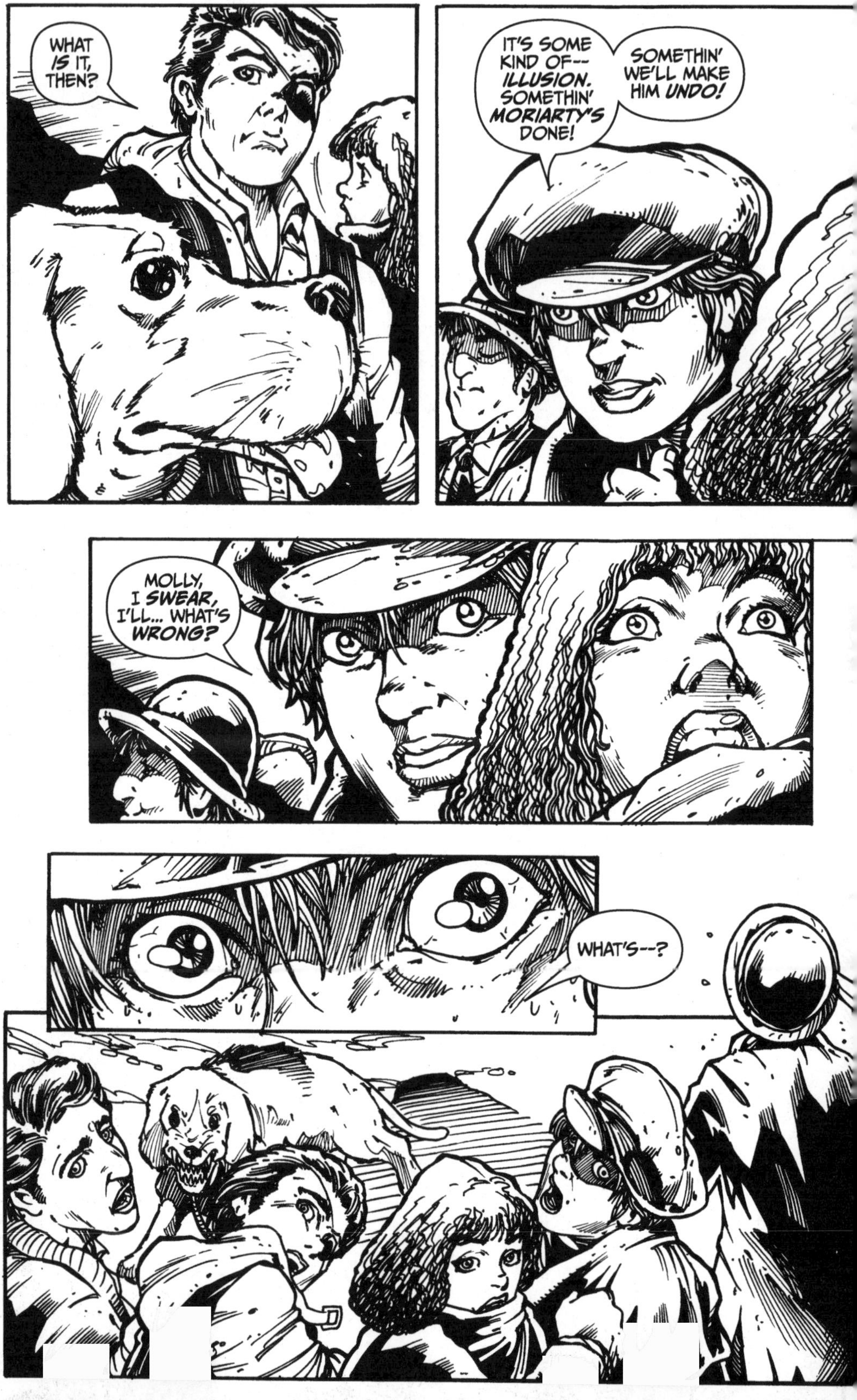
WHAT IS IT, THEN?
IT'S SOME KIND OF-- ILLUSION. SOMETHIN' MORIARTY'S DONE!
SOMETHIN' WE'LL MAKE HIM UNDO!
MOLLY, I SWEAR, I'LL... WHAT'S WRONG?
WHAT'S--?

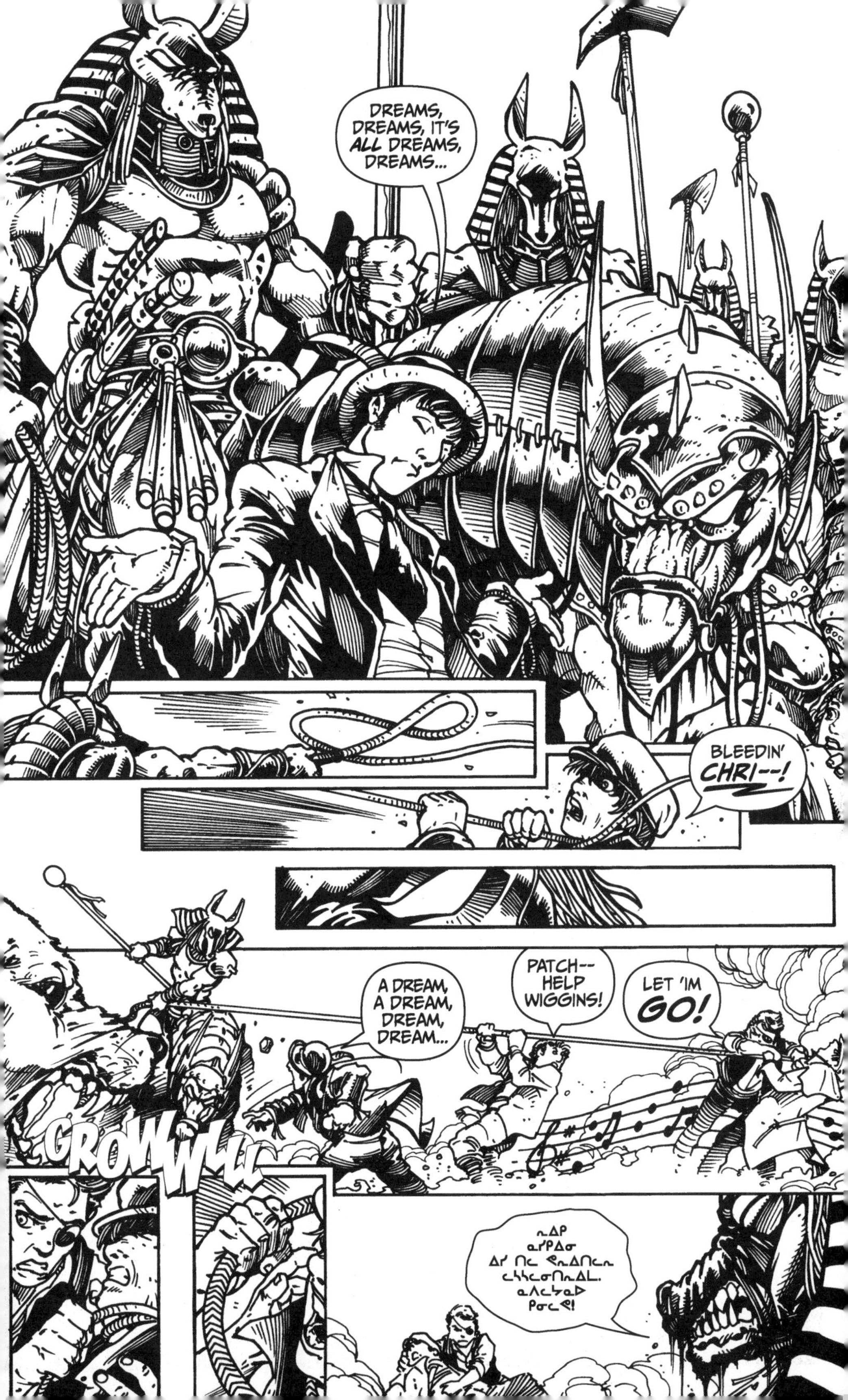
DREAMS, DREAMS, IT'S ALL DREAMS, DREAMS...
BLEEDIN' CHRI--!
A DREAM, A DREAM, DREAM, DREAM...
PATCH-- HELP WIGGINS!
LET 'IM GO!
GROWWLLL

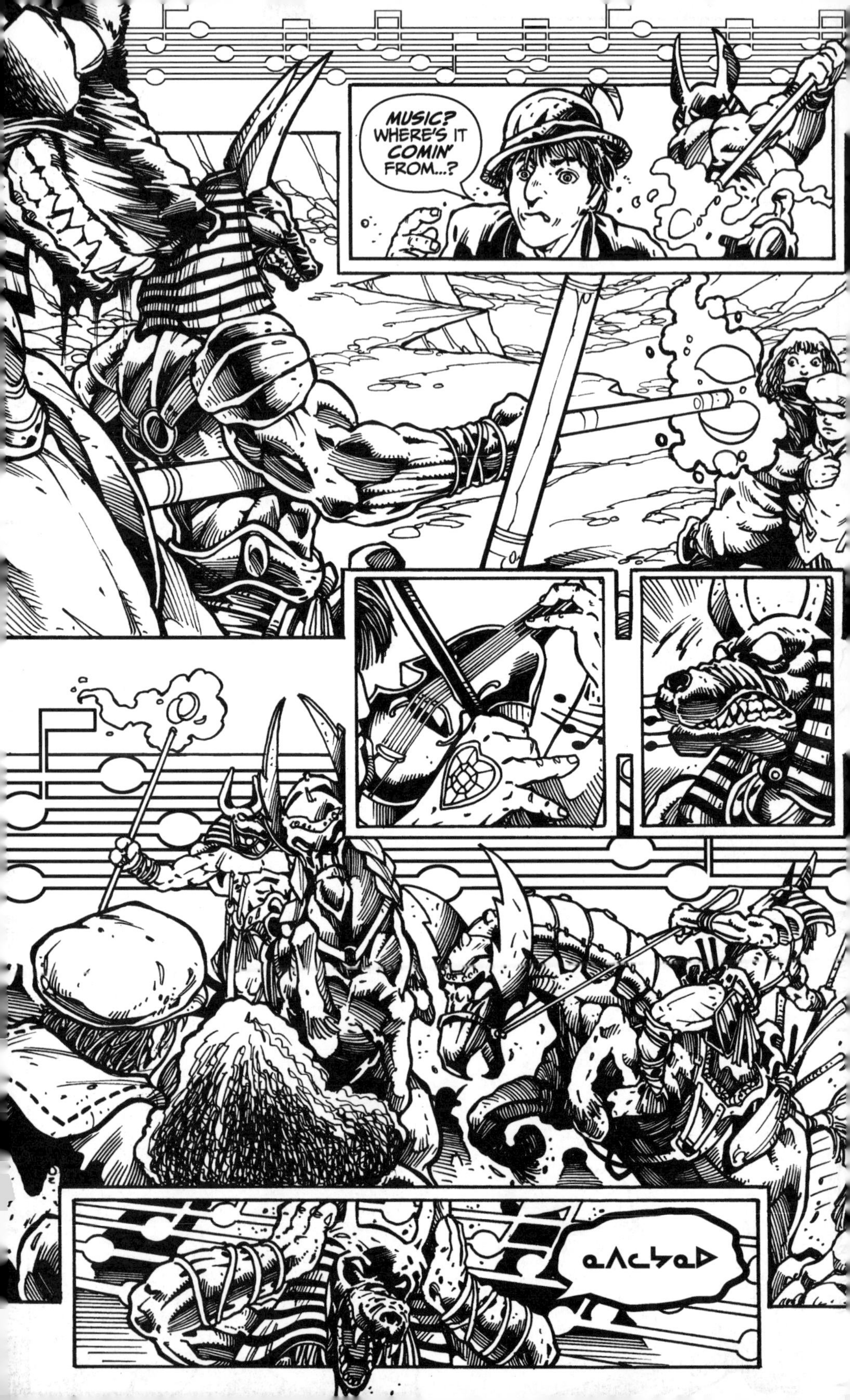
MUSIC? WHERE'S IT COMIN' FROM...?

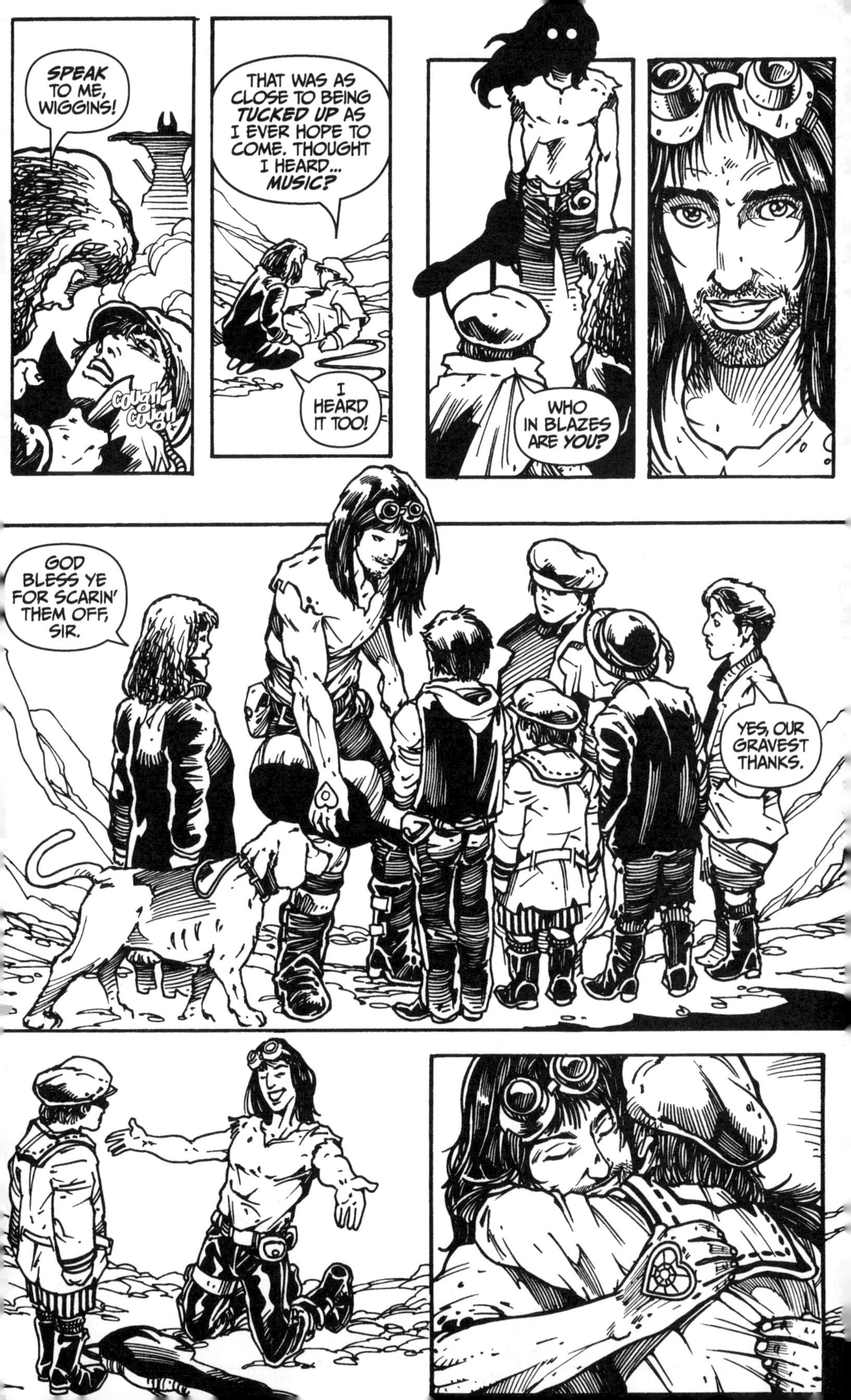

SPEAK TO ME, WIGGINS!
COUGH COUGH
THAT WAS AS CLOSE TO BEING TUCKED UP AS I EVER HOPE TO COME. THOUGHT I HEARD... MUSIC?
I HEARD IT TOO!
WHO IN BLAZES ARE YOU?
GOD BLESS YE FOR SCARIN' THEM OFF, SIR.
YES, OUR GRAVEST THANKS.

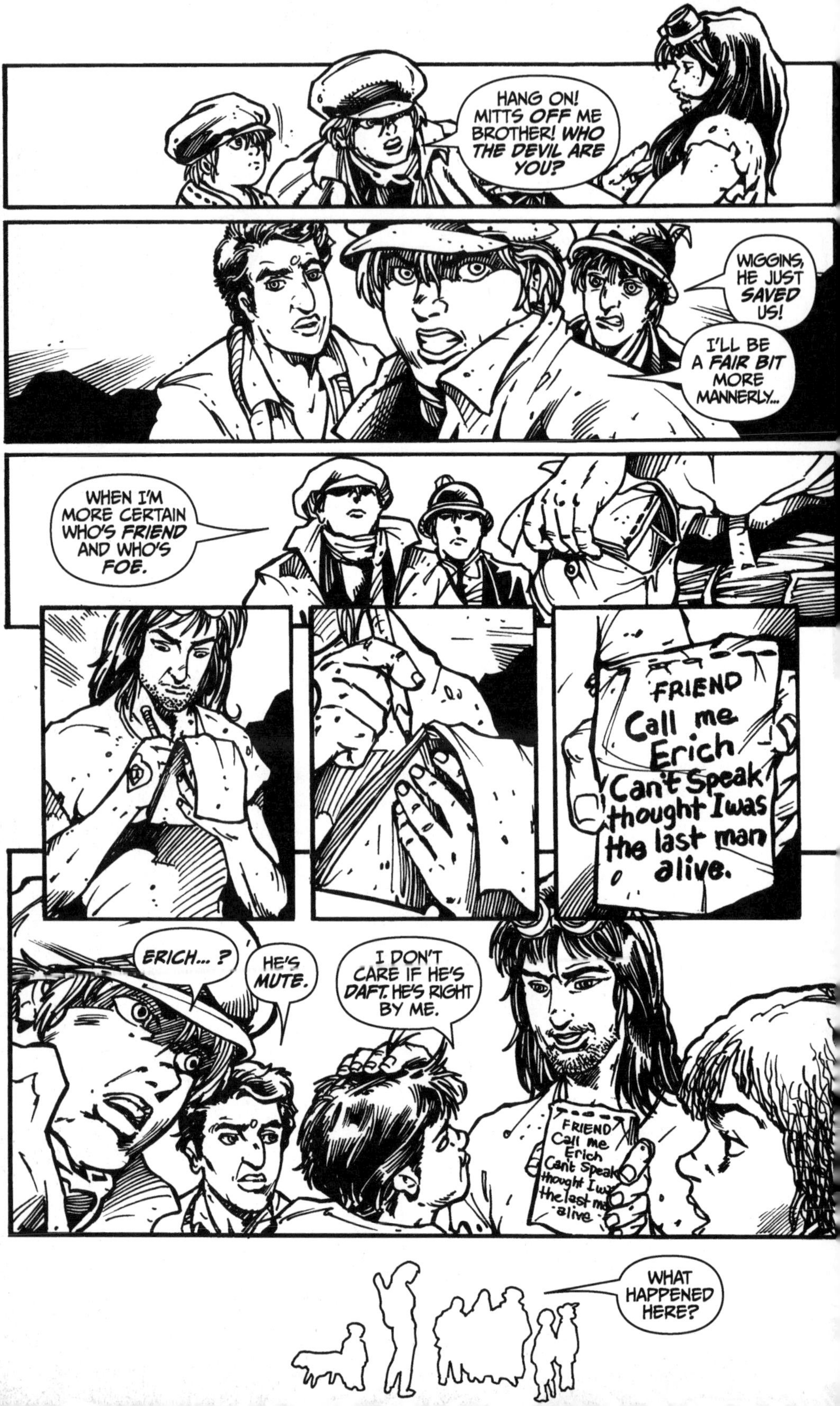
HANG ON! MITTS OFF ME BROTHER! WHO THE DEVIL ARE YOU?
WIGGINS, HE JUST SAVED US!
I'LL BE A FAIR BIT MORE MANNERLY...
WHEN I'M MORE CERTAIN WHO'S FRIEND AND WHO'S FOE.
FRIEND Call me Erich Can't Speak thought I was the last man alive.
ERICH... ?
HE'S MUTE.
I DON'T CARE IF HE'S DAFT. HE'S RIGHT BY ME.
FRIEND Call me Erich Can't Speak
WHAT HAPPENED HERE?

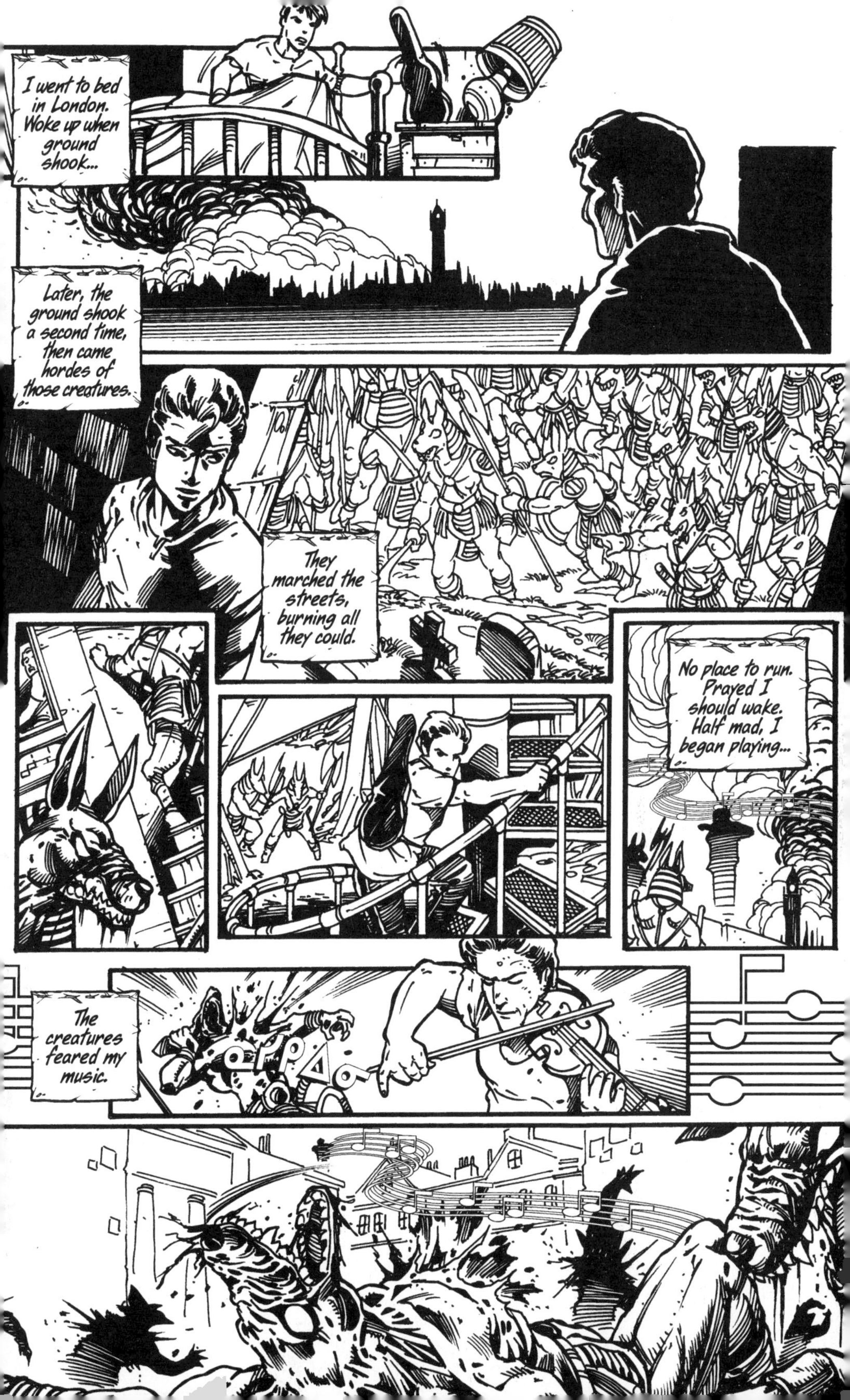
I went to bed in London. Woke up when ground shook...
Later, the ground shook a second time, then came hordes of those creatures.
They marched the streets, burning all they could.
No place to run. Prayed I should wake. Half mad, I began playing...
The creatures feared my music.

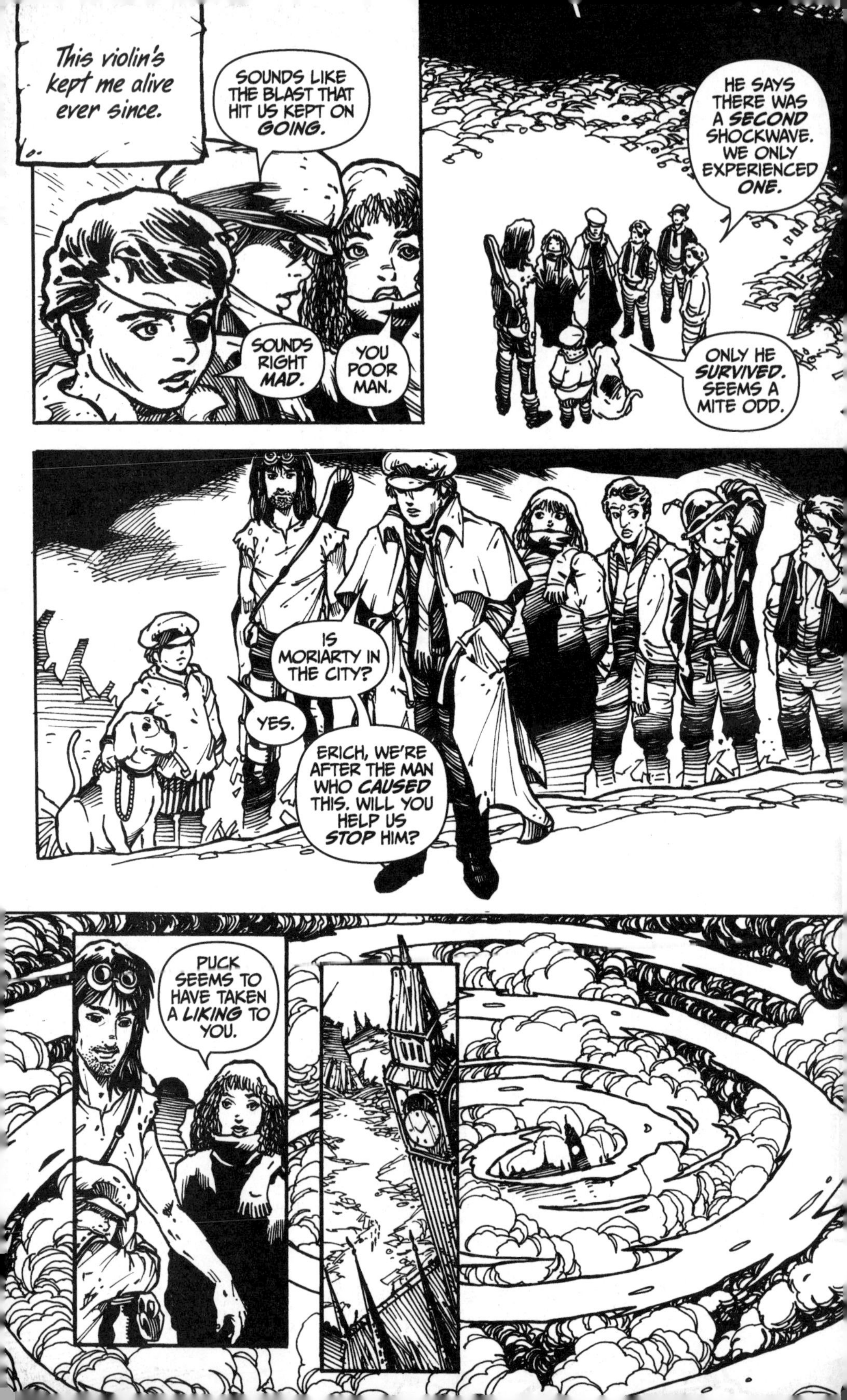

This violin's kept me alive ever since.
SOUNDS LIKE THE BLAST THAT HIT US KEPT ON GOING.
SOUNDS RIGHT MAD.
YOU POOR MAN.
HE SAYS THERE WAS A SECOND SHOCKWAVE. WE ONLY EXPERIENCED ONE.
ONLY HE SURVIVED. SEEMS A MITE ODD.
IS MORIARTY IN THE CITY?
YES.
ERICH, WE'RE AFTER THE MAN WHO CAUSED THIS. WILL YOU HELP US STOP HIM?
PUCK SEEMS TO HAVE TAKEN A LIKING TO YOU.

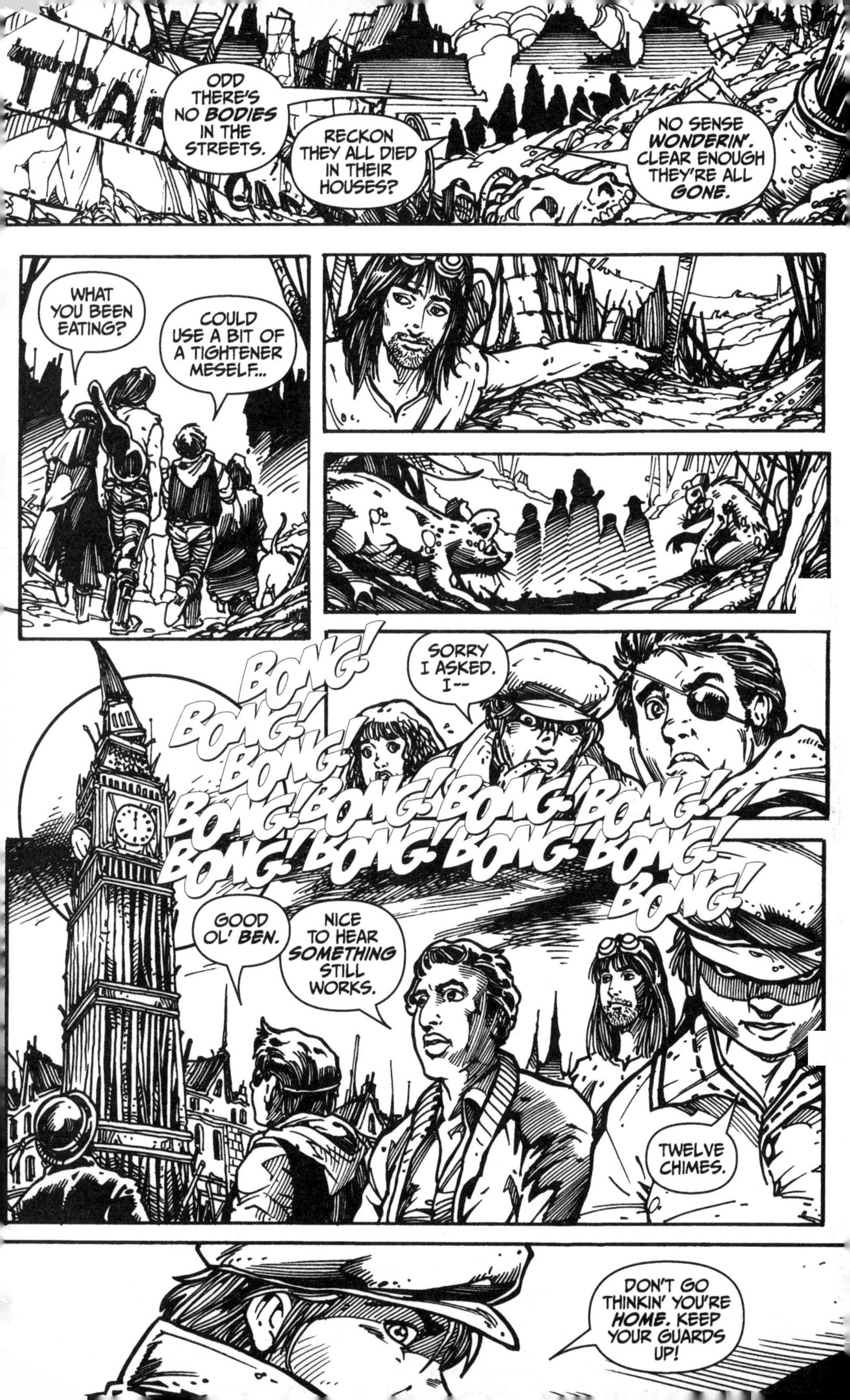
ODD THERE'S NO BODIES IN THE STREETS.
RECKON THEY ALL DIED IN THEIR HOUSES?
NO SENSE WONDERIN'. CLEAR ENOUGH THEY'RE ALL GONE.
WHAT YOU BEEN EATING?
COULD USE A BIT OF A TIGHTENER MESELF...
BONG! BONG! BONG! BONG! BONG! BONG! BONG! BONG! BONG! BONG! BONG! BONG!
SORRY I ASKED. I--
GOOD OL' BEN.
NICE TO HEAR SOMETHING STILL WORKS.
TWELVE CHIMES.
DON'T GO THINKIN' YOU'RE HOME. KEEP YOUR GUARDS UP!

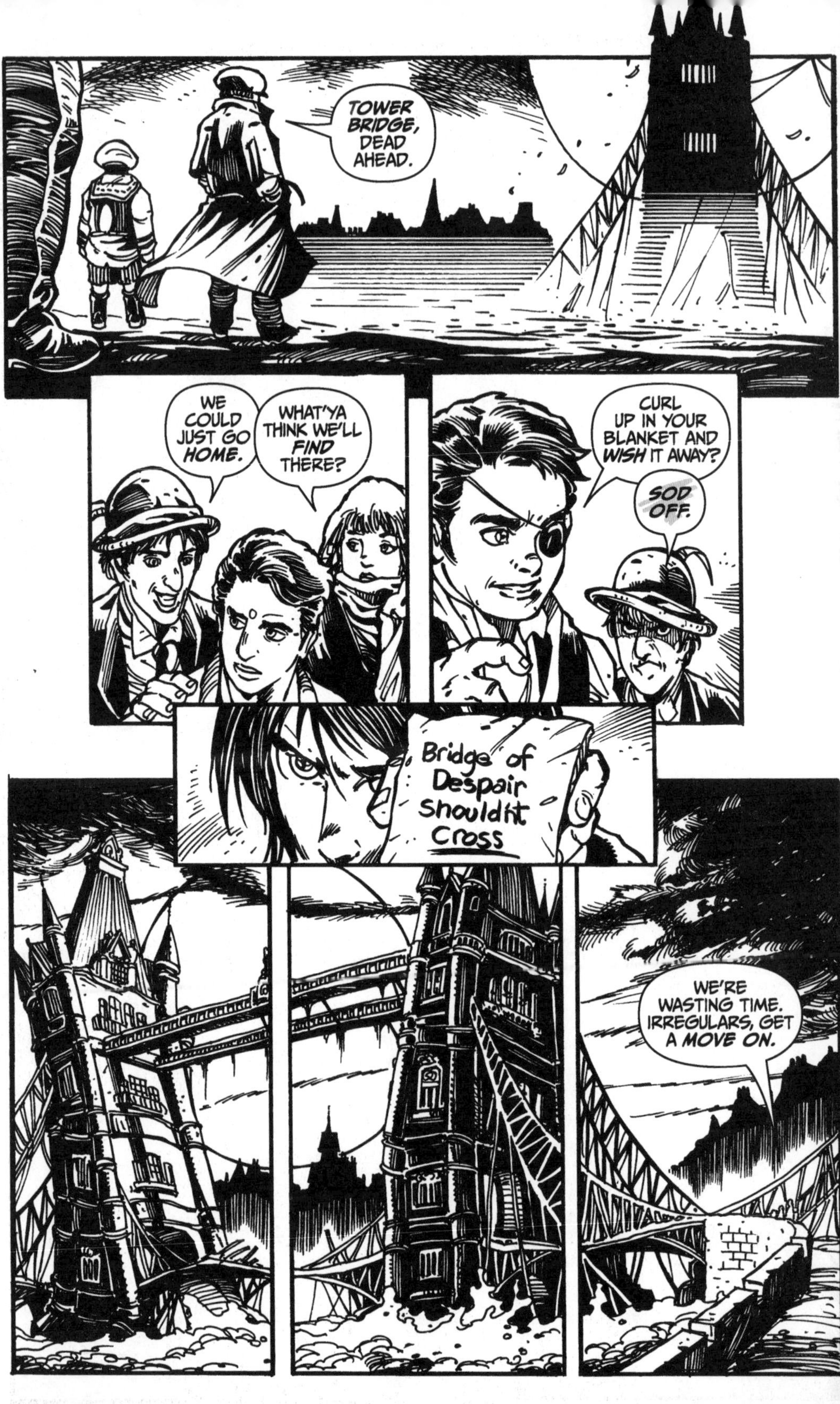
TOWER BRIDGE, DEAD AHEAD.
WE COULD JUST GO HOME.
WHAT'YA THINK WE'LL FIND THERE?
CURL UP IN YOUR BLANKET AND WISH IT AWAY?
SOD OFF.
Bridge of Despair Shouldn't Cross
WE'RE WASTING TIME. IRREGULARS, GET A MOVE ON.

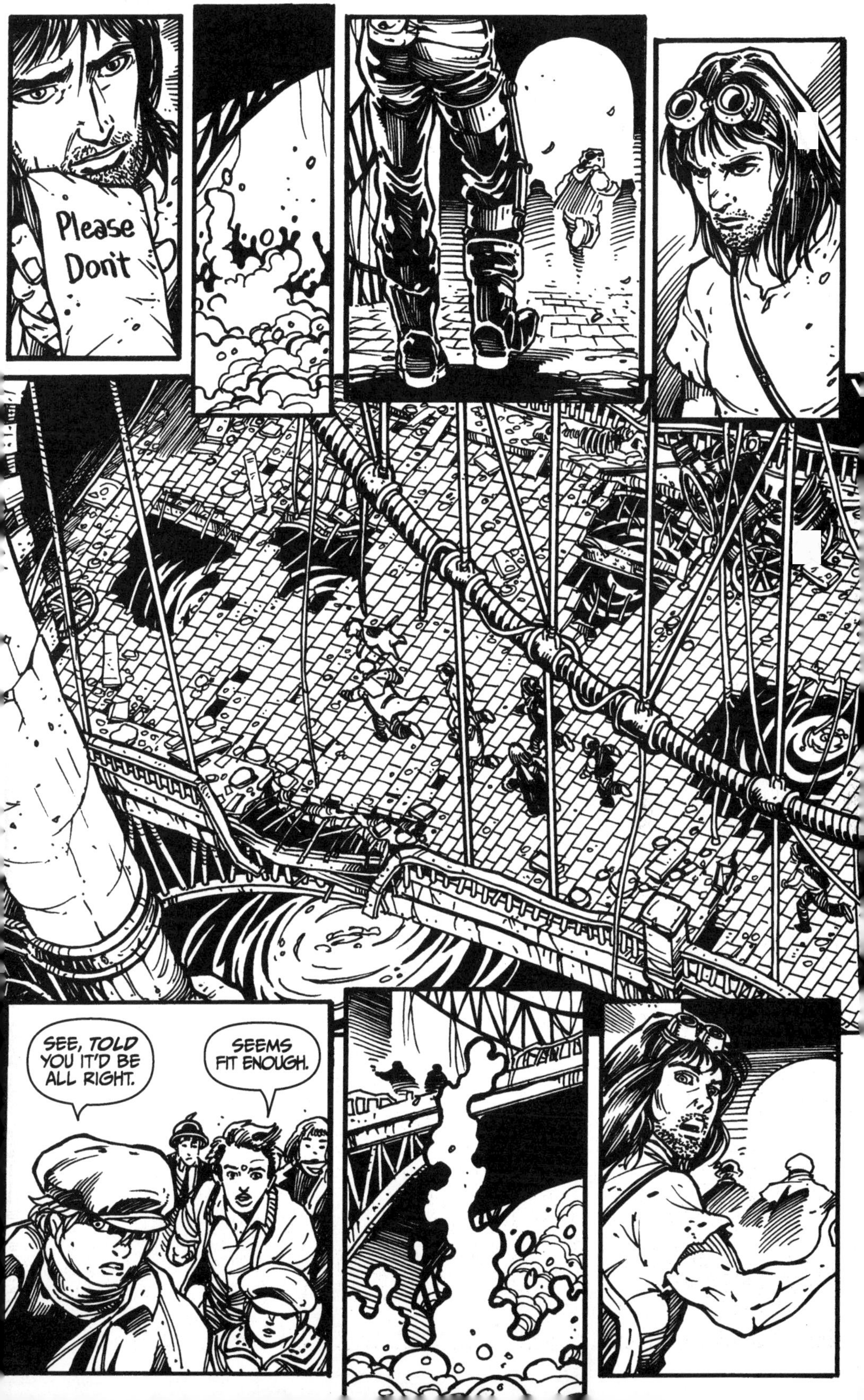
Please Don't
SEE, TOLD YOU IT'D BE ALL RIGHT.
SEEMS FIT ENOUGH.

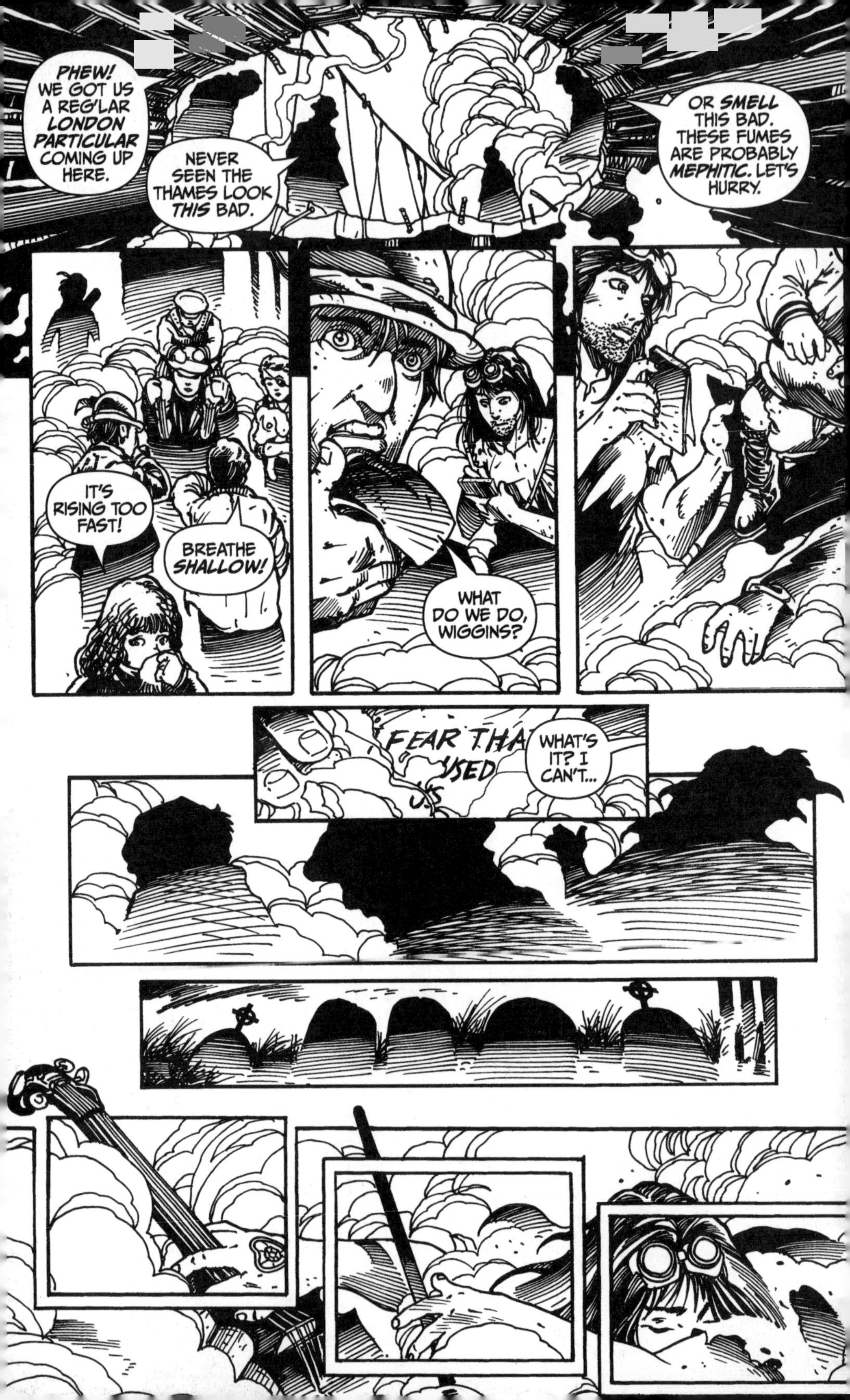
PHEW! WE GOT US A REG'LAR LONDON PARTICULAR COMING UP HERE.
NEVER SEEN THE THAMES LOOK THIS BAD.
OR SMELL THIS BAD. THESE FUMES ARE PROBABLY MEPHITIC. LET'S HURRY.
IT'S RISING TOO FAST!
BREATHE SHALLOW!
WHAT DO WE DO, WIGGINS?
WHAT'S IT? I CAN'T...

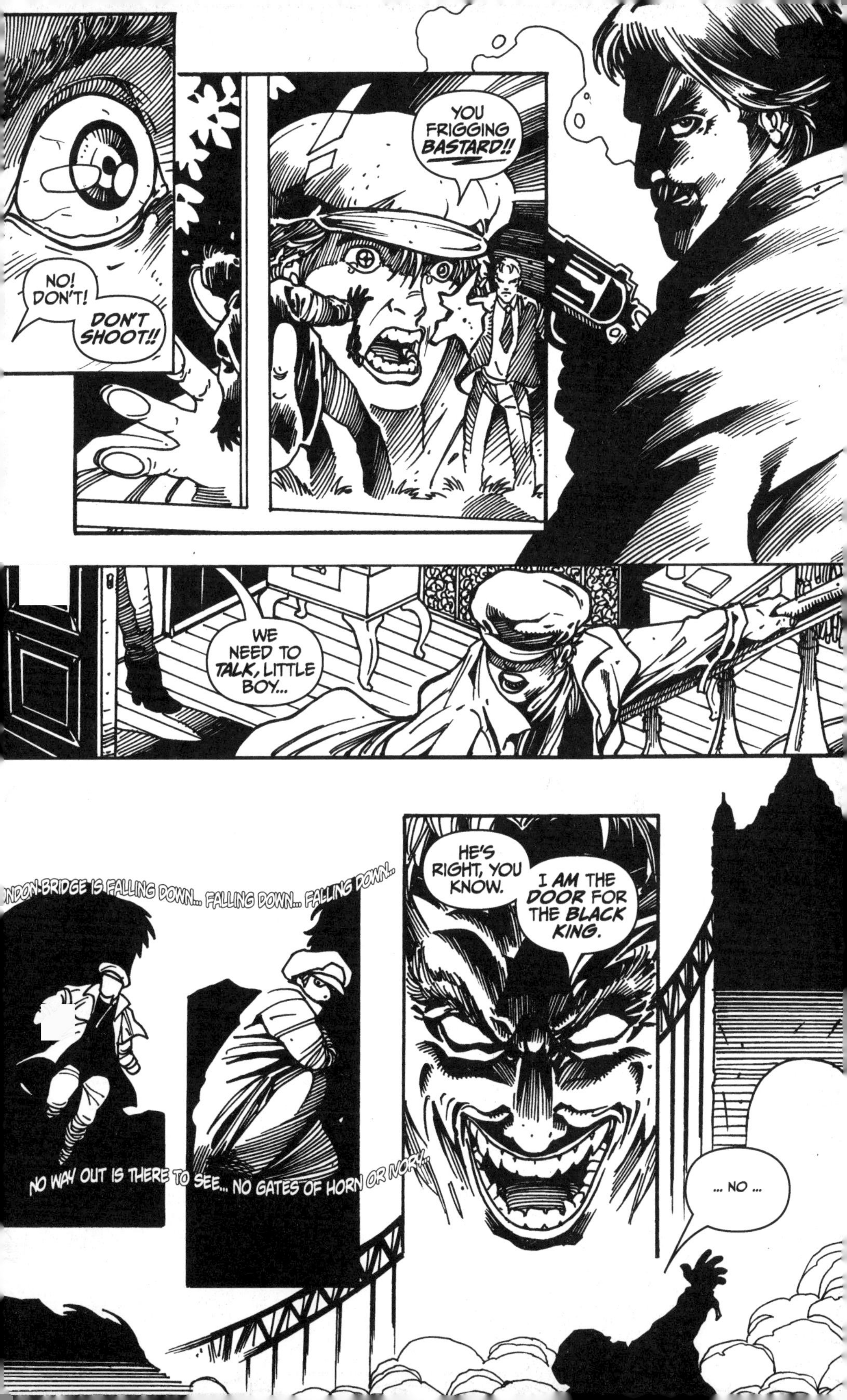
NO! DON'T!
DON'T SHOOT!!
YOU FRIGGING BASTARD!!
WE NEED TO TALK, LITTLE BOY...
NDON BRIDGE IS FALLING DOWN... FALLING DOWN... FALLING DOWN...
NO WAY OUT IS THERE TO SEE... NO GATES OF HORN OR IVORY...
HE'S RIGHT, YOU KNOW.
I AM THE DOOR FOR THE BLACK KING.
... NO ...

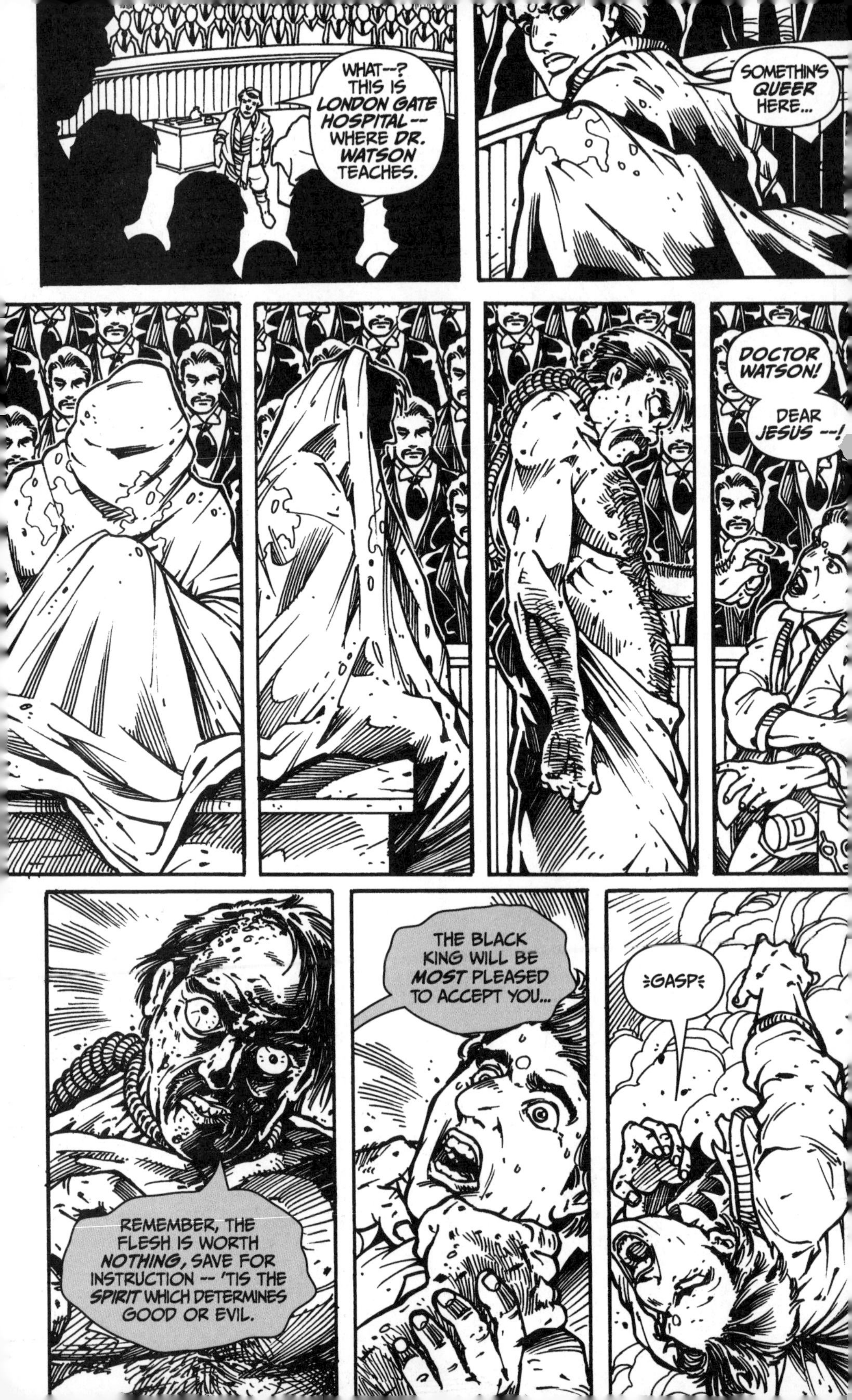
WHAT--? THIS IS LONDON GATE HOSPITAL-- WHERE DR. WATSON TEACHES.
SOMETHIN'S QUEER HERE...
DOCTOR WATSON!
DEAR JESUS --!
REMEMBER, THE FLESH IS WORTH NOTHING, SAVE FOR INSTRUCTION -- 'TIS THE SPIRIT WHICH DETERMINES GOOD OR EVIL.
THE BLACK KING WILL BE MOST PLEASED TO ACCEPT YOU...
GASP

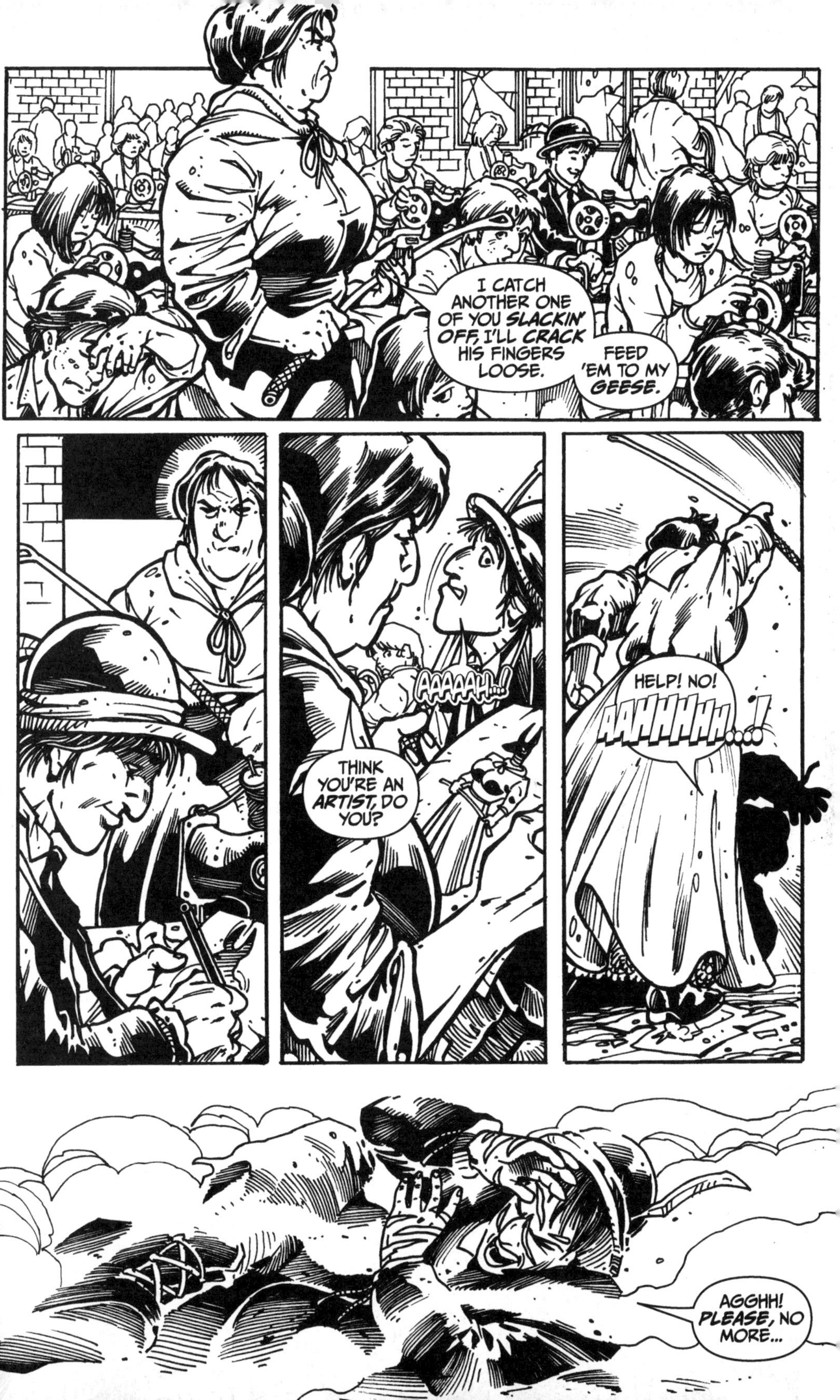
I CATCH ANOTHER ONE OF YOU SLACKIN' OFF, I'LL CRACK HIS FINGERS LOOSE.
FEED 'EM TO MY GEESE.
AAAAAH...!
THINK YOU'RE AN ARTIST, DO YOU?
HELP! NO!
AAHHHHH...!
AGGHH! PLEASE, NO MORE...

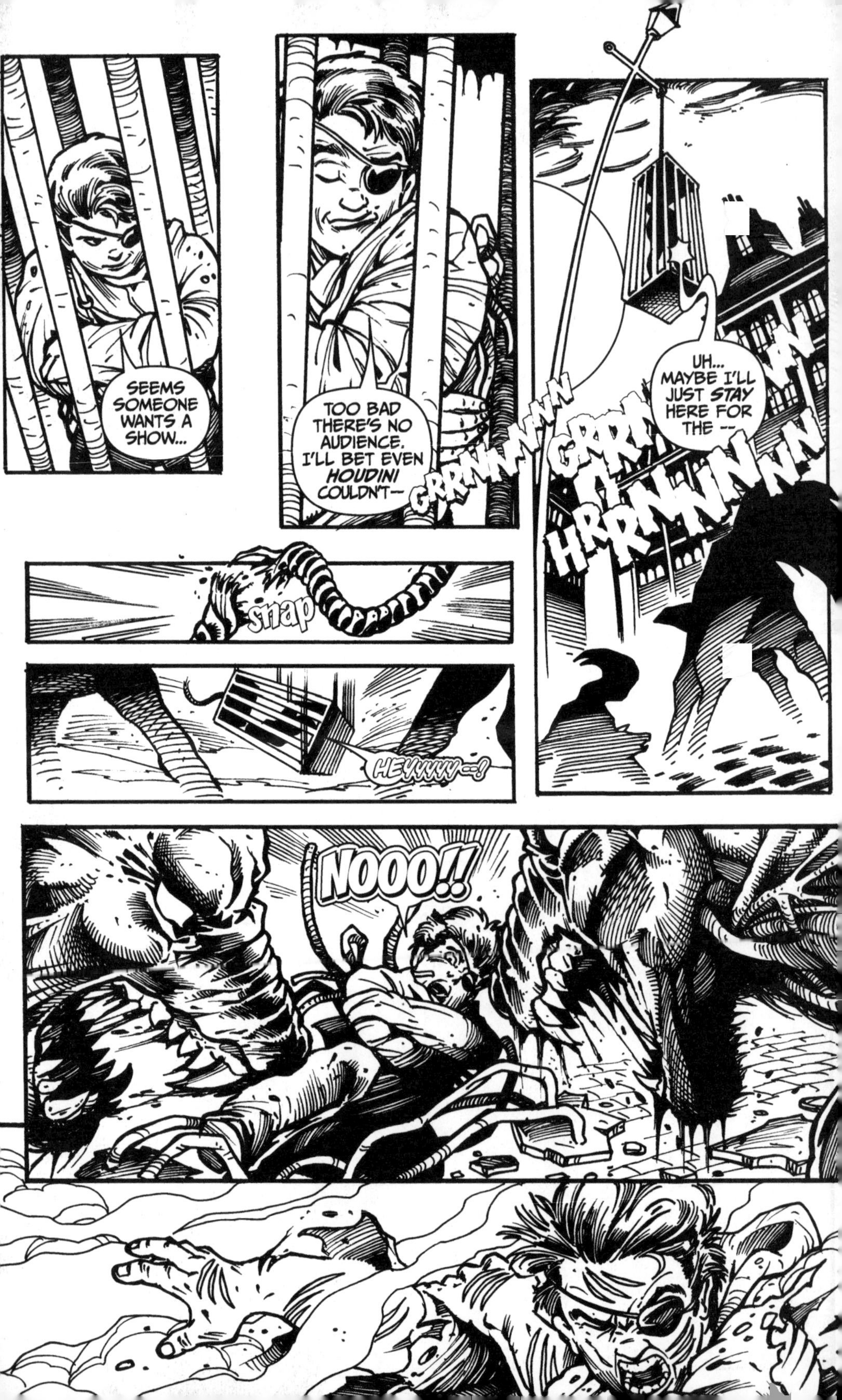

SEEMS SOMEONE WANTS A SHOW...
TOO BAD THERE'S NO AUDIENCE. I'LL BET EVEN *HOUDINI* COULDN'T--
GRRNNNNNN
GRRRNNNN
UH... MAYBE I'LL JUST *STAY* HERE FOR THE --
HRRNNNNNN
snap
HEYYYYY--!
NOOO!!

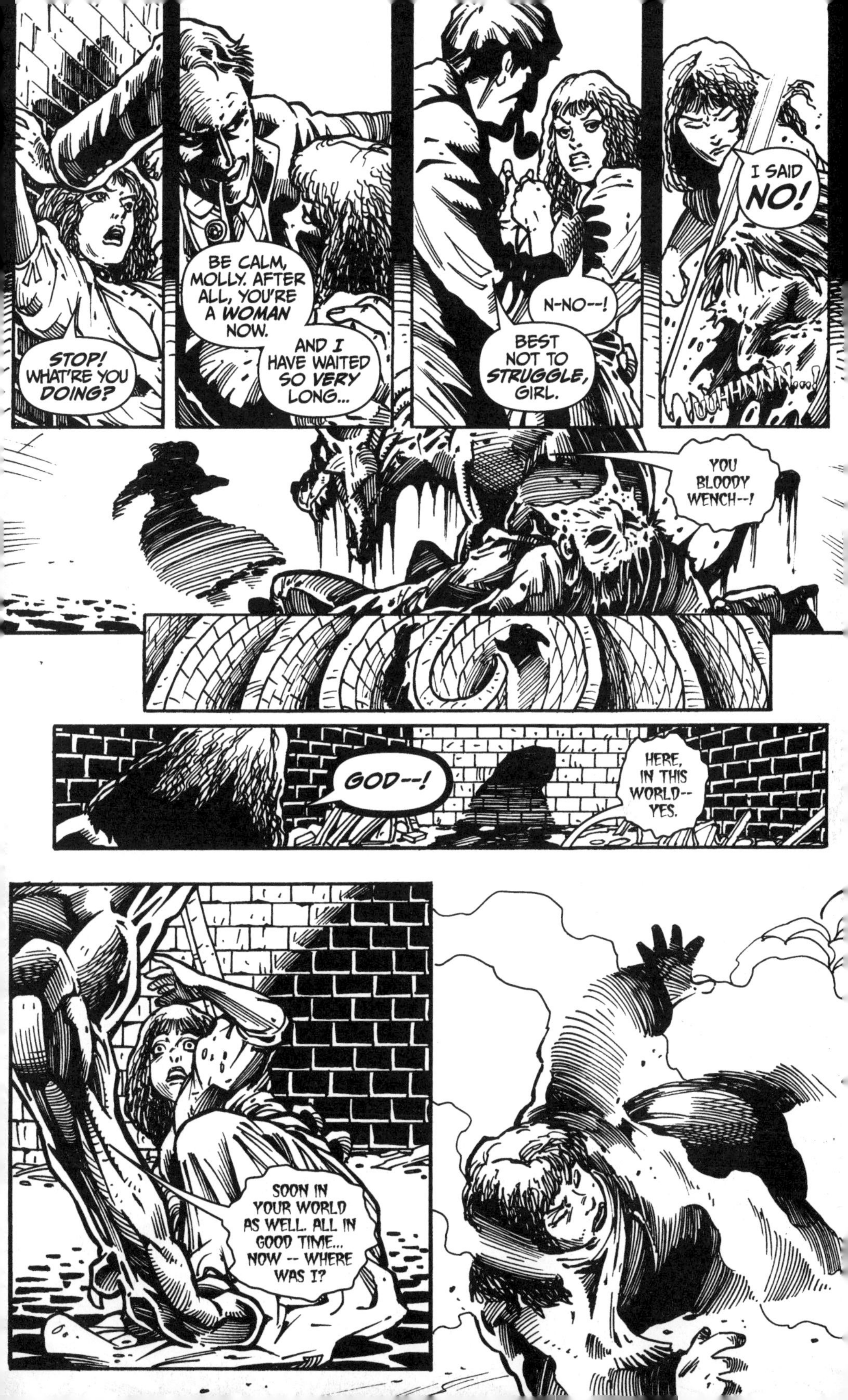
STOP! WHAT'RE YOU DOING?
BE CALM, MOLLY. AFTER ALL, YOU'RE A WOMAN NOW.
AND I HAVE WAITED SO VERY LONG...
N-NO--!
BEST NOT TO STRUGGLE, GIRL.
I SAID NO!
YOU BLOODY WENCH--!
GOD--!
HERE, IN THIS WORLD-- YES.
SOON IN YOUR WORLD AS WELL. ALL IN GOOD TIME... NOW -- WHERE WAS I?

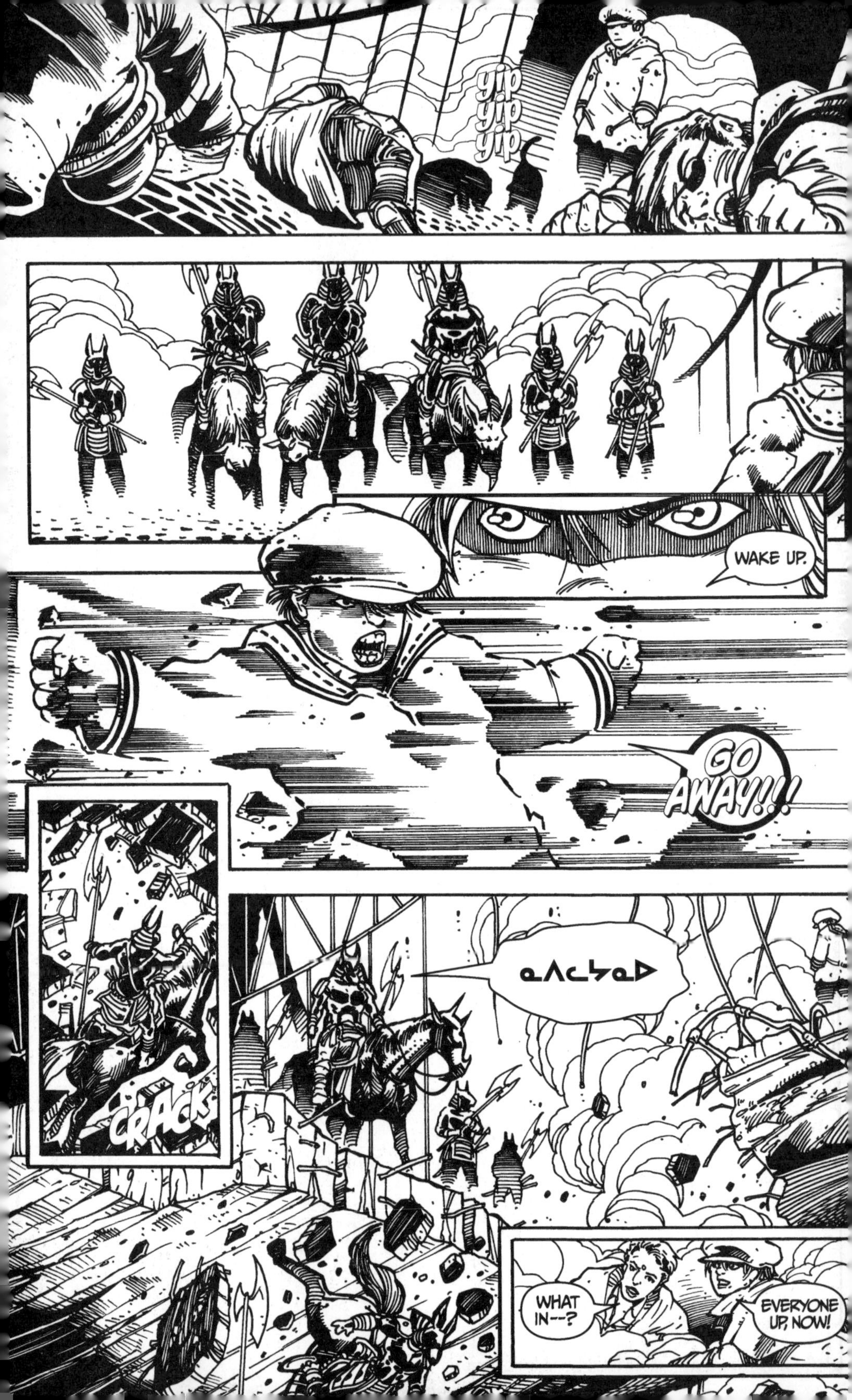
yip
yip
yip
WAKE UP.
GO AWAY!!!
CRACK
WHAT IN--?
EVERYONE UP, NOW!

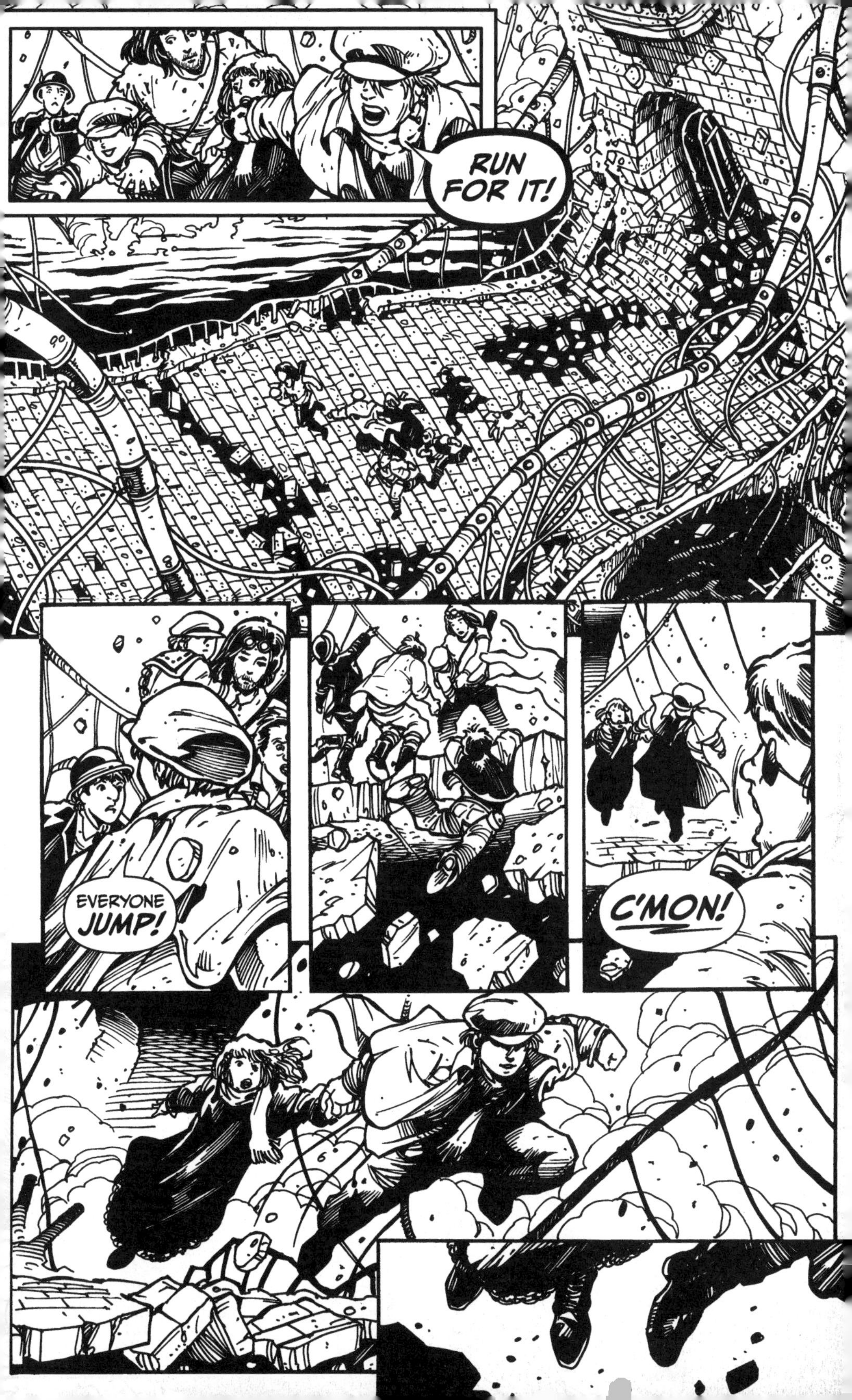
RUN FOR IT!
EVERYONE JUMP!
C'MON!

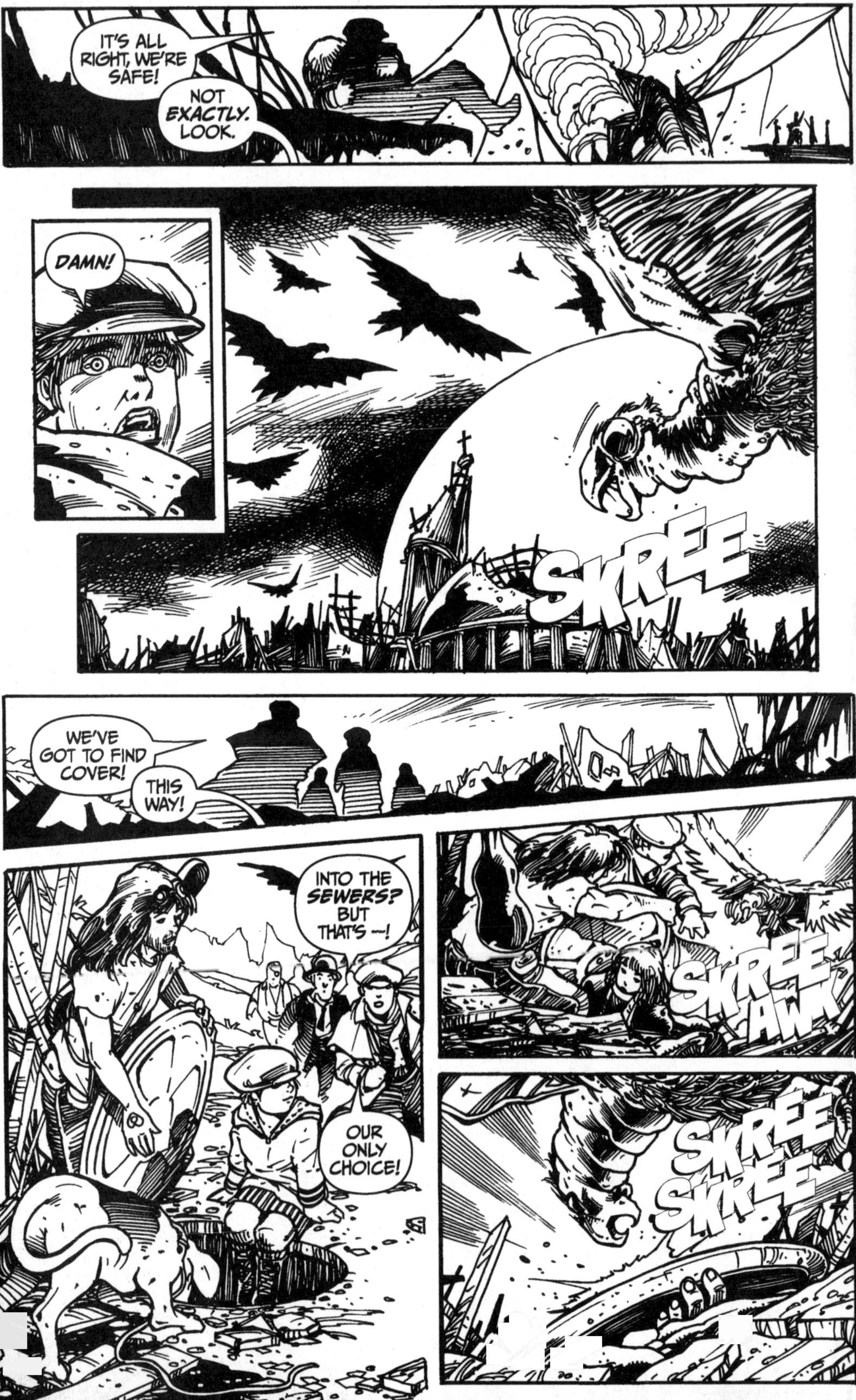
IT'S ALL RIGHT, WE'RE SAFE!
NOT EXACTLY. LOOK.
DAMN!
SKREE
WE'VE GOT TO FIND COVER!
THIS WAY!
INTO THE SEWERS? BUT THAT'S --!
OUR ONLY CHOICE!
SKREE AWK
SKREE SKREE

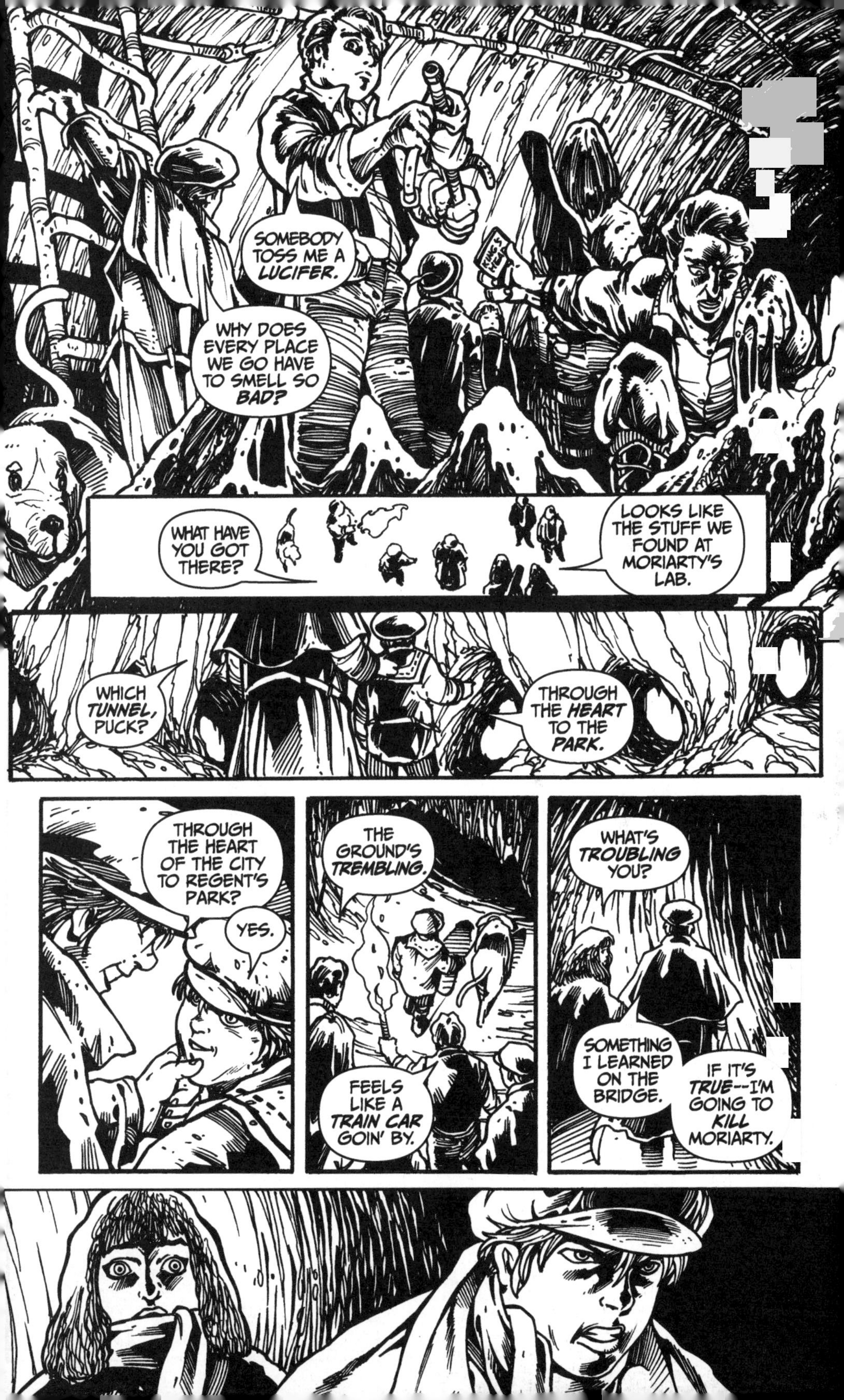
SOMEBODY TOSS ME A LUCIFER.
WHY DOES EVERY PLACE WE GO HAVE TO SMELL SO BAD?
KING'S HEAD
WHAT HAVE YOU GOT THERE?
LOOKS LIKE THE STUFF WE FOUND AT MORIARTY'S LAB.
WHICH TUNNEL, PUCK?
THROUGH THE HEART TO THE PARK.
THROUGH THE HEART OF THE CITY TO REGENT'S PARK?
YES.
THE GROUND'S TREMBLING.
FEELS LIKE A TRAIN CAR GOIN' BY.
WHAT'S TROUBLING YOU?
SOMETHING I LEARNED ON THE BRIDGE.
IF IT'S TRUE--I'M GOING TO KILL MORIARTY.

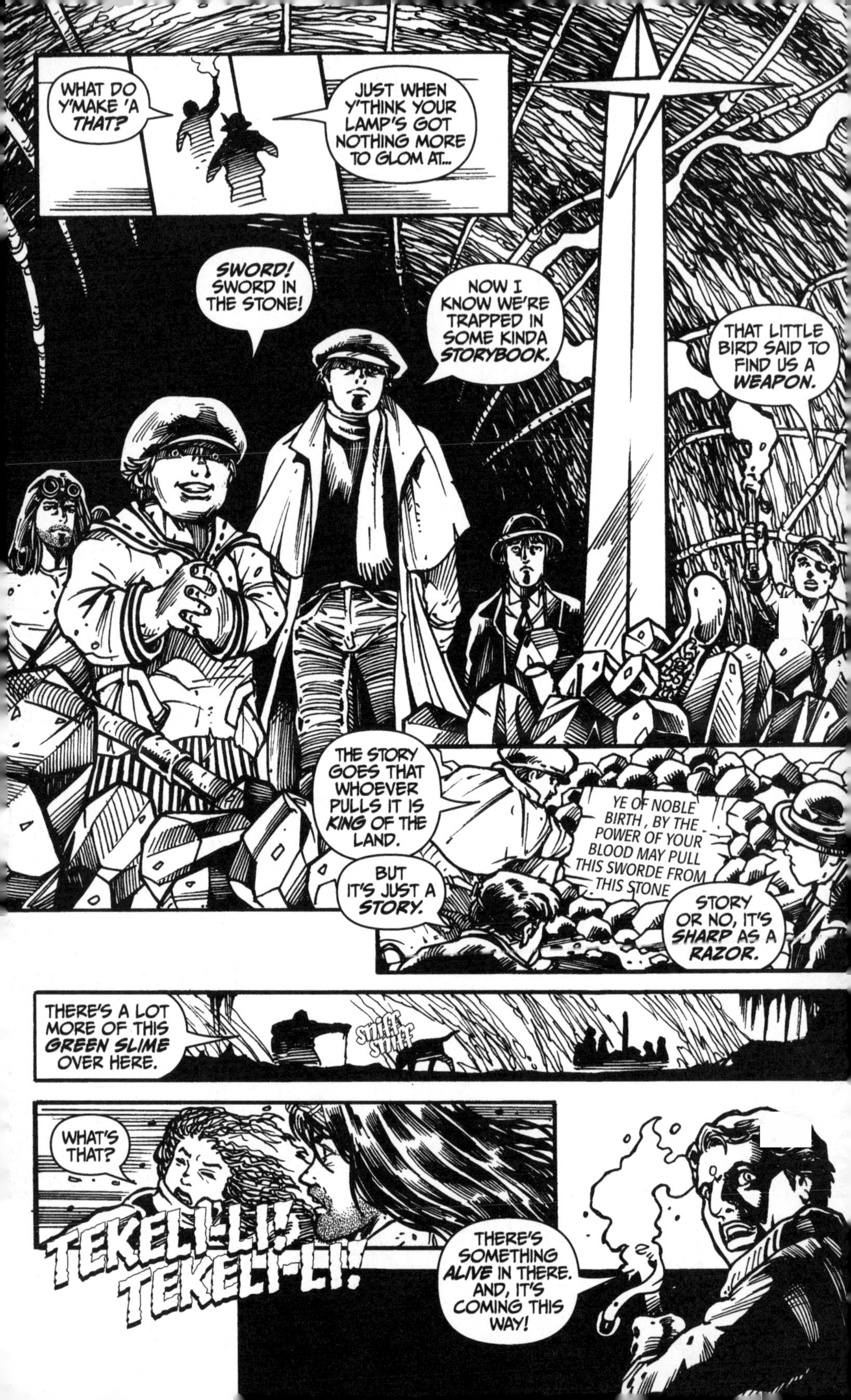
WHAT DO Y'MAKE 'A *THAT?*
JUST WHEN Y'THINK YOUR LAMP'S GOT NOTHING MORE TO GLOM AT...
SWORD! SWORD IN THE STONE!
NOW I KNOW WE'RE TRAPPED IN SOME KINDA *STORYBOOK.*
THAT LITTLE BIRD SAID TO FIND US A *WEAPON.*
THE STORY GOES THAT WHOEVER PULLS IT IS *KING* OF THE LAND.
BUT IT'S JUST A *STORY.*
YE OF NOBLE BIRTH, BY THE POWER OF YOUR BLOOD MAY PULL THIS SWORDE FROM THIS STONE
STORY OR NO, IT'S *SHARP* AS A *RAZOR.*
THERE'S A LOT MORE OF THIS *GREEN SLIME* OVER HERE.
SNIFF SNIFF
WHAT'S THAT?
TEKELI-LI! TEKELI-LI!
THERE'S SOMETHING *ALIVE* IN THERE. AND, IT'S COMING THIS WAY!

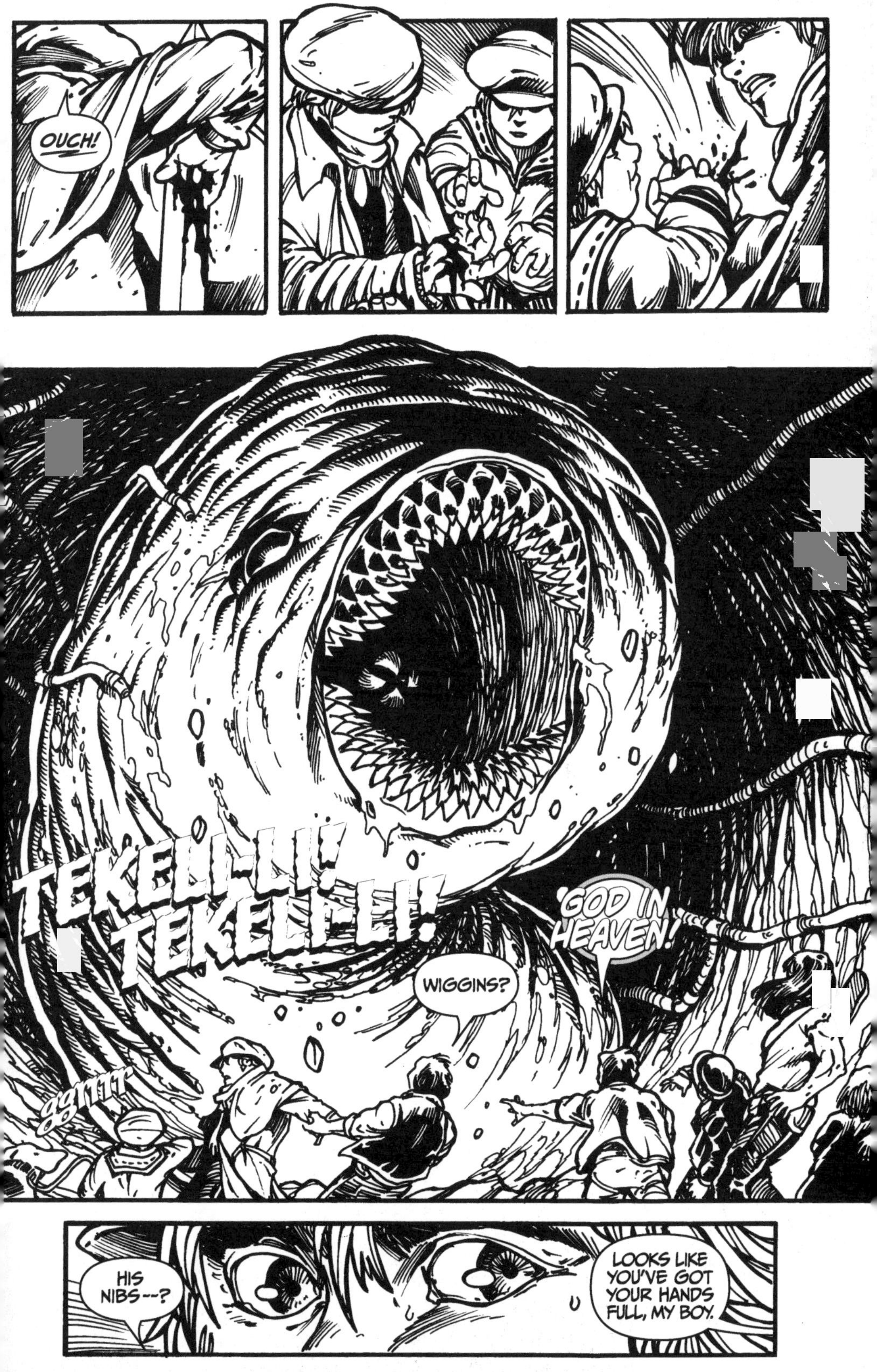
OUCH!
TEKELI-LI! TEKELI-LI!
GOD IN HEAVEN!
WIGGINS?
grrrr
HIS NIBS--?
LOOKS LIKE YOU'VE GOT YOUR HANDS FULL, MY BOY.

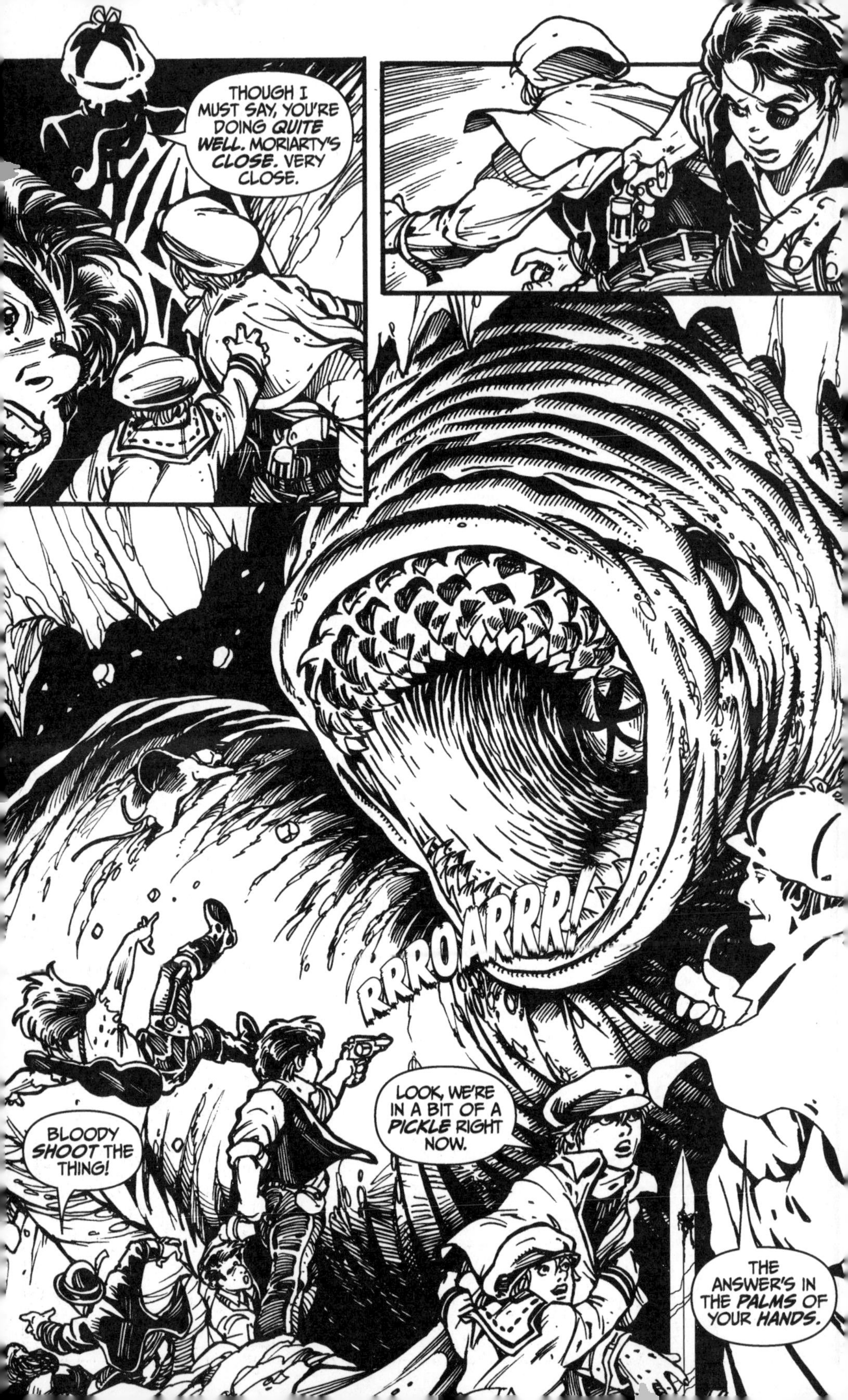
THOUGH I MUST SAY, YOU'RE DOING QUITE WELL. MORIARTY'S CLOSE. VERY CLOSE.
RRROARRR!
BLOODY SHOOT THE THING!
LOOK, WE'RE IN A BIT OF A PICKLE RIGHT NOW.
THE ANSWER'S IN THE PALMS OF YOUR HANDS.

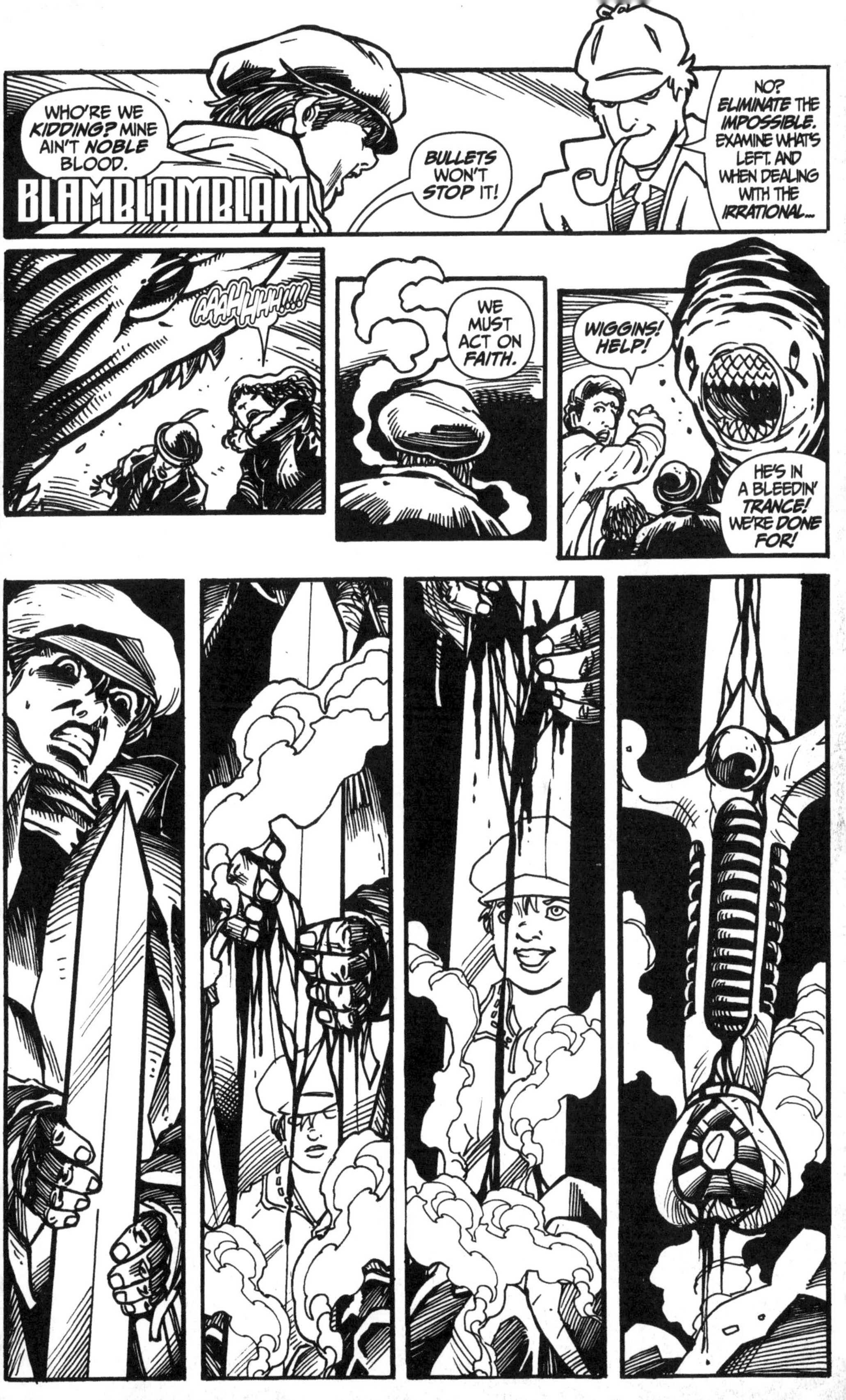
WHO'RE WE KIDDING? MINE AIN'T NOBLE BLOOD.
BLAMBLAMBLAM
BULLETS WON'T STOP IT!
NO? ELIMINATE THE IMPOSSIBLE. EXAMINE WHAT'S LEFT. AND WHEN DEALING WITH THE IRRATIONAL...
AAAHHHH!!!
WE MUST ACT ON FAITH.
WIGGINS! HELP!
HE'S IN A BLEEDIN' TRANCE! WE'RE DONE FOR!

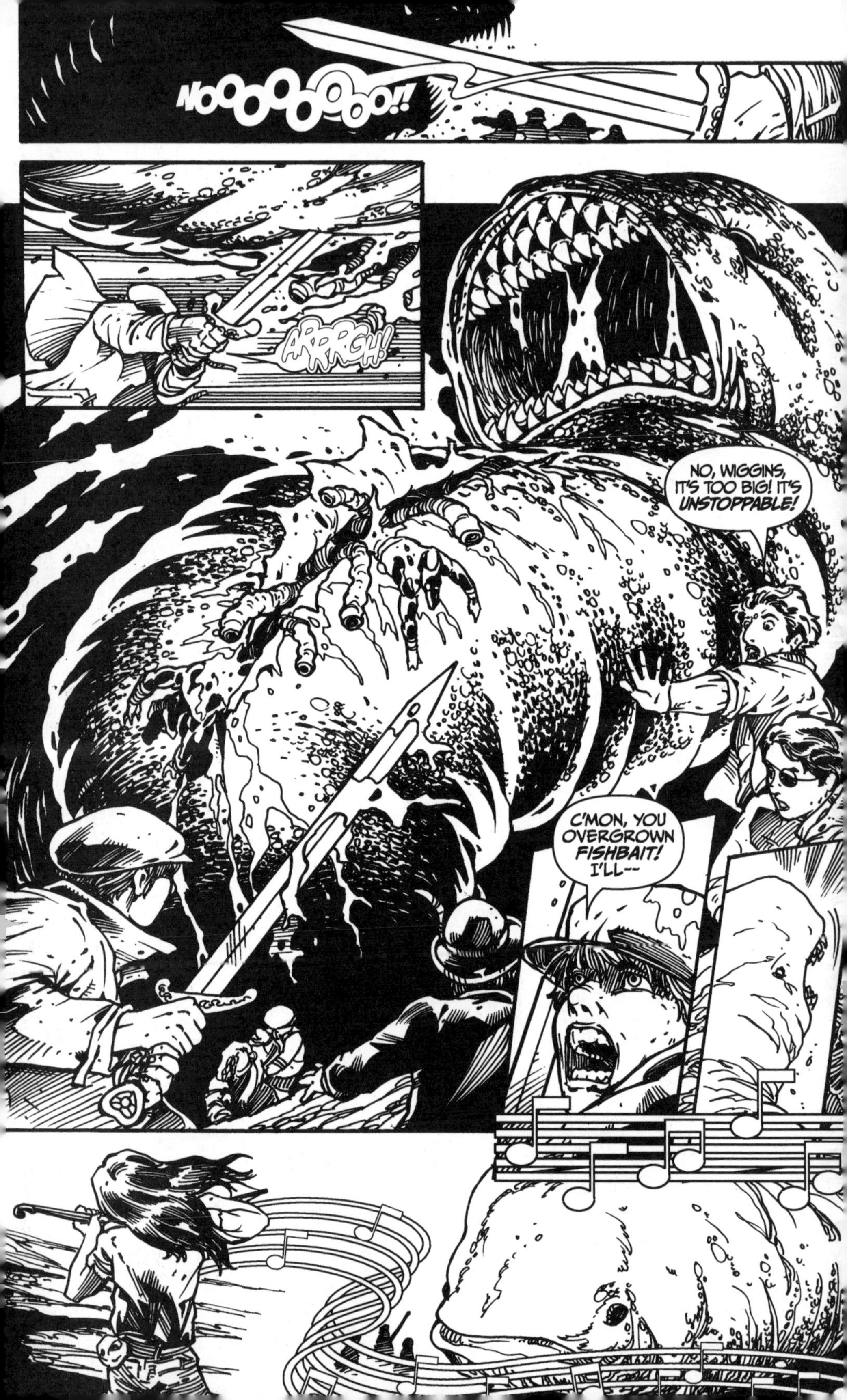
NOOOOOOOOO!!
ARRRGH!
NO, WIGGINS, IT'S TOO BIG! IT'S UNSTOPPABLE!
C'MON, YOU OVERGROWN FISHBAIT! I'LL--

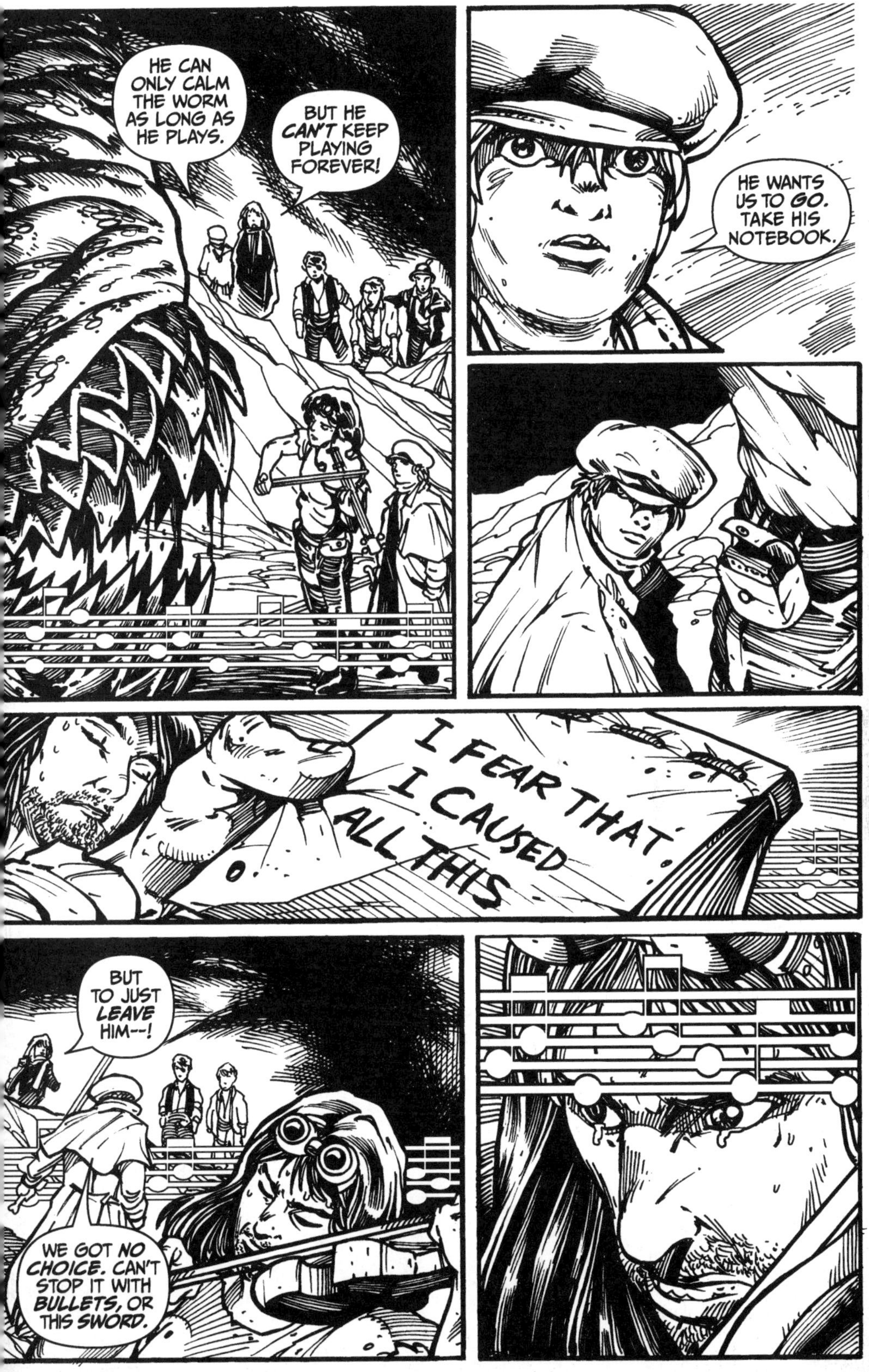
HE CAN ONLY CALM THE WORM AS LONG AS HE PLAYS.
BUT HE CAN'T KEEP PLAYING FOREVER!
HE WANTS US TO GO. TAKE HIS NOTEBOOK.
I FEAR THAT I CAUSED ALL THIS
BUT TO JUST LEAVE HIM--!
WE GOT NO CHOICE. CAN'T STOP IT WITH BULLETS, OR THIS SWORD.

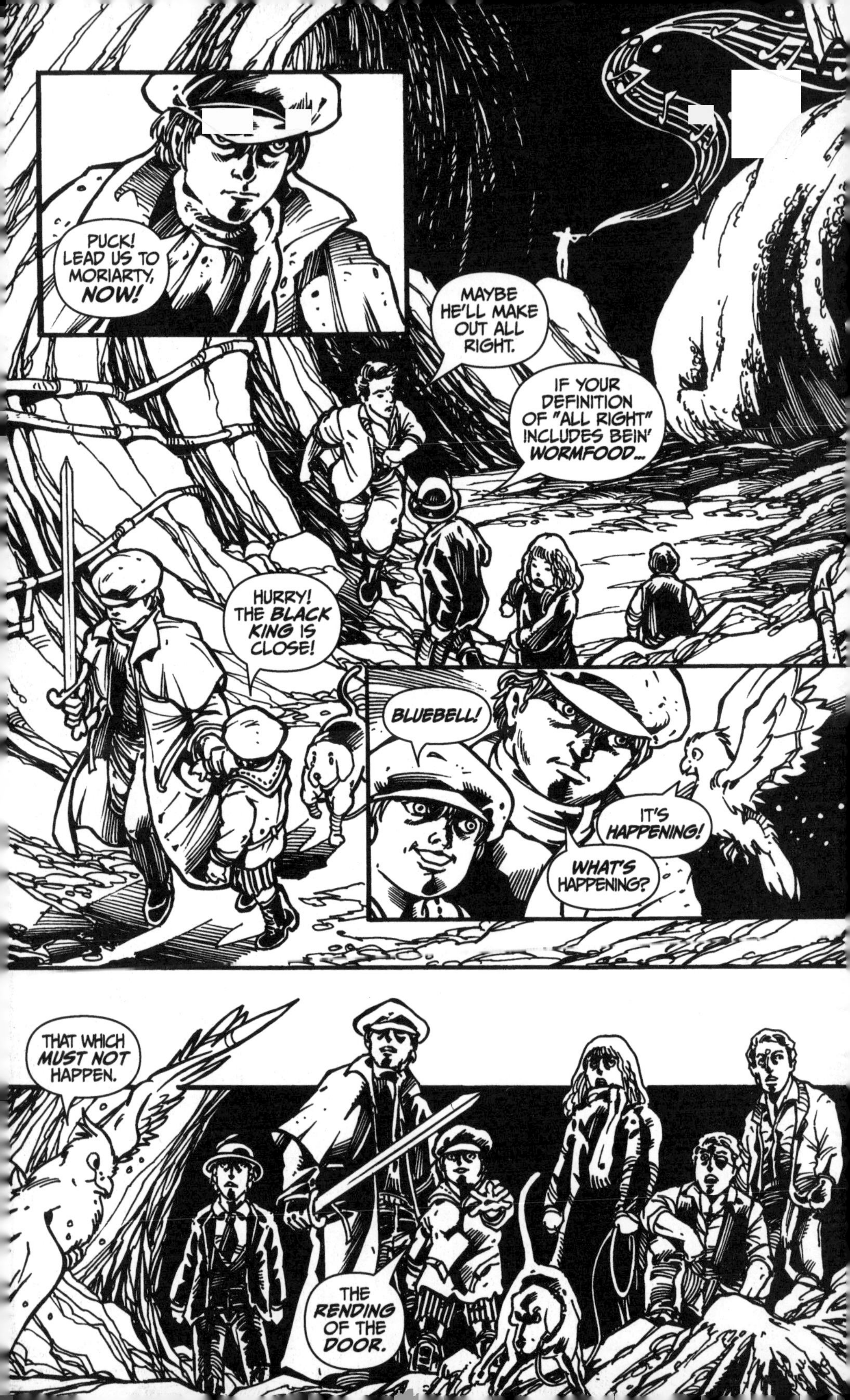
PUCK! LEAD US TO MORIARTY, *NOW!*
MAYBE HE'LL MAKE OUT ALL RIGHT.
IF YOUR DEFINITION OF "ALL RIGHT" INCLUDES BEIN' *WORMFOOD...*
HURRY! THE *BLACK KING* IS CLOSE!
BLUEBELL!
IT'S *HAPPENING!*
WHAT'S HAPPENING?
THAT WHICH *MUST NOT* HAPPEN.
THE *RENDING* OF THE *DOOR.*

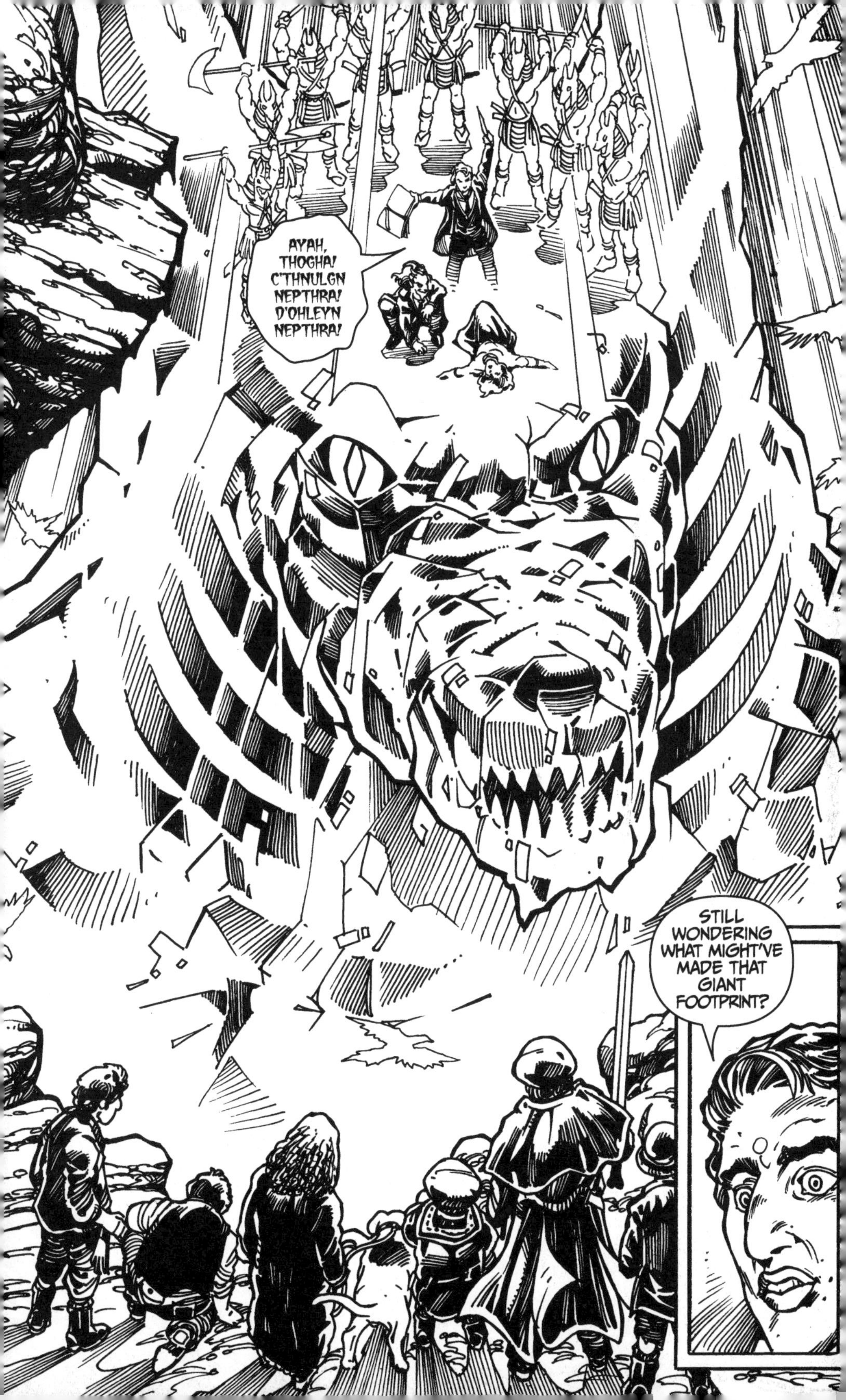
AYAH, THOGHA! C'THNULGN NEPTHRA! D'OHLEYN NEPTHRA!
STILL WONDERING WHAT MIGHT'VE MADE THAT GIANT FOOTPRINT?

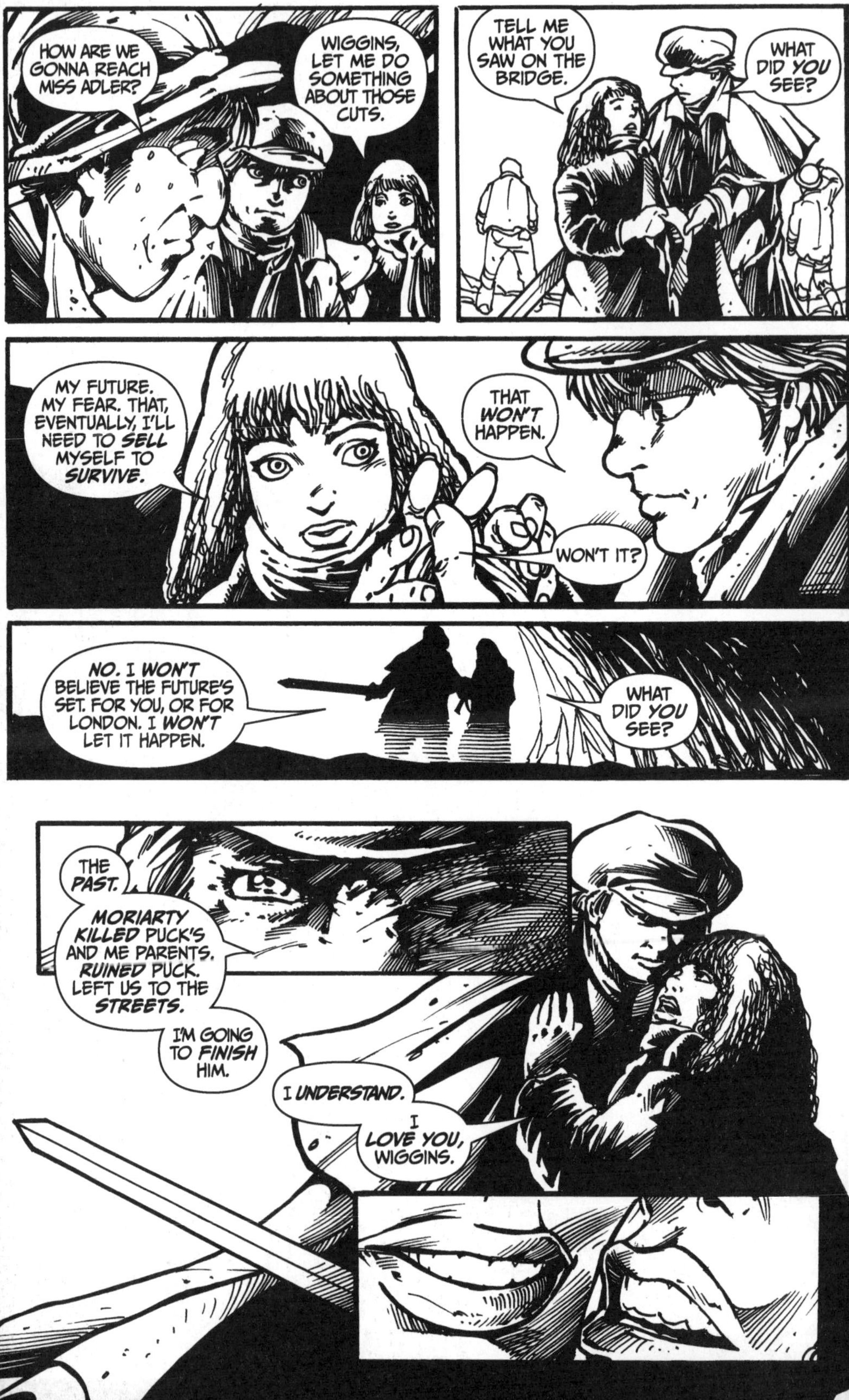
HOW ARE WE GONNA REACH MISS ADLER?
WIGGINS, LET ME DO SOMETHING ABOUT THOSE CUTS.
TELL ME WHAT YOU SAW ON THE BRIDGE.
WHAT DID *YOU* SEE?
MY FUTURE. MY FEAR. THAT, EVENTUALLY, I'LL NEED TO ***SELL*** MYSELF TO ***SURVIVE.***
THAT ***WON'T*** HAPPEN.
WON'T IT?
NO. I ***WON'T*** BELIEVE THE FUTURE'S SET. FOR YOU, OR FOR LONDON. I ***WON'T*** LET IT HAPPEN.
WHAT DID *YOU* SEE?
THE ***PAST.***
MORIARTY KILLED PUCK'S AND ME PARENTS. ***RUINED*** PUCK. LEFT US TO THE ***STREETS.***
I'M GOING TO ***FINISH*** HIM.
I ***UNDERSTAND.***
I ***LOVE YOU,*** WIGGINS.

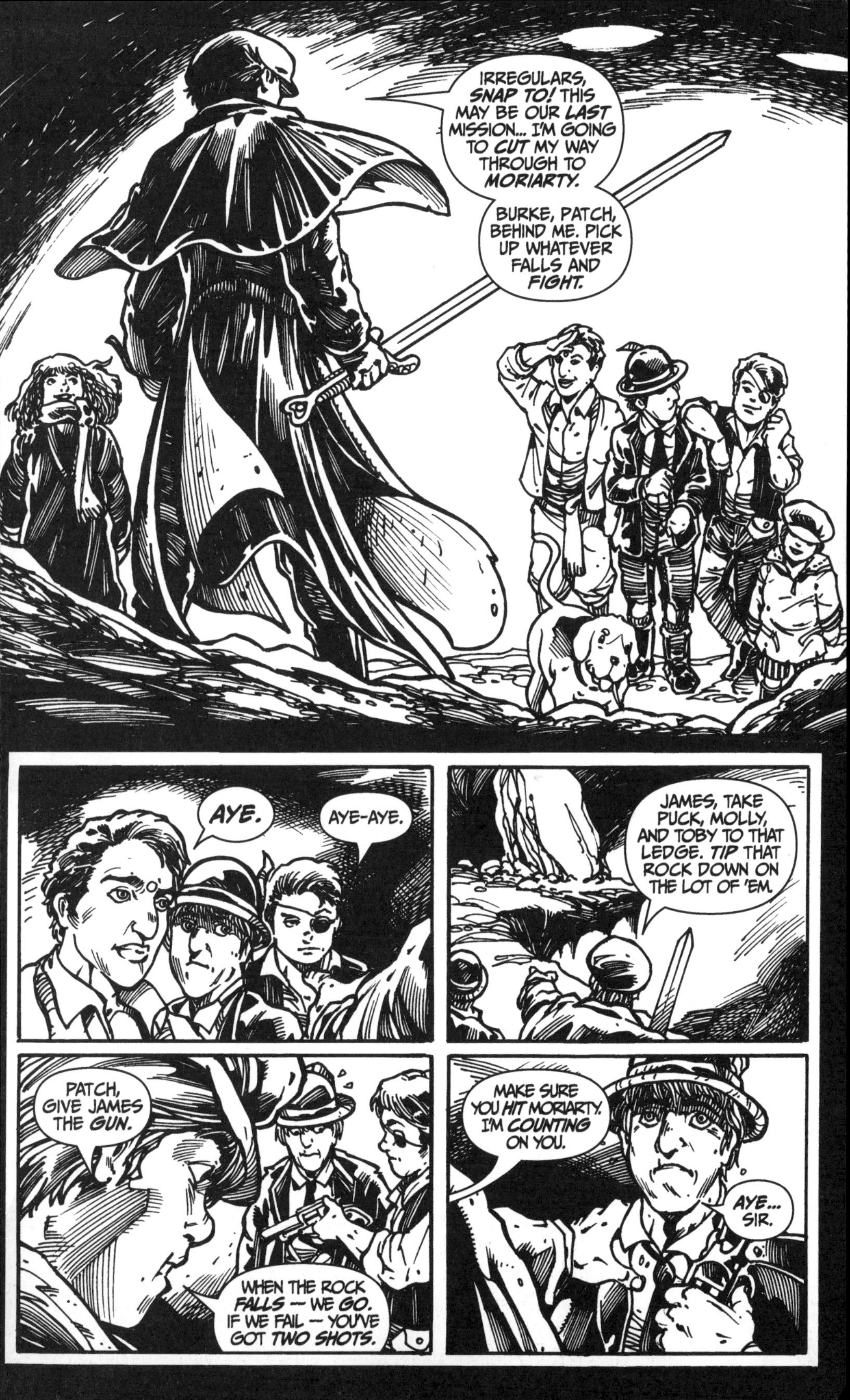
IRREGULARS, SNAP TO! THIS MAY BE OUR LAST MISSION... I'M GOING TO CUT MY WAY THROUGH TO MORIARTY.
BURKE, PATCH, BEHIND ME. PICK UP WHATEVER FALLS AND FIGHT.
AYE.
AYE-AYE.
JAMES, TAKE PUCK, MOLLY, AND TOBY TO THAT LEDGE. TIP THAT ROCK DOWN ON THE LOT OF 'EM.
PATCH, GIVE JAMES THE GUN.
WHEN THE ROCK FALLS -- WE GO. IF WE FAIL -- YOU'VE GOT TWO SHOTS.
MAKE SURE YOU HIT MORIARTY. I'M COUNTING ON YOU.
AYE... SIR.

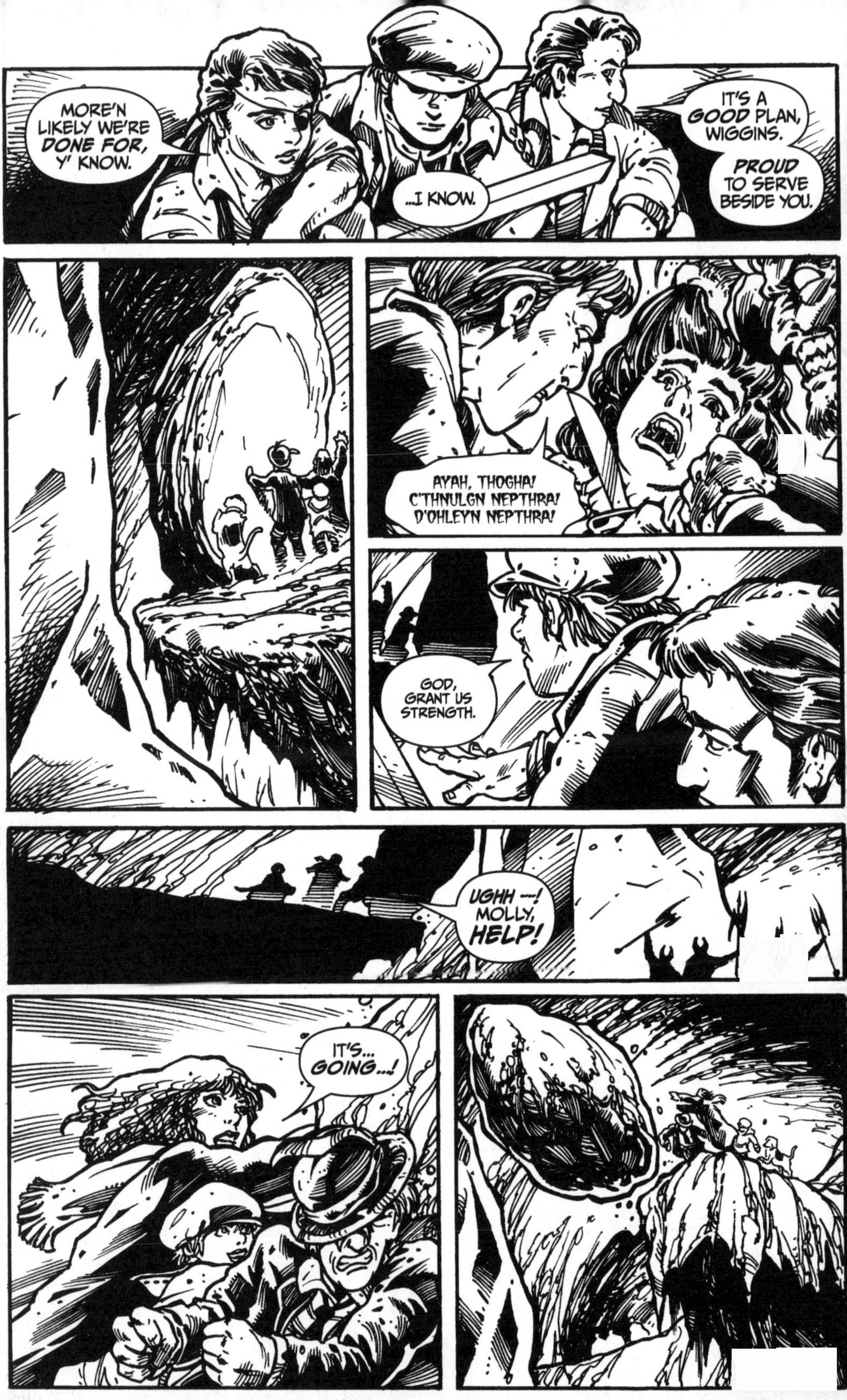
MORE'N LIKELY WE'RE DONE FOR, Y' KNOW.
...I KNOW.
IT'S A GOOD PLAN, WIGGINS.
PROUD TO SERVE BESIDE YOU.
AYAH, THOGHA! C'THNULGN NEPTHRA! D'OHLEYN NEPTHRA!
GOD, GRANT US STRENGTH.
UGHH --! MOLLY, HELP!
IT'S... GOING...!

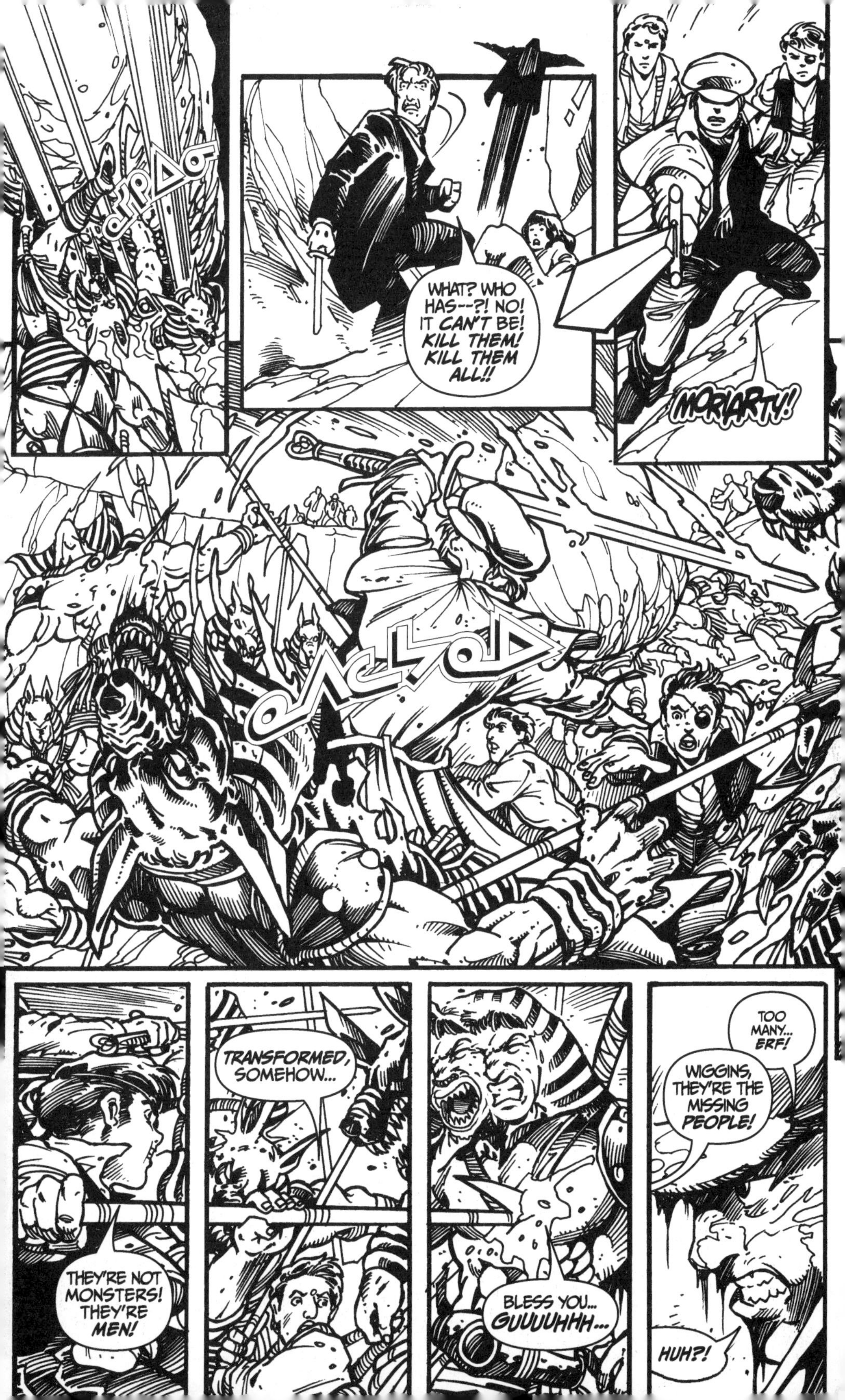
WHAT? WHO HAS--?! NO! IT CAN'T BE! KILL THEM! KILL THEM ALL!!
MORIARTY!
THEY'RE NOT MONSTERS! THEY'RE MEN!
TRANSFORMED, SOMEHOW...
BLESS YOU... GUUUUHHH...
TOO MANY... ERF!
WIGGINS, THEY'RE THE MISSING PEOPLE!
HUH?!

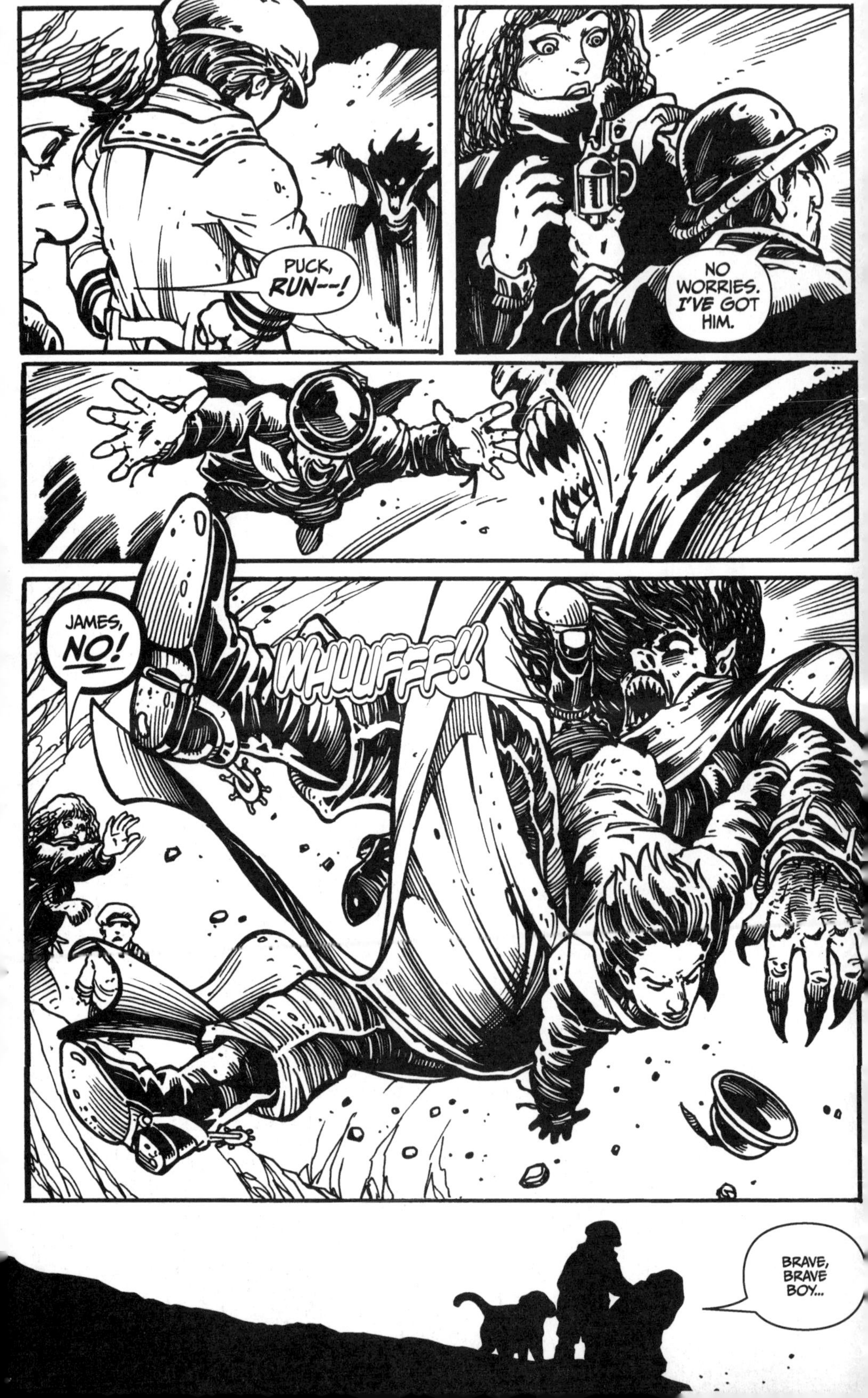
PUCK, RUN--!
NO WORRIES. I'VE GOT HIM.
JAMES, NO!
WHUUFFF!!
BRAVE, BRAVE BOY...

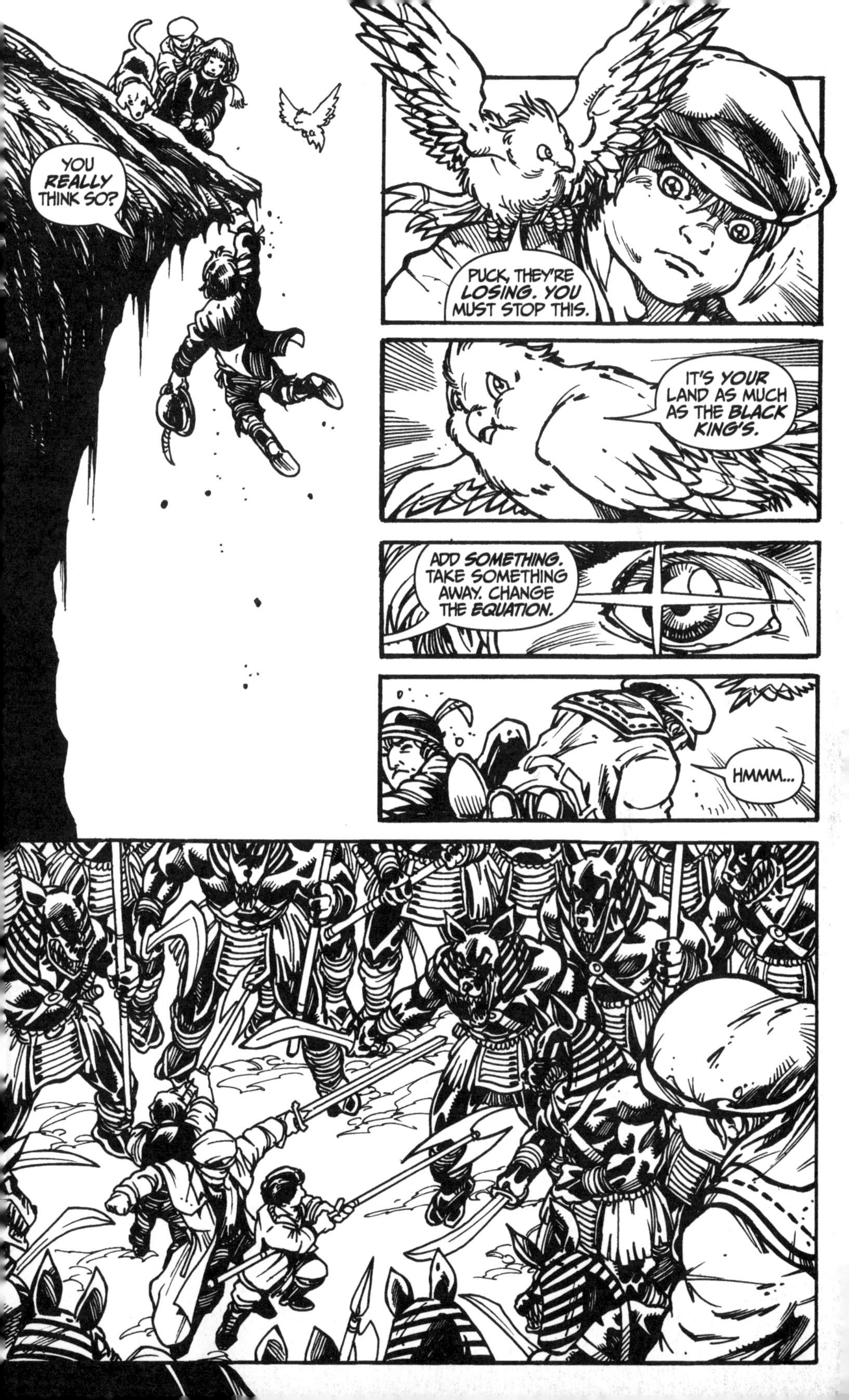
YOU REALLY THINK SO?
PUCK, THEY'RE LOSING. YOU MUST STOP THIS.
IT'S YOUR LAND AS MUCH AS THE BLACK KING'S.
ADD SOMETHING. TAKE SOMETHING AWAY. CHANGE THE EQUATION.
HMMM...

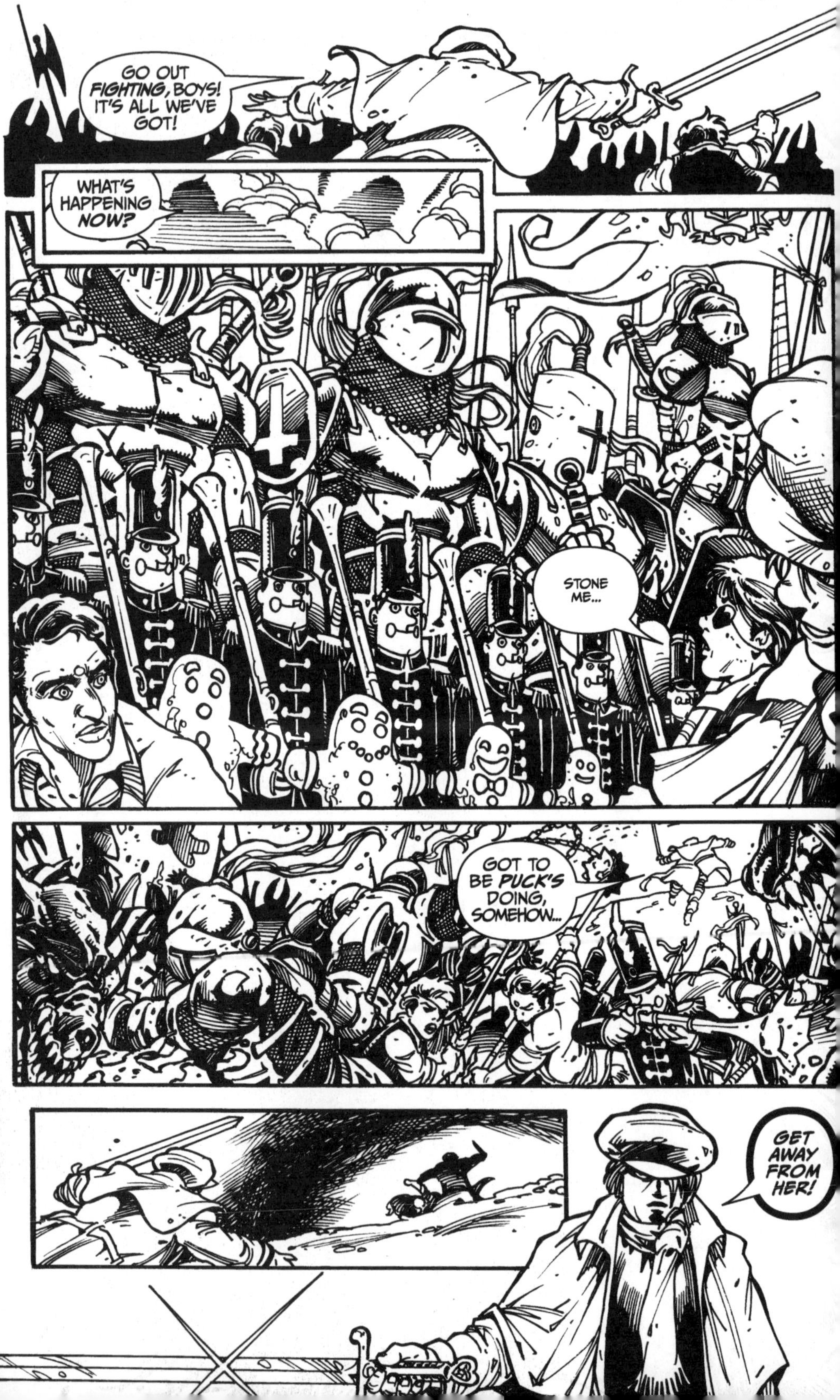
GO OUT FIGHTING, BOYS! IT'S ALL WE'VE GOT!
WHAT'S HAPPENING NOW?
STONE ME...
GOT TO BE PUCK'S DOING, SOMEHOW...
GET AWAY FROM HER!

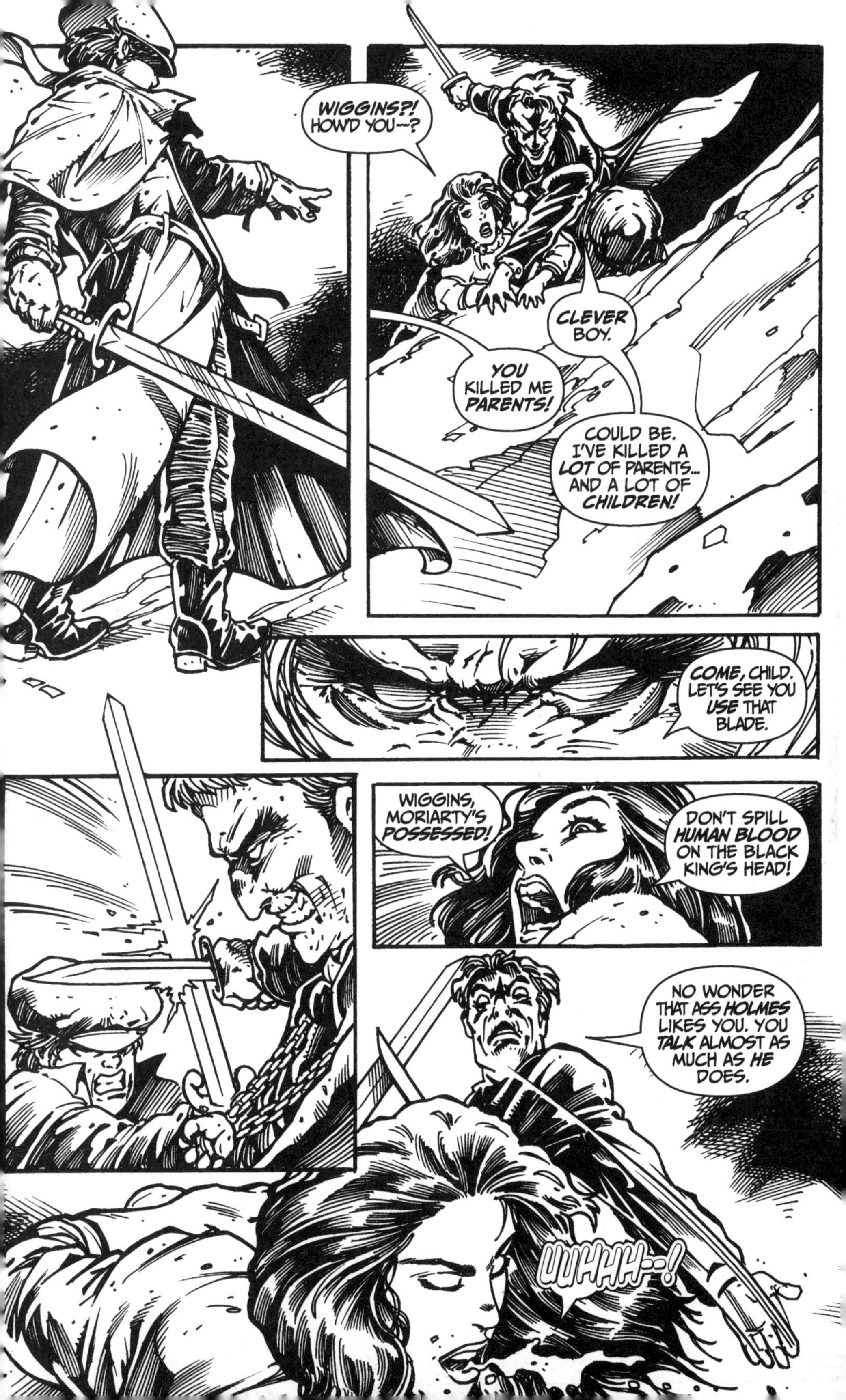
WIGGINS?! HOW'D YOU--?
YOU KILLED ME PARENTS!
CLEVER BOY.
COULD BE. I'VE KILLED A LOT OF PARENTS... AND A LOT OF CHILDREN!
COME, CHILD. LET'S SEE YOU USE THAT BLADE.
WIGGINS, MORIARTY'S POSSESSED!
DON'T SPILL HUMAN BLOOD ON THE BLACK KING'S HEAD!
NO WONDER THAT ASS HOLMES LIKES YOU. YOU TALK ALMOST AS MUCH AS HE DOES.
UUHHH--!

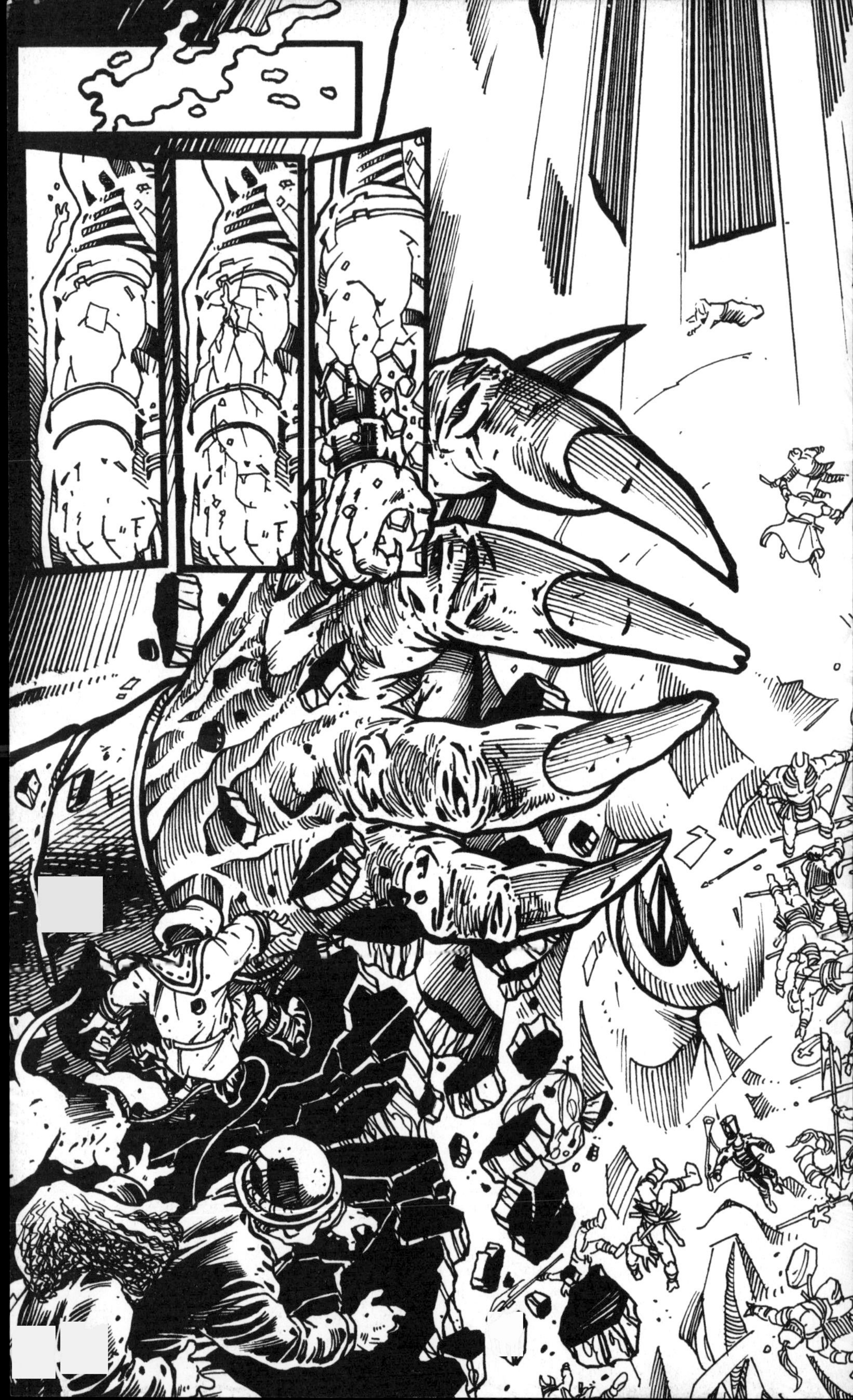

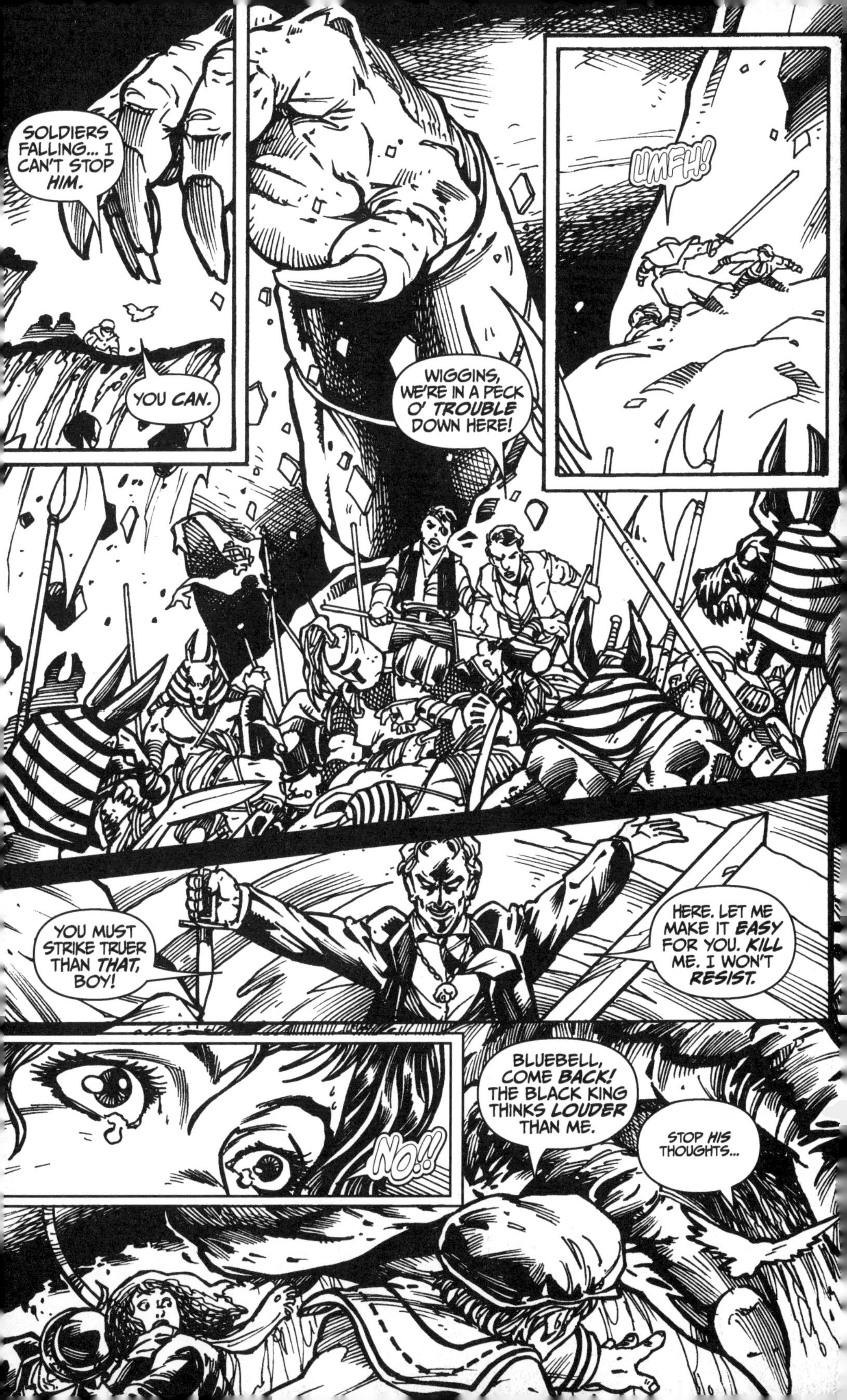
SOLDIERS FALLING... I CAN'T STOP HIM.
YOU CAN.
WIGGINS, WE'RE IN A PECK O' TROUBLE DOWN HERE!
UMFH!
YOU MUST STRIKE TRUER THAN THAT, BOY!
HERE. LET ME MAKE IT EASY FOR YOU. KILL ME. I WON'T RESIST.
NO!!
BLUEBELL, COME BACK! THE BLACK KING THINKS LOUDER THAN ME.
STOP HIS THOUGHTS...

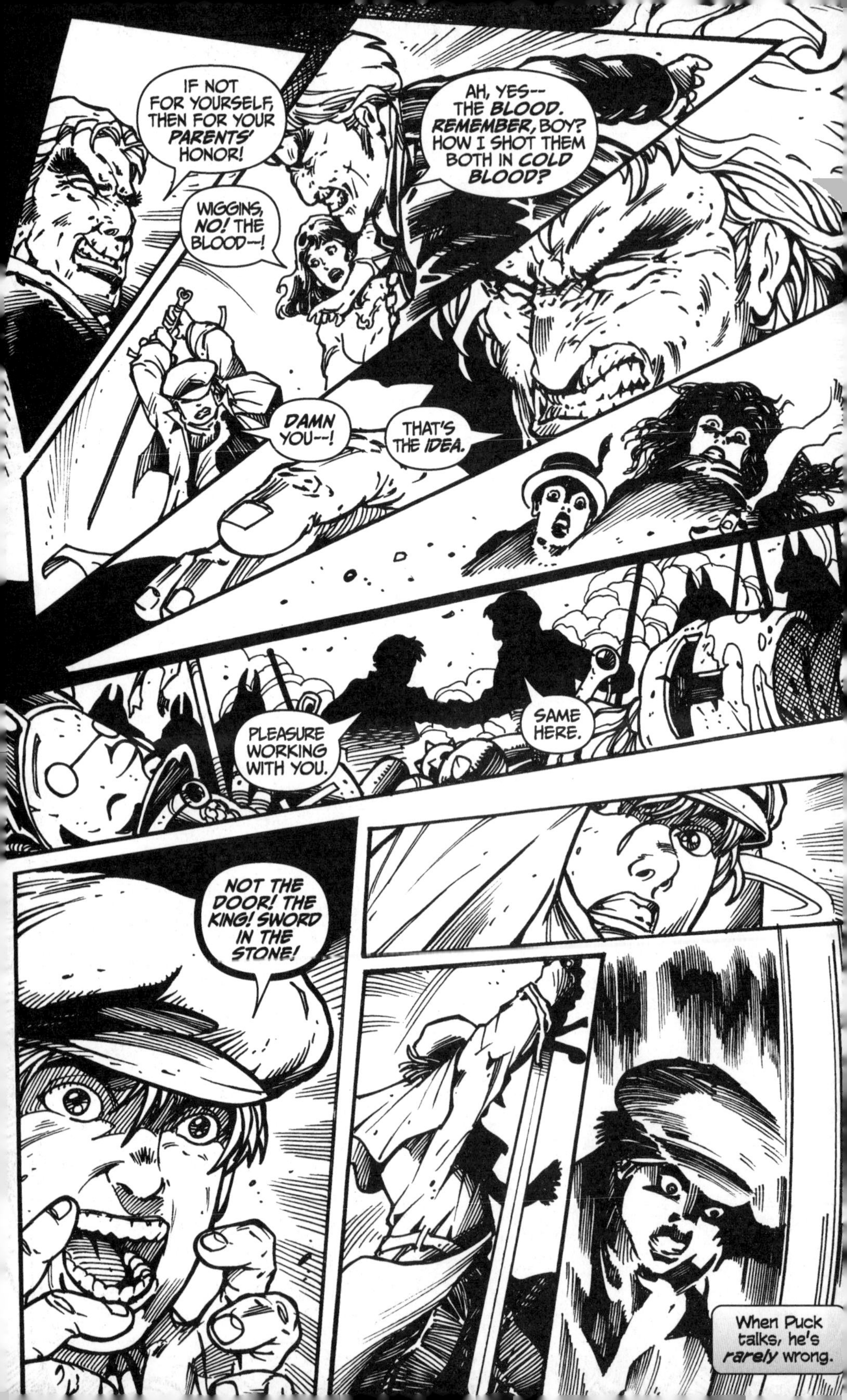
IF NOT FOR YOURSELF, THEN FOR YOUR PARENTS' HONOR!
AH, YES-- THE BLOOD. REMEMBER, BOY? HOW I SHOT THEM BOTH IN COLD BLOOD?
WIGGINS, NO! THE BLOOD--!
DAMN YOU--!
THAT'S THE IDEA.
PLEASURE WORKING WITH YOU.
SAME HERE.
NOT THE DOOR! THE KING! SWORD IN THE STONE!
When Puck talks, he's rarely wrong.

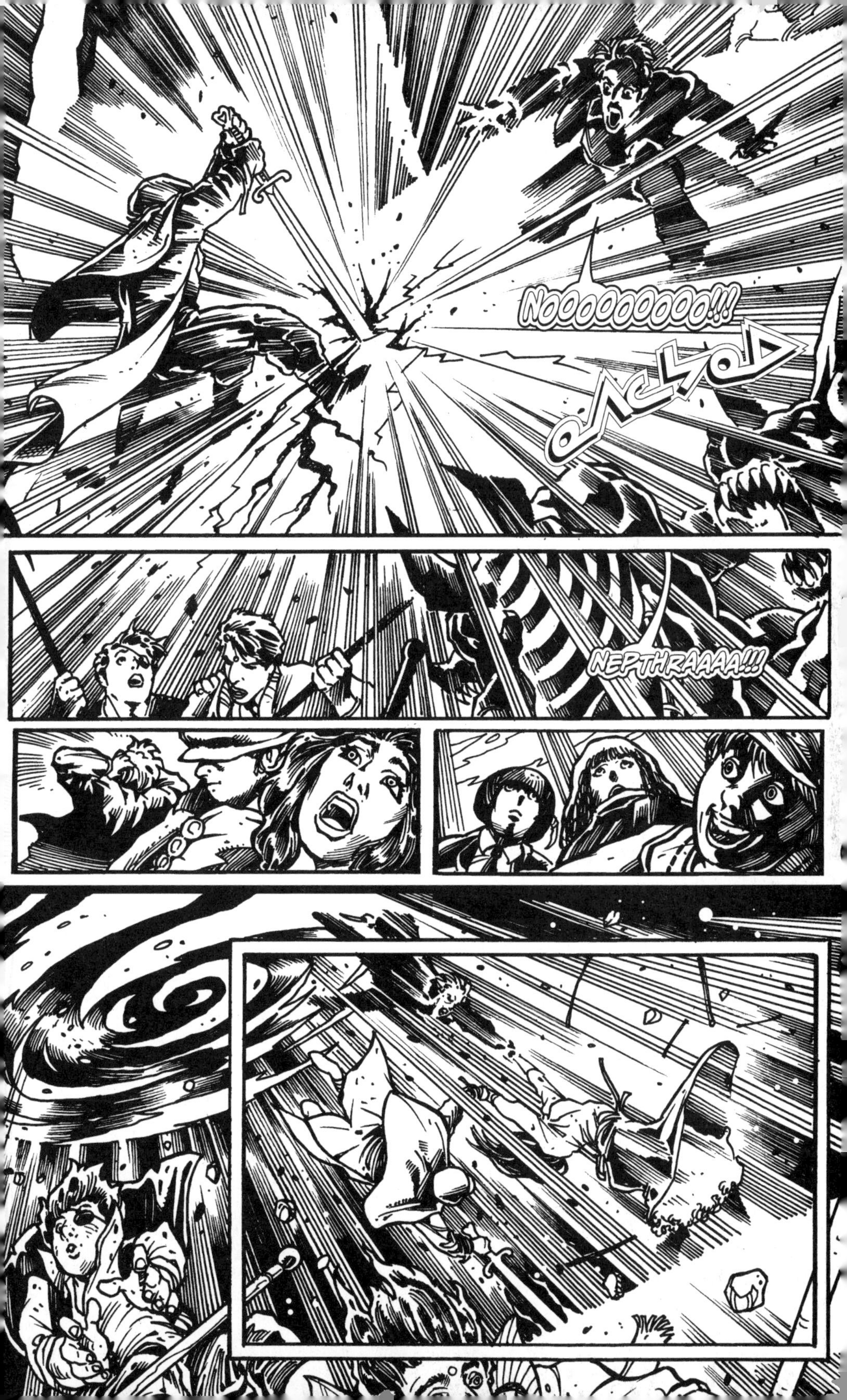
NOOOOOOOOOO!!!
NEPTHRAAAA!!!

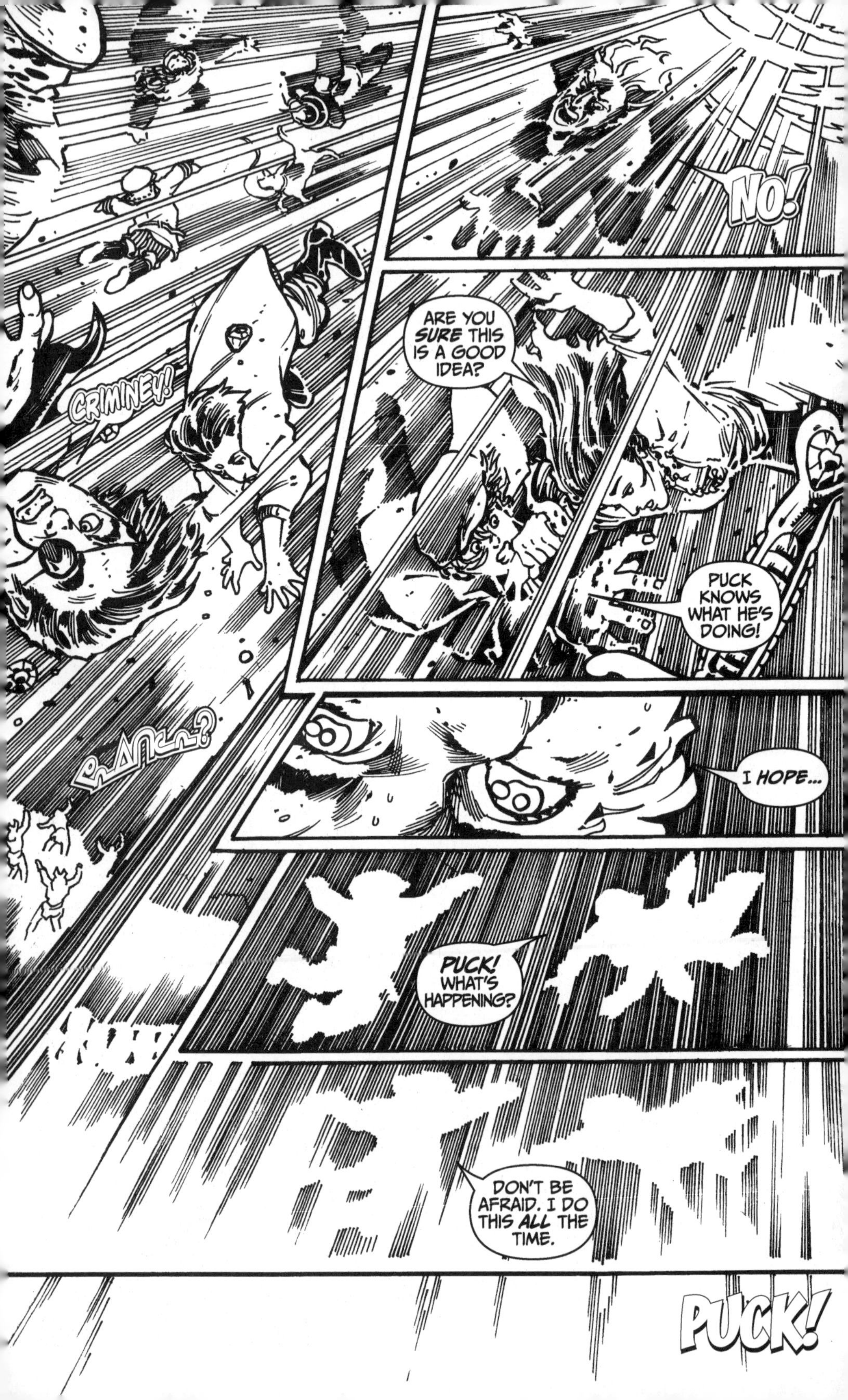
NO!
CRIMINEY!
ARE YOU SURE THIS IS A GOOD IDEA?
PUCK KNOWS WHAT HE'S DOING!
I HOPE...
PUCK! WHAT'S HAPPENING?
DON'T BE AFRAID. I DO THIS ALL THE TIME.
PUCK!

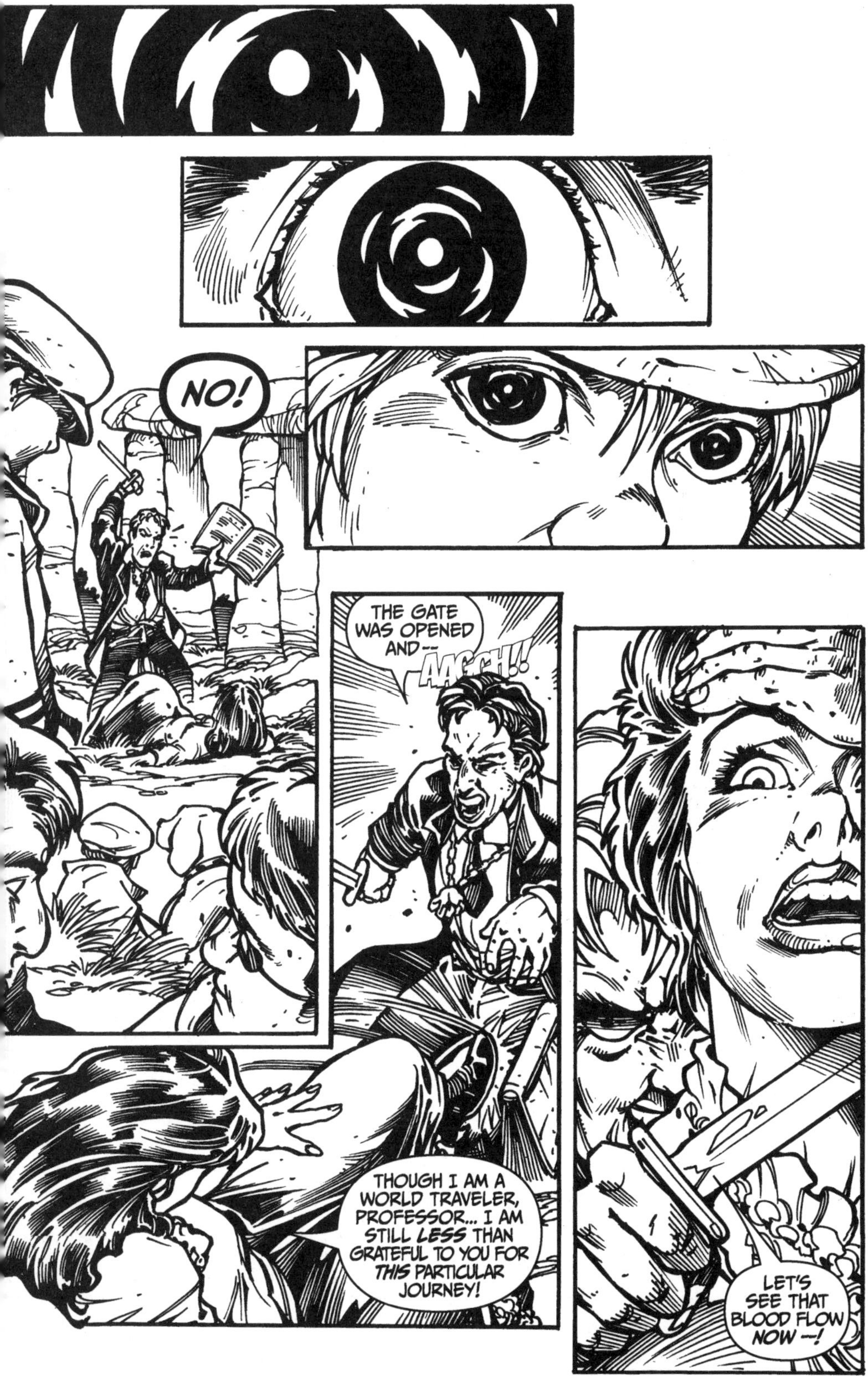
NO!
THE GATE WAS OPENED AND--
AAGGH!!
THOUGH I AM A WORLD TRAVELER, PROFESSOR... I AM STILL *LESS* THAN GRATEFUL TO YOU FOR *THIS* PARTICULAR JOURNEY!
LET'S SEE THAT BLOOD FLOW *NOW* --!

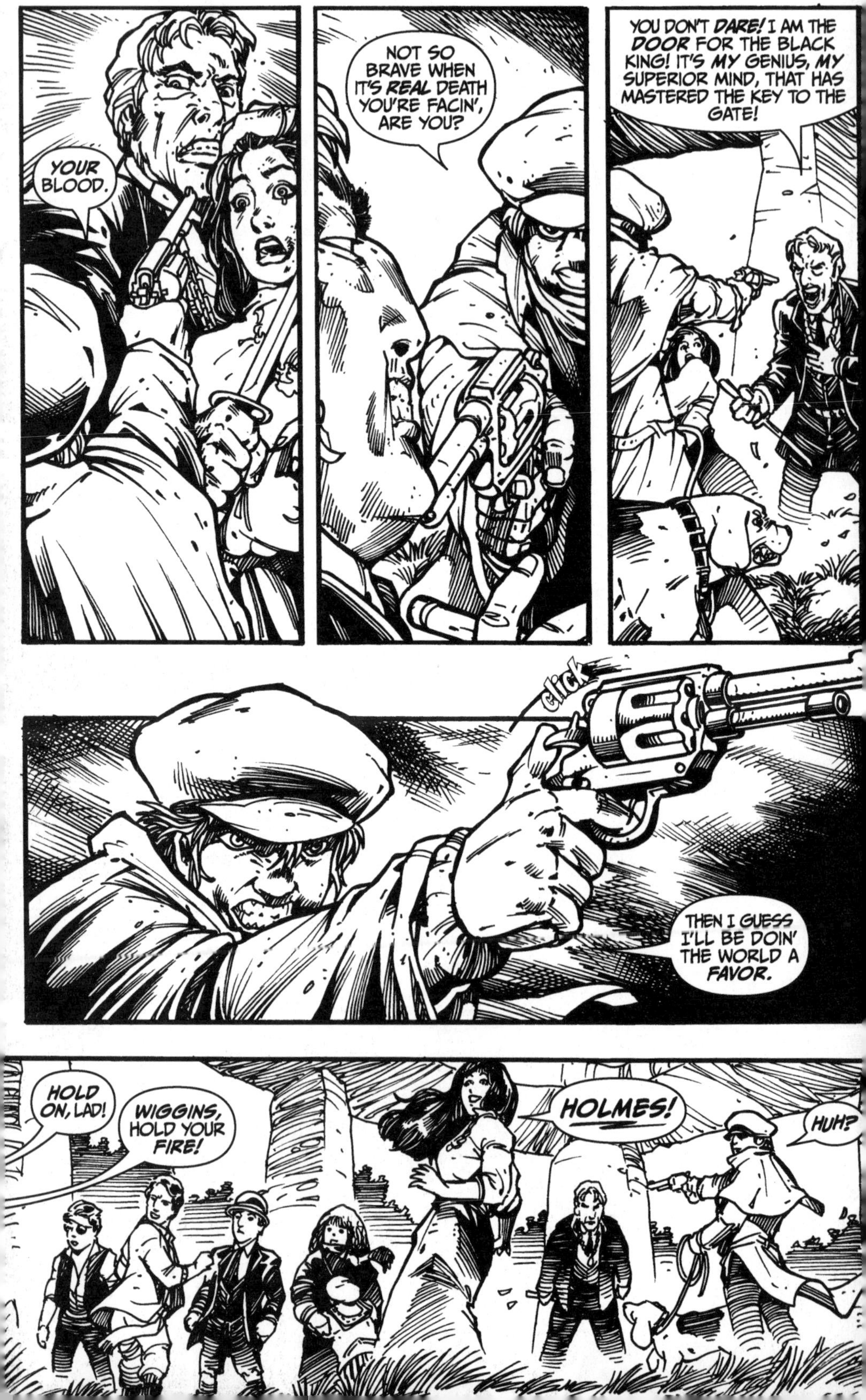
YOUR BLOOD.
NOT SO BRAVE WHEN IT'S REAL DEATH YOU'RE FACIN', ARE YOU?
YOU DON'T DARE! I AM THE DOOR FOR THE BLACK KING! IT'S MY GENIUS, MY SUPERIOR MIND, THAT HAS MASTERED THE KEY TO THE GATE!
click
THEN I GUESS I'LL BE DOIN' THE WORLD A FAVOR.
HOLD ON, LAD!
WIGGINS, HOLD YOUR FIRE!
HOLMES!
HUH?

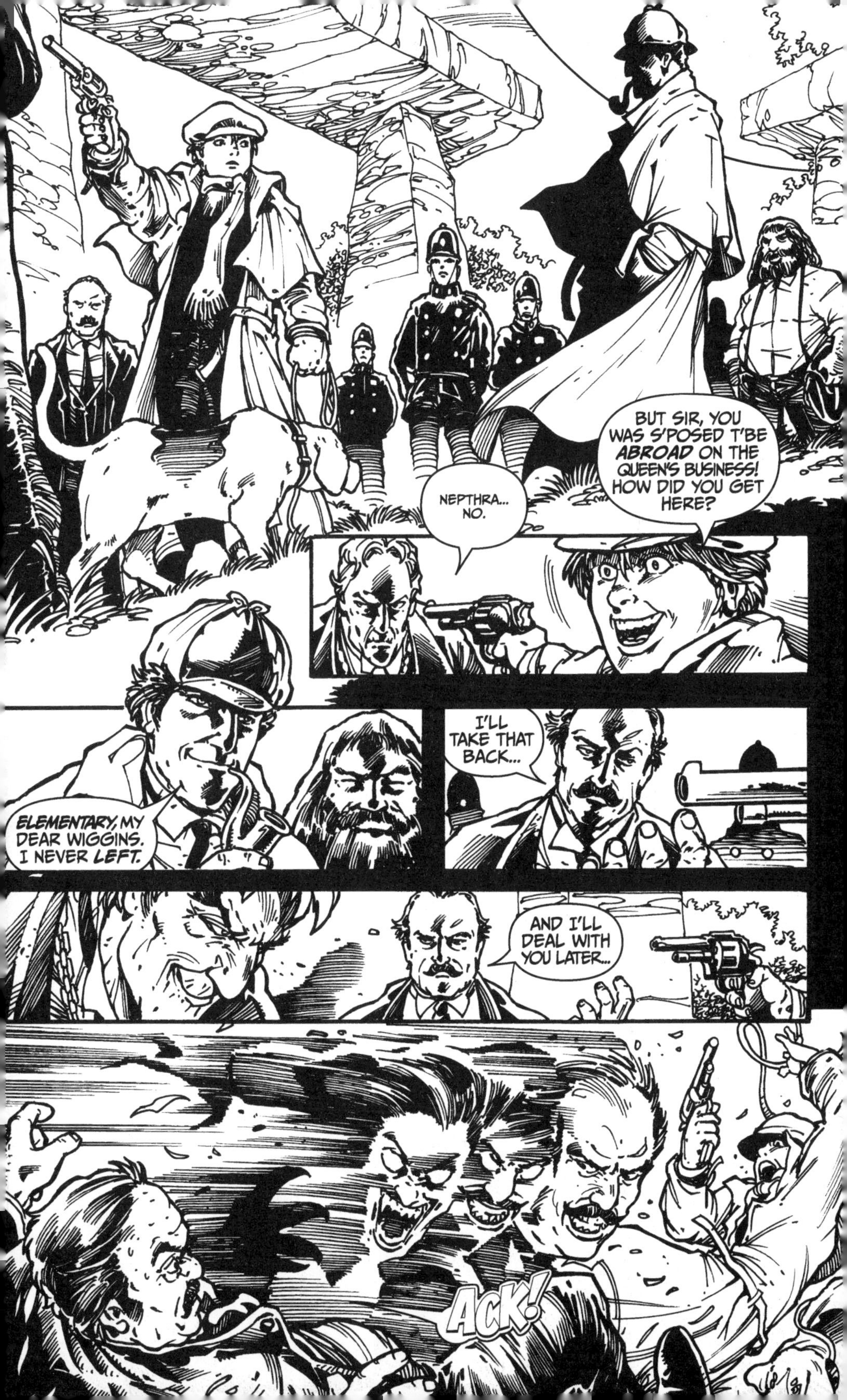
BUT SIR, YOU WAS S'POSED T'BE ABROAD ON THE QUEEN'S BUSINESS! HOW DID YOU GET HERE?
NEPTHRA... NO.
ELEMENTARY, MY DEAR WIGGINS. I NEVER LEFT.
I'LL TAKE THAT BACK...
AND I'LL DEAL WITH YOU LATER...
ACK!

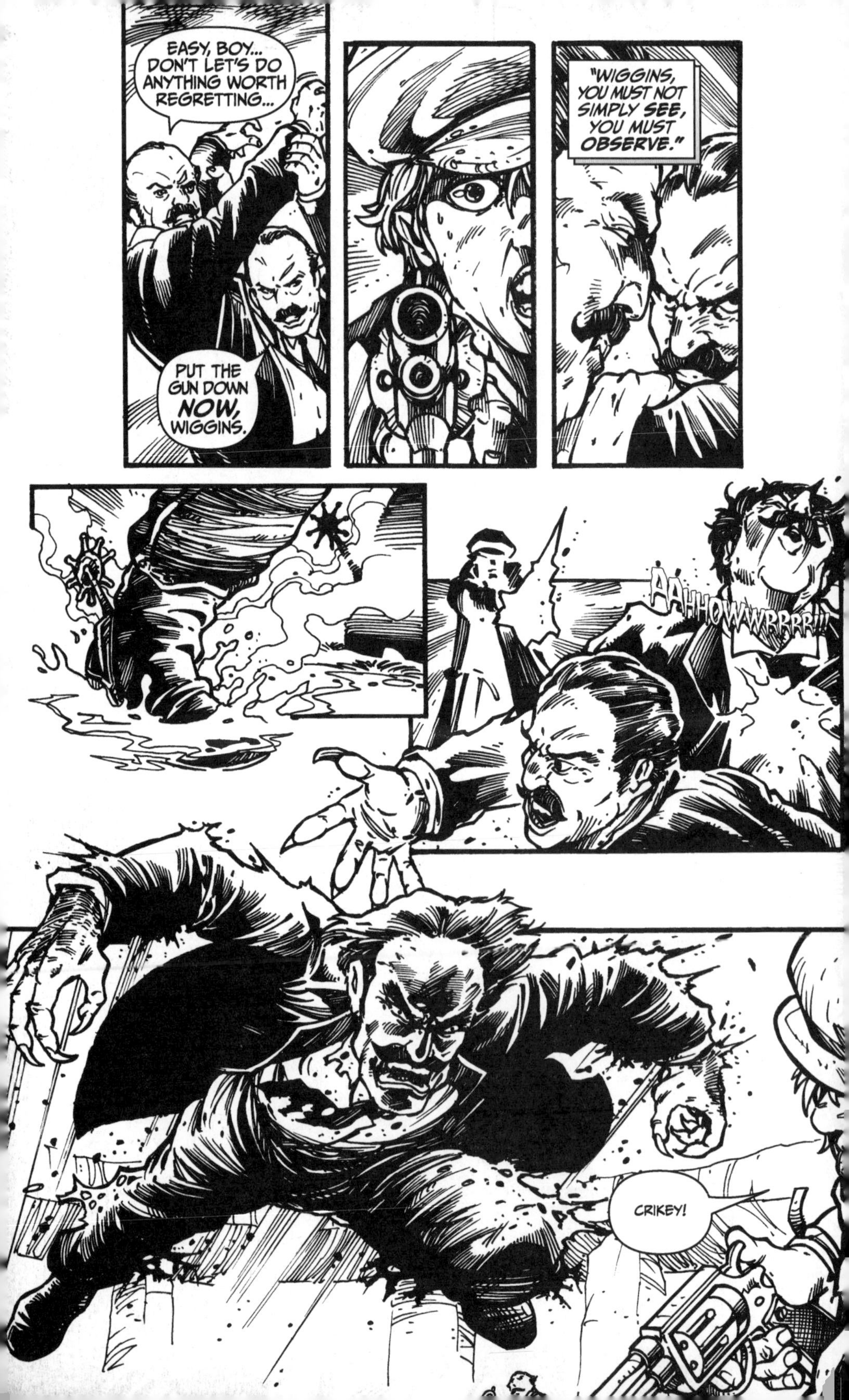
EASY, BOY... DON'T LET'S DO ANYTHING WORTH REGRETTING...
PUT THE GUN DOWN NOW, WIGGINS.
"WIGGINS, YOU MUST NOT SIMPLY SEE, YOU MUST OBSERVE."
AAHHOWWRRRR!!
CRIKEY!

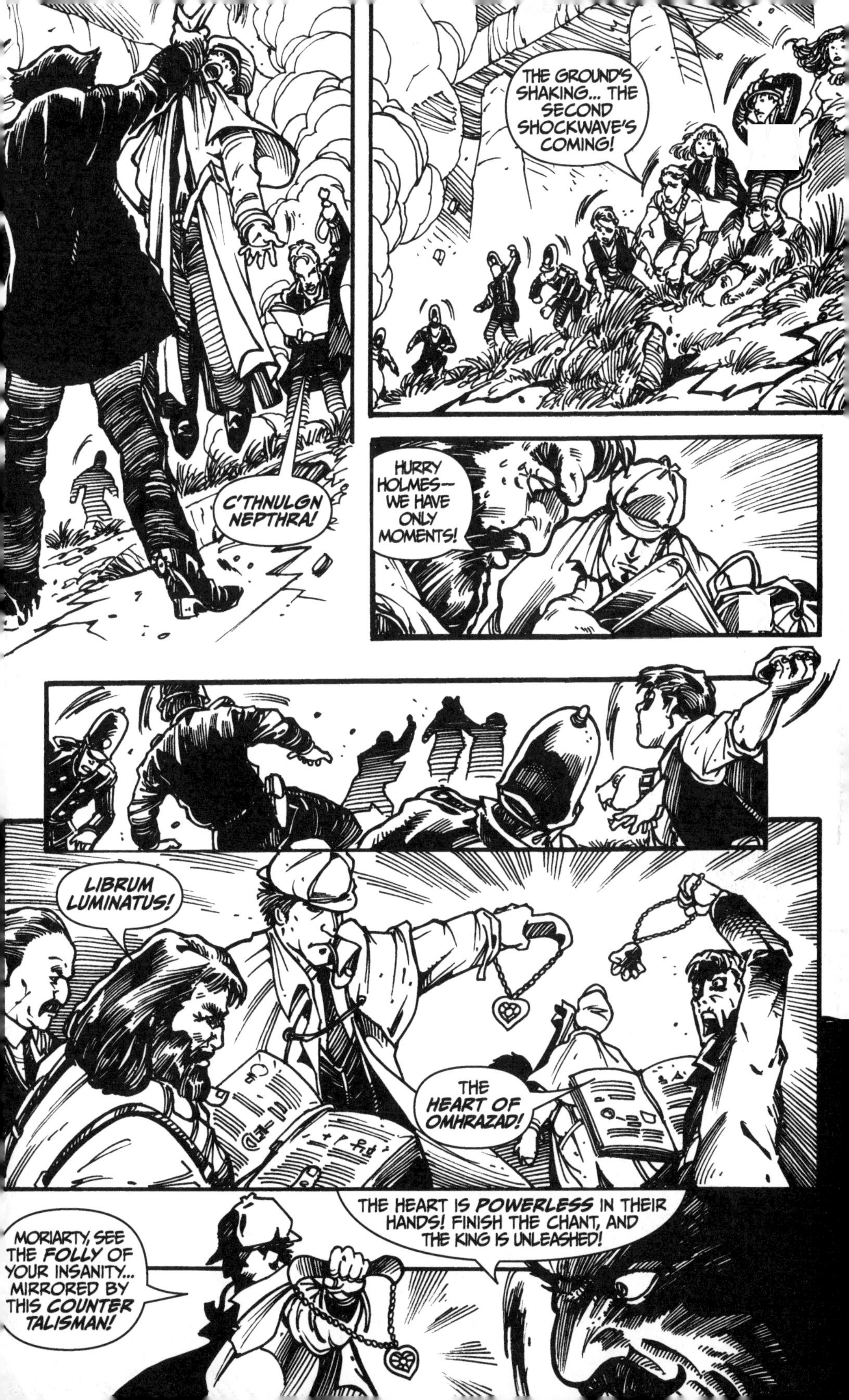
C'THNULGN NEPTHRA!
THE GROUND'S SHAKING... THE SECOND SHOCKWAVE'S COMING!
HURRY HOLMES-- WE HAVE ONLY MOMENTS!
LIBRUM LUMINATUS!
THE HEART OF OMHRAZAD!
MORIARTY, SEE THE FOLLY OF YOUR INSANITY... MIRRORED BY THIS COUNTER TALISMAN!
THE HEART IS POWERLESS IN THEIR HANDS! FINISH THE CHANT, AND THE KING IS UNLEASHED!

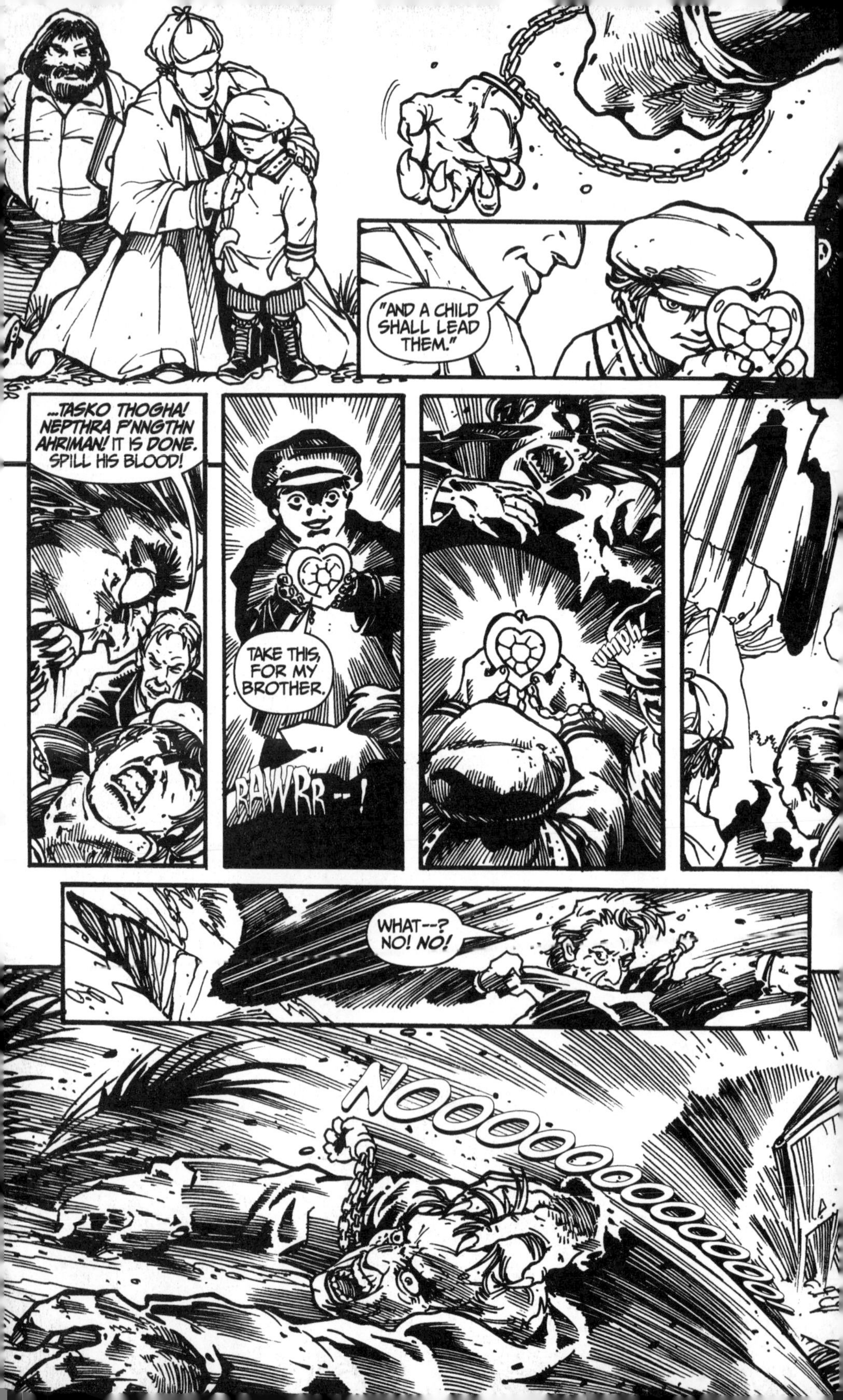
"AND A CHILD SHALL LEAD THEM."
...TASKO THOGHA! NEPTHRA F'NNGTHN AHRIMAN! IT IS DONE. SPILL HIS BLOOD!
TAKE THIS, FOR MY BROTHER.
RAWRR--!
UMPH!
WHAT--? NO! NO!
NOOOOOOOOOOOOO

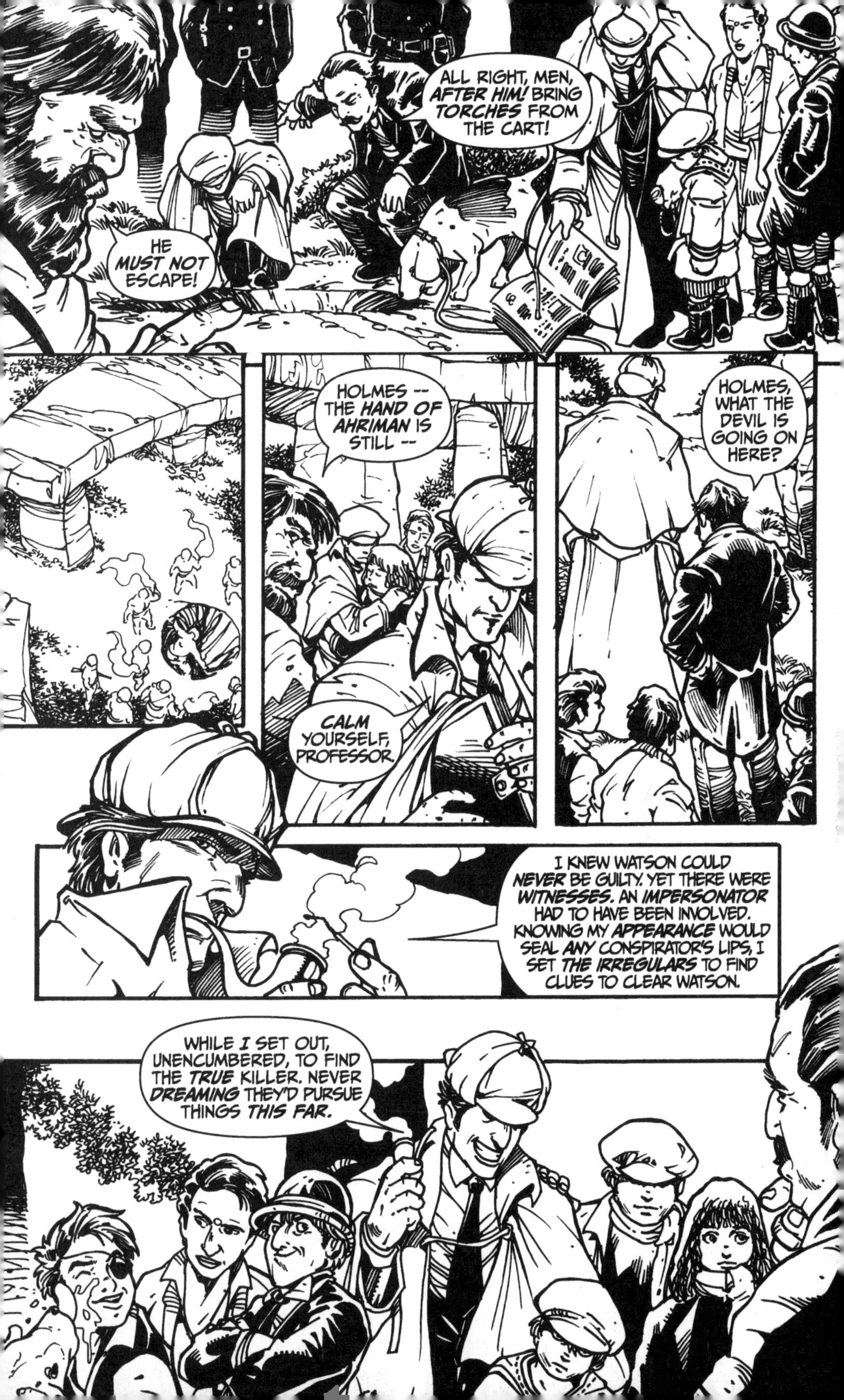
ALL RIGHT, MEN, AFTER HIM! BRING TORCHES FROM THE CART!
HE MUST NOT ESCAPE!
HOLMES -- THE HAND OF AHRIMAN IS STILL --
CALM YOURSELF, PROFESSOR.
HOLMES, WHAT THE DEVIL IS GOING ON HERE?
I KNEW WATSON COULD NEVER BE GUILTY. YET THERE WERE WITNESSES. AN IMPERSONATOR HAD TO HAVE BEEN INVOLVED. KNOWING MY APPEARANCE WOULD SEAL ANY CONSPIRATOR'S LIPS, I SET THE IRREGULARS TO FIND CLUES TO CLEAR WATSON.
WHILE I SET OUT, UNENCUMBERED, TO FIND THE TRUE KILLER. NEVER DREAMING THEY'D PURSUE THINGS THIS FAR.

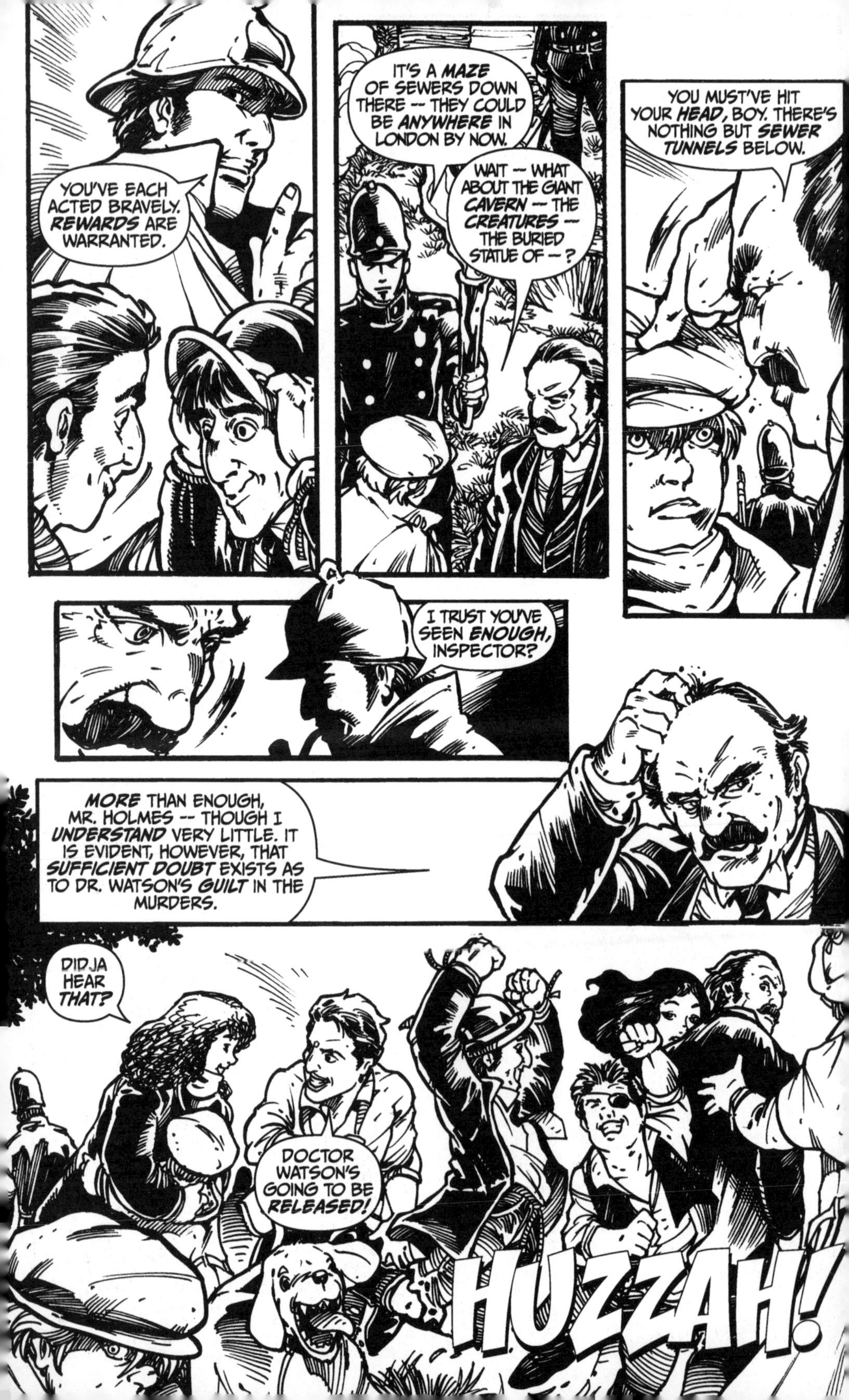
YOU'VE EACH ACTED BRAVELY. REWARDS ARE WARRANTED.
IT'S A MAZE OF SEWERS DOWN THERE -- THEY COULD BE ANYWHERE IN LONDON BY NOW.
WAIT -- WHAT ABOUT THE GIANT CAVERN -- THE CREATURES -- THE BURIED STATUE OF -- ?
YOU MUST'VE HIT YOUR HEAD, BOY. THERE'S NOTHING BUT SEWER TUNNELS BELOW.
I TRUST YOU'VE SEEN ENOUGH, INSPECTOR?
MORE THAN ENOUGH, MR. HOLMES -- THOUGH I UNDERSTAND VERY LITTLE. IT IS EVIDENT, HOWEVER, THAT SUFFICIENT DOUBT EXISTS AS TO DR. WATSON'S GUILT IN THE MURDERS.
DIDJA HEAR THAT?
DOCTOR WATSON'S GOING TO BE RELEASED!
HUZZAH!

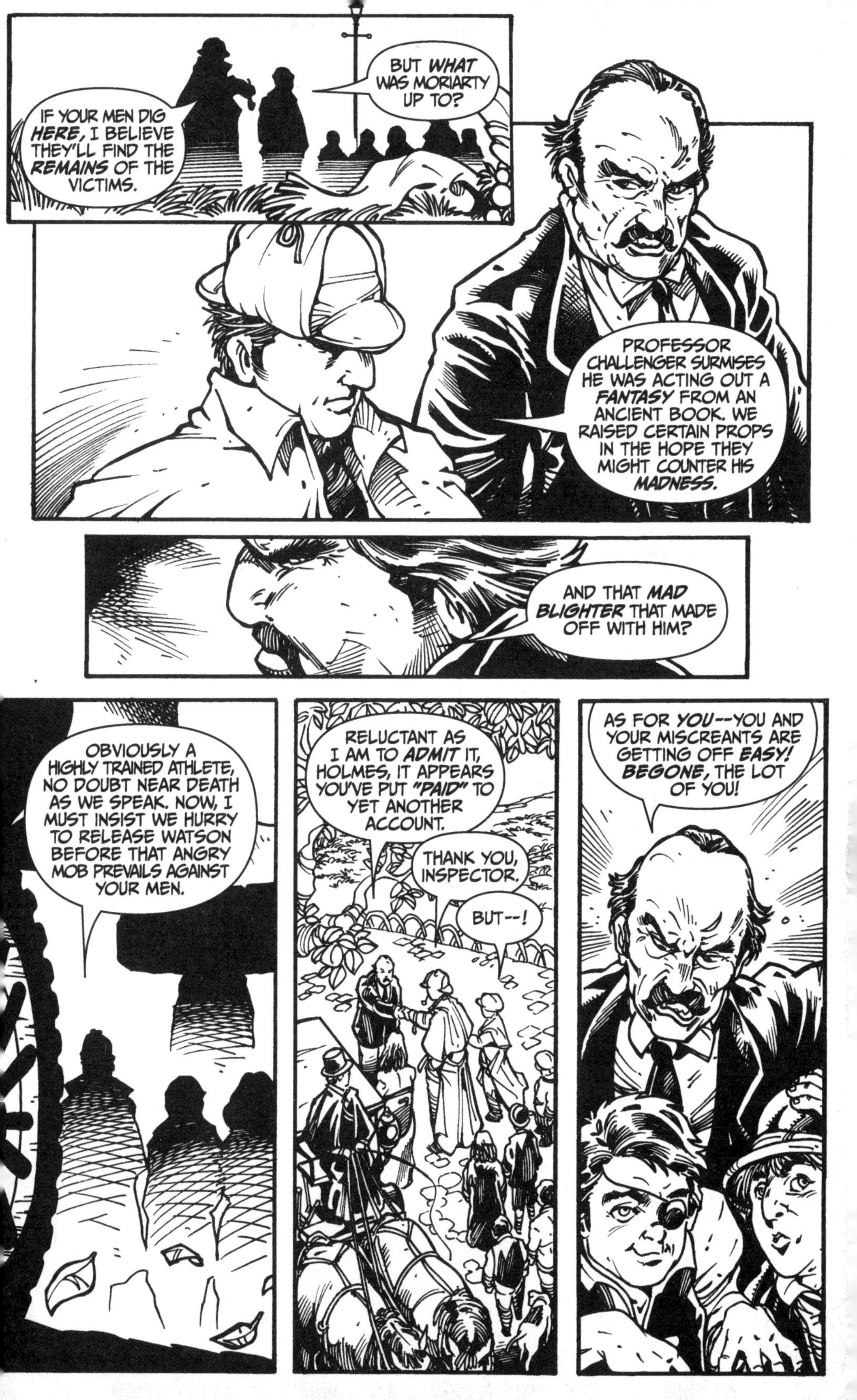
IF YOUR MEN DIG *HERE*, I BELIEVE THEY'LL FIND THE *REMAINS* OF THE VICTIMS.
BUT *WHAT* WAS MORIARTY UP TO?
PROFESSOR CHALLENGER SURMISES HE WAS ACTING OUT A *FANTASY* FROM AN ANCIENT BOOK. WE RAISED CERTAIN PROPS IN THE HOPE THEY MIGHT COUNTER HIS *MADNESS*.
AND THAT *MAD BLIGHTER* THAT MADE OFF WITH HIM?
OBVIOUSLY A HIGHLY TRAINED ATHLETE, NO DOUBT NEAR DEATH AS WE SPEAK. NOW, I MUST INSIST WE HURRY TO RELEASE WATSON BEFORE THAT ANGRY MOB PREVAILS AGAINST YOUR MEN.
RELUCTANT AS I AM TO *ADMIT* IT, HOLMES, IT APPEARS YOU'VE PUT *"PAID"* TO YET ANOTHER ACCOUNT.
THANK YOU, INSPECTOR.
BUT--!
AS FOR *YOU*--YOU AND YOUR MISCREANTS ARE GETTING OFF *EASY*! *BEGONE*, THE LOT OF YOU!

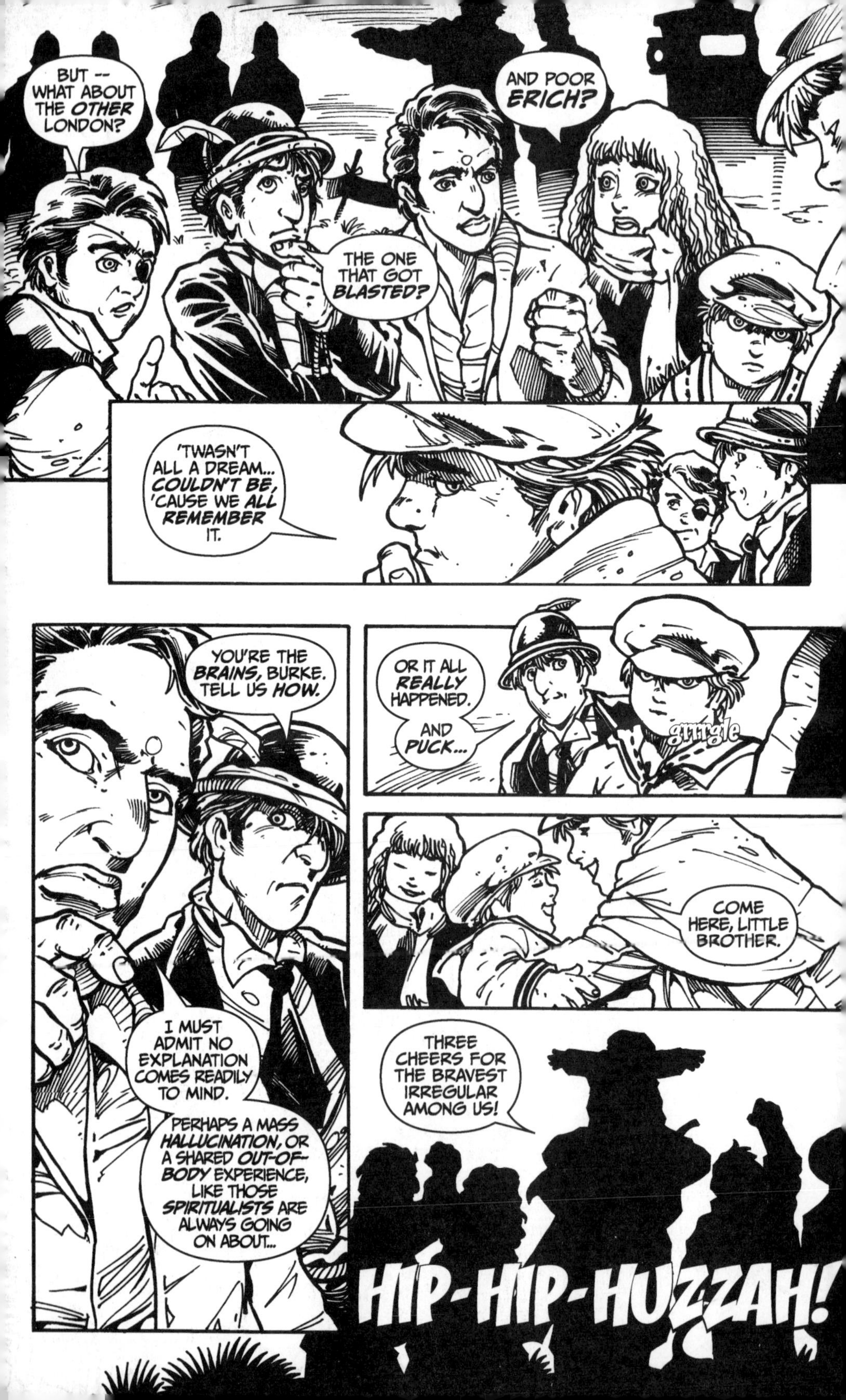
BUT -- WHAT ABOUT THE OTHER LONDON?
AND POOR ERICH?
THE ONE THAT GOT BLASTED?
'TWASN'T ALL A DREAM... COULDN'T BE, 'CAUSE WE ALL REMEMBER IT.
YOU'RE THE BRAINS, BURKE. TELL US HOW.
I MUST ADMIT NO EXPLANATION COMES READILY TO MIND.
PERHAPS A MASS HALLUCINATION, OR A SHARED OUT-OF-BODY EXPERIENCE, LIKE THOSE SPIRITUALISTS ARE ALWAYS GOING ON ABOUT...
OR IT ALL REALLY HAPPENED.
AND PUCK...
grrrgle
COME HERE, LITTLE BROTHER.
THREE CHEERS FOR THE BRAVEST IRREGULAR AMONG US!
HIP-HIP-HUZZAH!